The Mongol Period

Jingiz Khan receives Muslim dignitaries from Bukhara.

The Mongol Period

History of the Muslim World

Bertold Spuler

Introduction by Arthur N. Waldron

Markus Wiener Publishers
Princeton

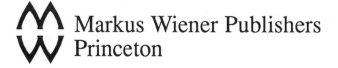

For information write to: Markus Wiener Publishers
114 Jefferson Road, Princeton, NJ 08540

Library of Congress Cataloging-in-Publication Data

Spuler, Bertold, 1911-
[Geschichte der islamischen Lander. English]
History of the Muslim world/Bertold Spuler: with a new introduction by Jane Hathaway.
Vol. [2} has new introd. by Arthur Waldron.
Previously published:The Muslim World. Leiden: E.J. Brill, 1960-<1969 >
Inclides bibliographical references and indexes.
ISBN 1-55876-095-4 (v.1)
ISBN 1-55876-079-2 (v. 2)
1. Islamic Empire—History. I. Title.
DS35.63S68 1994 94-11585
909'.097671—dc20 CIP

The photographs and drawings in the text are reproduced courtesy of the Galerie und Verlag Neshe, Munich.

Printed in the United States of America on acid-free paper.

CONTENTS

Introduction vii
Translator's Preface xxxiv
The Mongol empire 1
The Īlkhāns in Persia 25
The Mongols in Central Asia 43
The Golden Horde 47
Egypt: The Baḥrī Mamlūks 56
India before Tīmūr 60
Tīmūr 65
India: From Tīmūr to Bābar 71
Qara Qoyunlu and Aq Qoyunlu 74
Egypt: The Burjī Mamlūks 77
The Muslims in East Europe 80
Russian rule on the Volga 88
The Crimea 95

TABLES

The Posterity of Jingiz Khān 102
The Posterity of Tīmūr 103
Dynastic Tables 104

Bibliography 109
Indices 111

MAPS

Turkish States in the Middle East: 125

Turkish States in the Middle East (11th- 12th cents.). — Jingiz Khān 1155 (1167?)-1227 and the Mongol empires of the 13th cent. — Western Asia under Tīmūr (c. 1400).

The enthronement of Jingiz Khan at the 1206 Khuriltai.

INTRODUCTION*

Where should one begin the study of modern history? The soundest answer is probably with the Mongols. The great states of Eurasia today—China, Russia, and India, as well as most of the Middle East—all were once incorporated into Mongol empires, and changed by that experience. The modern history of those states, moreover, began when the Mongol empires ended then the component parts reconstituted themselves, emerging as successor states that, although independent, nevertheless bore an unmistakable Mongol stamp. Study the Mongol empires and their gradual breakdown, then, and you have the basis for an integrated understanding of contemporary Eurasia.

To make such a study, however, is difficult even today, which is why the book reprinted here is of such great importance. Most scholars approach the study of world history—implicitly at least—as if it were essentially a matter of accumulating national histories. Thus many books deal individually with the histories of Russia and India and China, but scarcely any look at their shared history, common institutions, and cultural features—many of which are legacies of Mongol conquest.[1] This way of portioning out the past in turn reflects the political reality of nineteenth century Europe, as well as the idea of nationalism, the key ideology for Europe then and most of the rest of the world now.

As for the pan-Eurasian Mongol empires and their historical consequences—the real beginnings of much of modern history—few books have yet been written that deal with them authoritatively, comprehensively, and in a way that is accessible to a non-specialist reader. So for now, this thin volume, by the great German orientalist Bertold Spuler (1911—1990), is a very good place to start. It provides a lucid account of the empires of the two greatest Mongol empire builders, Jingiz Khan (1162?-1227: his name is more commonly transliterated as Chinggis or Genghis) and Tīmūr (1336-1405, or Temür, known in the West as Tamerlane), and their successor states in Western Eurasia. The story is remarkable and dramatic, and it poses many questions about which scholars today continue to disagree.

---

*The author would like to thank Professor Morris Rossabi for his criticisms of drafts of this essay, and the reference department of the Naval War College Library, Mrs. Alice K. Juda in particular, for assistance with research.

Jingiz Khan

Before Jingiz, the Mongols were a scattered nomadic people, having no empire and only the most rudimentary organization; indeed, even the name "Mongol" was then limited to a single tribal group. Jingiz, however, changed that: galvanizing his people—historians still debate exactly how—he made himself, by 1206, overlord of a vast and militarily potent confederation, which he then led on unprecedented campaigns of conquest. When he died twenty-one years later, Jingiz had created an empire that included North China and much of Central Asia; his subordinate generals had reached as far as Georgia and the Crimea. With periodic interruptions owing to internal struggles, his successors as khan continued to expand a more-or-less unified empire until 1259, when the death of his grandson, Möngke, led to the division—but not the disintegration—of the empire Jingiz had founded.[2]

The second great conqueror Spuler discusses is Tīmūr, born a little over a century after Jingiz's death, in Transoxiana, the part of Central Asia that lies east of the Oxus (or Amu Darya) river. This had been part of the inheritance assigned Jingiz's second son Jagatai (or Chaghadai, c.1185-1242). Tīmūr was of Mongol descent, although not related to the royal house of Jingiz; like other members of the Mongol ruling class in western Asia, he spoke Turkic. But like Jingiz he made a meteoric ascent to power: by 1370 he had seized control of the domains of Jagatai; then he embarked on campaigns that took him into what today are Iran, Afghanistan, Azerbaijan, Georgia, Armenia, Russia, India, and the Middle East. In the process he constructed a renewed and revived Turkic-Mongol empire that stretched from Delhi to Moscow; when he died in 1405, he was on the way to conquer China. Tīmūr was personally feared for his ferocity, but his dynasty—the Timurids—presided over "a period of exceptional cultural brilliance" in Iran and Central Asia. And in 1526, as the Central Asian heartland of their empire was falling to others, Bābar (or Babur, 1483-

Jingiz Khan pursuing his enemies (from a Persian impression)

1530), who claimed Timurid descent, conquered India and founded the Mughal dynasty, which would endure there until 1857.[3]

At their apogees, these empires dazzled the world. Qara Qorum (or Karakorum), which Jingiz founded as a tent city on the Orkhon river, southwest of the capital of present-day Mongolia, was transformed into a populous capital and center of trade by his third son Ögedei (or Ögödei, 1186-1241), who built walls and a palace, and invited skilled craftsmen from all over the world to ply their trades.[4] Samarqand (or Samarkand) was even more splendid. It had been besieged and largely destroyed by Jingiz, but recovered when Tīmūr chose it as his capital in 1369; its population grew to perhaps 150,000, including many skilled artisans and merchants, and was embellished by the Timurids with palaces, Islamic colleges, and a famous astronomical observatory.[5]

Even in decline, moreover, the Mongol empires provided the frameworks from which new states emerged, and many of the institutions they adopted. Thus the last native-Chinese dynasty, the Ming (1368-1644), based its structure of government not on the model of earlier Chinese states such as the T'ang or the Sung, but rather on the example of the Mongol Yüan (1279-1368), founded by one of Jingiz's grandsons, Qubilai (or Khubilai, 1215-1294).[6] The rise of Muscovy in the fourteenth and fifteenth centuries and the so-called throwing off of the "Tatar Yoke" was a similarly complex political process; not a simple expulsion of the Mongols, but rather a multi-sided political process; a power struggle among Russians and others that grew more and more heated as the once-united and dominant Mongolian Golden Horde (the territories promised by Jingiz to his eldest son Jochi) itself divided and lost power. Even so, contending Russian princes initially looked (as their Chinese counterparts had when the Yuan declined) to the successors of the Mongols—and not to their fellow Russians or Chinese—for legitimation. Iran may seem to be the exception to this pattern. There the victory of the Safavid dynasty (1501-1722) over the Timurids was owed, according to Spuler, less to military luck than to the religious power of the form of Shi'ite Islam that it embraced. But even in this process, the importance of the conversion of Mongol military commanders should not be overlooked.

To these and many other political events, Spuler provides an excellent guide. He narrates the successes and failures of Mongol conquest and empire building, and its consequences for neighboring states. He traces the ruling lineages, of Jingiz and Tīmūr, as well as Mamluk Egypt (which the Mongols never ruled directly), and the Muslim rulers of India. Finally, he

After the capitulation to the Mongols, the citizens are permitted to leave the town of Balkh.

follows the fragments of the Mongol world empire in the West almost to the present—the book ends with the forcible expulsion of the last remnant of the Golden Horde, the Crimean Tatars, from their Black Sea homeland to Siberia by Joseph Stalin in 1944 (today they are trying to return).

Furthermore, Spuler is thoroughly aware of the way that his story of the Mongol empire and its disintegration prepares the ground for the more familiar narratives and themes of "modern" history. He stresses the importance for subsequent global politics, of the emergence, from the ruins of the Timurid empire, of a Persian state not politically connected to Central Asia and with Shi'a as its creed. He notes its rivalry with the Sunni-believing Ottoman empire, which displaced it as ruler of the Mongol legacy in the Middle East. He describes the progress of Islam into the Indian subcontinent, some of the most important background to understanding present disuptes there. He is fascinated by the question of how much Mongol influence shaped Russia, a state which for Germany traditionally, and most importantly for Germans of Spuler's generation, was a primary rival and adversary.

But Spuler also leaves out a lot. His primary interest is Islam[7]; he writes about the Mongols first because Jingiz and Tīmūr conquered existing Islamic states, and second, because many Mongols adopted Islam and spread it; he does not discuss places where Mongol conquest and Islam did not coincide. For that reason he does not treat either Mongol rule in China and Korea or Mongol invasions of Vietnam, Burma, Java, and Japan. By the same token, however, he provides marvelously clear accounts of the confusing history of Central Asia, where Turkic language and Islamic culture rapidly overwhelmed most of what Jingiz would have found familiar. He is excellent on Russia, showing that the Mongol factor was absolutely integral to the development of the state there—even though that state, like the Ming in China, ultimately would deny any relationship to the Mongols whatsoever.

Still, Spuler concentrates on political history, and in particular on the tracing of dynasties, mentioning issues of culture and society only briefly. For the contemporary reader, however, certain basic questions about the origins and legacies of the great Mongol empires are likely to be at least as interesting as the names of their rulers and dates of their conquests (although these are indispensable).

Take, for instance, the very basic question of how and why the Mongols succeeded. The Mongol empire founded by Jingiz was "the largest contiguous land-based empire in human history."[8] The Mongols set out to conquer it militarily: as a number of sources make clear, Jingiz asserted early on that he possessed a divine mandate that "the Tatars should conquer every country in the world"; his clear enunciation of this belief seems furthermore to have been a key to his ability to unify the Mongols.[9] Furthermore, Mongol warfare was remarkable. Thus, Allsen observes that the campaigns of Hūlāgū (or Hülegü) which created the Ilkhānid dynasty, and those of Möngke against China, "have a character that is undeniably akin to the modern concept of total war"; the scale of these operations of the 1250s, "in terms of the number of troops engaged and the distances involved was not again equaled until the wars of the Napoleonic era and

Tartar cavalry fighting an oriental army.

not surpassed until the World Wars of the twentieth century."[10]

Yet admiration for Mongol martial skills should not be overdone. Scholars have long since abandoned the idea that some edge in military technology was the key to the success of Jingiz and his successors. It was true that Mongols defeated adversary after adversary, helped always by their mastery of cavalry tactics and mounted archery. But the Mongols were not invincible: Jingiz's grandson Hūlāgū, for example, was stopped decisively in 1260 by the Mamluks at 'Ayn Jālūt (near Nazareth in what today is Israel).[11] So to explain Mongol victories, scholars today look now to a combination of military and administrative skills, and an ability to marshal sheer numbers. Mongol armies were organized on a decimal basis, in units nominally of one thousand and ten thousand, a system that had repeatedly been used by steppe nomads in the past and contributed to their regular victories over sedentary neighbors.[12] The decimal system's appeal as a means of creating a powerful army evidently outweighed its great disadvantage from the point of view of most Mongols: the way it undercut tribal and clan loyalties.[13] Initially a tool to organize the Mongols themselves, this system was quickly extended to conquered peoples. The result was that the huge Mongol armies, although international in character, did not contain the sorts of mercenary and slave soliders previously

Hülegü besieges and bombards Baghdad.

common in the forces of earlier empires. "The great size and ethnic diversity of Mongol field armies was achieved in the main by imposing something akin to a 'national-service obligation' on all subject peoples immediately upon their incorporation into the empire."[14]

By the middle of the thirteenth century, the Mongol great khan probably had at his command more resources than any other ruler in human history up to that time. How they were applied can be seen in the example of the great campaign into the Middle East. "Troops for Hūlāgū's assault on the Assassins and Abbāsids came from Mongolia, Turkestan, Iran, the Transcaucasus, and the Golden Horde. Food to sustain these armies came from Armenia, Georgia, and central Asia. Technical specialists to operate the catapults and siege equipment were sent from China to undertake the difficult task of neutralizing the mountain strongholds of the Assassins and destroying the formidable fortifications of Baghdad."[15]

These campaigns may have begun with Jingiz's world-conquering purpose and the charismatic leadership, but carrying them out and sustaining the empire they created, required far more. To prepare for the sorts of campaigns the Mongols regularly waged demanded resources, both in manpower and wealth, far beyond what the Mongols themselves—perhaps 700,000 at the time—could provide; to fight them demanded superb strategic coordination and tactical abilities; to hold what was taken demanded the creation of administrative insitutions that would encompass most of Eurasia, something never seen before. It was in the first and last of these areas—mobilization of resources and creation of administration—that the Mongols made their most important contribution to subsequent history.

Until the death of Möngke in 1259, the Mongols ruled the closest history had yet witnessed to a centralized world empire. It is true that the territory Jingiz conquered had been partitioned among his sons at his death in 1227, but central authority over the empire nevertheless remained strong, although just how strong is a matter of scholarly debate. In theory, authority was exercised by the great khan, chosen by a consensus of Jingiz's descendants, gathered at a *quryltai* (or *quriltai*), the assembly of princes and high officials. The great khan retained extensive powers over foreign relations, military operation, taxation, and population registration, and played a major role, through the system of joint administration, in the running of the regional khanates.

Thus, foreign rulers wishing to deal with the Mongols seem to have gone directly to Qara Qorum rather than treat with the regional authorities.

Batu, of the Golden Horde, enjoyed very substantial autonomy in administering his realm. But when the king of lesser Armenia went to him in 1254 seeking submission to the Mongols, Batu sent him and his entourage directly to Qara Qorum. When friar William of Rubruck sought from Batu first permission to enter, and later to remain, in the territory of the Golden Horde, he was told that the permission of the great khan Möngke was required.[16]

The great khan also personally vetted and invested with the regalia of authority the Mongols' dependent or vassal rulers—those previously independent kings that were sometimes left in power after conquest. Such ceremonies took place in a large tent in the imperial camp; the emperor placed robes of office on the ruler, then gave him a patent of investiture and three badges of authority, as well as the seals of office "whose imprint on all official documents was mandatory." Political residents, usually Mongols or central Asian Turks, were posted to the courts of such tributaries, and hostages were also regularly required; they usually served in the imperial guard.[17]

Central authority over the territorial khans was also asserted through officials representing the center, and by the presence, in territorial administrations, of representatives of the families of Jingiz's four eldest sons. In the Hūlāgu's Ilkhanate, and in Qubilai's Chinese domains, major administrative posts were filled by officials named by the center; the same was true for military commanders. Thus, although Hūlāgū was in charge of the conquest of the Middle East, the generals who led the Mongol armies against the Assassins, Baghdad, and Egypt, were all named by the great khan.[18]

The center also had a good deal of authority over the material resources of the regions. The basis of standardized administration was the periodic census carried out in the territories the Mongols conquered. Jingiz ordered the first such enumeration in 1206, with records to be kept in a book called the "blue register." This system developed, so that by the time of Möngke, "the results would have been recorded in several languages: one copy in the local language of administration (for example, Chinese in China) and another in Mongolian or Uighur for the use of the emperor and the central secretariat." Non-Mongol sources confirm the efficacy of the process. The *Chronicle of Novgorod* records that "the accursed ones [the Mongol officials] began to ride through the streets, writing down the Christian houses [the equivalent of the tents by which Mongols were counted]." The census was, broadly speaking, "an inventory of the talent and wealth of the empire

. . . the *Georgian Chronicle* relates that it recorded everything 'from men to animals, from cultivated fields to vineyards, from gardens to orchards.' " Census enumerations were sent to Qara Qorum as soon as they were completed.[19]

The census was joined, in the mid thirteenth century, by a new system of taxation that greatly increased the efficiency of Mongol administration. This was based on the creation of two fundamental categories, one a poll tax on adult males, paid in cash every year, the other an agricultural tax, collected in kind. This system better suited the needs of the settled peoples of the Mongol empire, both in China and in Central Asia and the Middle East, than had the previous multiple exactions. Associated with these developments were increased use of money within the Mongol realms and monetization of taxes: coins stamped with the great khan's name appear in quantity only under Möngke (although coins of Jingiz and Göyük are also known).[20]

The succession of khans, from Jingiz to Möngke, adds up to not quite fifty years of something approaching unified central power. Thereafter the descendants of Jingiz never agreed completely about who should have primacy. In China, Qubilai proclaimed himself the "Great Khan," a title accepted in Persia by the Īlkhans, but contested by others, some of whom, like Aryq Böge (or Arigh Böke), fought him from the steppe. At the other end of the empire, in the Golden Horde, Berke broke away. He had already converted to Islam, the first Mongol ruler to do so, and in the campaign against Egypt, "for the first time combined with a foreign power against brother Mongols" (page 22). Once initiated, this process of division was never fully reversed, even by Tīmūr. The subsequent history of the Mongol lands—and certainly most of what Spuler discusses—concerns a divided and dividing Mongol inheritance.

What accounted for the breakup? Before considering that problem, it is worth asking some questions about the origins of the inheritance itself. How is the rise of the Mongol empire to be understood in the most general historical terms? So far we have mentioned Mongol military and administrative prowess, but have not underlined how astonishing the whole story is: a people unknown to history, and numbering only in the hundreds of thousands, suddenly rises to dominate all of Eurasia, including settled civilizations far richer, more established, and more sophisticated. And indeed, the problem of the origin of the nomadic state is one of the most interesting in social theory. It asks why peoples like the Mongols, nor-

Mongols setting up camp.

mally scattered and seemingly content on the margins of human civilization, periodically give themselves state structures, launch wars, and build empires.

Nomads have been a puzzle to their neighbors, in modern as well as in ancient times.[21] Ancient descriptions, from the Mediterranean to China, make them cruel and vicious: the Chinese *Han shu* describes the Hsiung-nu (who are sometimes identified with the Huns) as "covetous for gain, human-faced but animal-hearted."[22] Moderns, by contrast, have tended to think of nomadism as mankind's original way of life, from which others developed. Modern Mongolia, or any other nomadic territory, was thought of as a kind of museum of prehistory.[23] To travel there was to be swept far back into the past, so that one could see, at the start of the twentieth century, a "natural economy."[24] Today, however, both views are generally rejected. Nomads are neither particularly cruel nor particularly primitive (in the root sense of the word). Rather, anthropologists and others have come to understand that they are, above all, particularly adapted to survive in the marginal territories they have made their homes. In the Middle East, these are deserts and desert margins; in Eurasia they are the steppe, where rainfall is not sufficient to support settled agriculture.

Recent anthropological work—based, of course, on nomadic societies

Waggons and huts of Medieval Tartars.

that exist today or have existed until recently—has shown how every aspect of the nomadic way of life is turned to the narrow purpose of exploiting the thin margin of subsistence available in such arid areas. Judged by the strictest economic criteria, moreover, in terms of capital and inputs, nomadic herding and production turn out to be very efficient.[25]

Even social structure seems to have been adapted to suit the environment. Property in traditional Mongolia, for instance, was divided into private herds, held by families having only limited claims on one another, in a way that makes sense best when one understands that dispersal provides insurance against catastrophe. When disaster strikes, some family units will be so hungry that they will reduce their flock to below the level required for it to sustain itself. But others will not, so while some herds will perish (and with them their owners), others will not. Closer kinship or common property would not permit this.[26]

But this last point in particular only deepens the mystery about the origin of the sorts of nomadic polities—the Mongols are the best example—that proved cohesive and strong enough to conquer their neighbors and much of the world. For if even kinship is limited in what it can require, what possible glue is there to form a nomadic conquest state?

Most theories of the state associate its initiation with some technical breakthrough in agriculture. This makes a "surplus" available, which the state then emerges to seize, and its subsequent development and differentiation are thought of as resting on one or another similar sort of economic foundation. Given this, the emergence of the nomadic state at all has long been a puzzle. Nomads do regularly form states, but considering the long-term stability of the nomadic economy, it has been very hard to find their origins in internal economic development.

This has not been for want of trying. Scholars have repeatedly attempted to find economic differentiation in nomadic societies, and thereby to bring their pattern of change more or less into line with the European derived main sequence. Thus some have argued for shifts in the property relations among nomads, and the consequent development of a "nomadic feudalism . . . which differed little from feudalism in Western Europe."[27] Spuler indirectly mentions this sort of theory when he talks about the struggle between Temujin and his former friend Jamukha (page 3): "Whether these struggles denote the emergence of two movements, one based on the broad masses supporting Jamukha, and the other aristocratic under Jingiz Khan, as recent research, particularly in Russia, has claimed, is a question which must remain doubtful in the light of the existing sources." In fact, although long influential, the argument for nomadic feudalism and class differentiation has proved difficult to sustain. Some internal processes of nomadic societies do make for social differentiation, but as Khazanov points out, they prove to be

> reversible, and, most importantly, not too intensive. In specific, fairly rare cases they can make for a stratified society, but never a state. At any rate I know no examples of a state emerging as the result of the internal development of a nomadic society.[28]

So the search for the origins of the nomadic state has finally led scholars to examine not the nomadic society itself so much as its relationship to neighboring societies, in particularly wealthy settled societies which provide an opportunity for enrichment by trade and conquest. The nomadic state, so the most recent argument has it, emerges in order to exploit this opportunity.[29]

What this means is that the development of the state is a precondition for improvement in the nomadic standard of living, and that when improvement comes it is the result not of increases in productivity within the nomadic system, but (at best) of trade and comparative advantage or (at worst) of simple extraction. We tend to assume economic primacy in settled states, but political and military processes appear to be basic in the nomadic case. As a result, the nomadic state has a fundamentally different logic than the state built on agrarian foundations. As Khazanov puts it:

> In this society, the main differences between the different strata and classes consisted not in their relation to key resources, but in their relation to power and government. Those direct obligations which the rulers imposed on the ruled were not the cause, but the consequence of the emergence of the rulers.[30]

Such state-formation would not, furthermore, have been possible had not nomads, for much of history, commanded a military technology which gave them advantages over their settled neighbors. Elsewhere in Eurasia internal economic development made possible the elaboration of ever more complex state structures. Among the nomads the opposite was true: it was the elaboration of such structures that made possible the extraction of resources from elsewhere that filled economic needs which, for environmental reasons, the nomadic economy itself could not meet. Politics was a substitute for economics, and political enterprise offered the way out of an economic dead end.

Hence the growing (but by no means complete) consensus among students of nomadism that nomadic states were created for the express purpose of extracting wealth from neighboring states. The argument is perhaps best worked out for the Chinese case: the rise and fall of nomadic states beyond the frontier correlates well with the strength and weakness of the Chinese dynasties, and the demands and policies of the nomads, to the extent they can be recovered from ancient sources, are compatible with a desire not so much to conquer as to exploit.[31]

Against this, however, can be raised numerous cautions. The ancients—the Greeks, for example—tended to lack the sorts of concepts of economically rational war (or indeed economic rationality at all) that have developed over the last century or so in the West. Therefore it is almost certainly a mistake to seek the "underlying economic reasons" when we look at their wars. The same may be true *a fortiori* for nomads.

John Masson Smith, Jr. argues—against most of the scholars we have cited—that economic issues did not lie at the root of nomadic warfare. Rather, he maintains that in some cases nomadism was not so much an ecological adaptation as a strategic decision, dictated by the fact that mobility made one less likely to be attacked. The warrior culture that developed in response to that strategic imperative offered certain political possibilities. In particular, the summons to conquest, convincingly issued, could lead to political power and organization, as Jingiz showed. Successful conquest, of course, created the problems of administration, with which Jingiz's successors grappled, and even brought economic benefits. But those were not the initial impulse. "For the nomads," Smith has written "war was the end, not the means . . . of policy."[32] This view would be in keeping with Spuler's explanation of why, having achieved power among the Mongols, Jingiz did not simply stop there: "Temujin's dynamic energy reached out for more distant goals" (page 3).

Compared to the question of origin, the problem of the breakup of the Mongol empire seems almost simple. The explanations are multiple. Arguably the most important is succession practices. As we have seen, and as Spuler chronicles, the Mongol world empire was repeatedly shaken by conflicts among members of the royal family, including sons and brothers of the khan, for the succession. The late Joseph Fletcher has argued that the practice of fighting for primacy—"tanistry" is the technical term—undermined the long-term stability of rule in the Mongol empire, and in those successor states that took it as a model. Against this, Thomas Allsen maintains that Jingiz intended a system of succession by nomination: the problem was that certain members of the clan would not obey. Whichever interpretation is correct, the effect was the same: repeated struggle for the throne that undermined both the Mongol empire and its inheritors.[33]

But other, less specific, reasons may be given as well. There was distance and the consequent impossibility of enforcing unity; the distinct regional interests of the various parts of the empire and of the cultures subsumed within it; the interests of the individuals concerned, many of whom chose to rule one part securely rather than to contest the whole. As the process of division worked, rulers became more and more local and less and less distinctly Mongol. The result was that instead of being overthrown and expelled, like many empire builders, the Mongols were absorbed into their empire and almost disappeared, so that, by a sort of historical process of *cire-perdue*, successor states emerged from the mold of the Mongol polity. Transition was dynastic, not structural. And although Spuler would not have expressed it as I have, that is the process he recounts in the present volume. It is not a study of the founding of the Mongol empire, but rather of something equally, or even more, important: namely, how that empire did not shatter, but rather slowly separated into successor states, in India, Persia, Russia, and the Middle East (he might have added China), leaving a heritage whose influence is still felt today.

Like the structure of the original Mongol empire, the weight of its subsequent influence is assessed differently by various historians. Nationalistically-inclined writers tend to give it short shrift, as the examples of Russia and China make clear. Mongol rule in each is customarily portrayed as an episode of barbarism. Russia is thought of as being under the *Tatarskoe igo*—the "Tatar Yoke"—from the fall of Kiev in 1240 until 1480 when Ivan III managed to slip out. China's predicament is seen in much the same way: Qubilai's completion in 1279 of the subjugation his grandfather Jingiz had begun humiliated China until 1368 when Chu Yüan-chang, sometimes portrayed as a leader of national resistance, expelled the alien Yüan rulers and founded the Ming dynasty (1368-1644). Such an approach, however, seriously distorts the history of both states. For neither China nor Russia in their modern forms can be understood without considertaion of the Mongol impact.

It is true that, in order to rule China, the Mongols had to make many concessions to and accommodations with both the Chinese population and their culture. But by the same token the Chinese changed too. Indeed, Ming China, in its initial period, is best understood as a successor state to the Yüan: one that perpetuated many Mongol institutions under Chinese rule. As Mongol succession struggles weakened the Yüan in the early fourteenth century, Chinese would-be successors regularly asserted their loyalty to the dynasty, even as they attempted to seize real power.[34] Once the Ming had succeeded, they created an administrative system that followed the Mongol pattern far more than it restored any earlier Chinese model. Military institutions, for example, were Mongol in form (despite the claim of the dynastic history that they followed T'ang precedents), and many Mongol customs and linguistic usages survived in the north. Some are still evident today.[35]

Early Ming rulers, moreover, seem to have taken as their models not the palace-bound sovereigns of the Southern Sung, but rather the Mongol khans. Chu Yüan-chang's generals repeatedly campaigned deep in the steppe, while his son Chu Ti (r.1403-1424) personally led his forces against the Mongols. The purpose of Chu Yüan-chang's campaigns is instructive: they aimed at Qara Qorum, a fact which would suggest that in the early Ming, at least, definitions of territory to be ruled and more generally of national security followed Mongol conceptions at least as much as earlier Chinese ones.[36] This residual Mongol influence diminished substantially by the late fifteenth century; the Ch'ing conquest in 1644, however, brought Inner Asian administration once again to China. Therefore it is probably fair to conclude, with Fletcher, that the whole later Chinese empire—Ming and Ch'ing alike—cannot be understood outside of the pan-Eurasian context.[37]

Much the same argument can be made for Russia. As Charles J. Halperin has shown, the Russia that emerges from Mongol domination is permeated by Mongol influences, practices, and concepts: to argue otherwise is to project later concepts of nation and nationalism into the past.[38] In Ivan III's ambition we may find an echo of that of Jingiz: "His goal was the union of all Russia—of Great, Little and White Russia—under the independent leadership of the grand prince of Moscow, and the creation of a centralized state."[39] His maneuvers in a military and diplomatic world where the Mongols are still powerful bear more than passing resemblance to those of the Ming founder.[40] Mongol influences persisted in Moscow, even after the arrival as Ivan III's second wife of Sofia, or Zoe, the niece of Constantine XI, the last emperor of Constantinople, which some historians have taken as marking the revival of Byzantine influences in the emerging Russian state.[41] Although the "stand on the Ugra river" in 1480 has commonly been taken as marking the end of the Tatar yoke, this interpretation of the event only entered historiography three quarters of a century later.[42] Its real consequences were more limited and ambiguous. "Though no khan ever again tried to assert Mongol power in the Russian forest zone . . . The Grand Princes of Moscow continued to collect tribute for the Tatars; in his will, Ivan III allocated tribute (admittedly smaller sums than before) to [the various khanates]."[43]

Spuler mused about the Mongol influence on subsequent Russian history in lectures he gave at the University of Bordeaux during the winter of 1959-60. It was abundantly clear, he stated, "that certain Tatar characteriztics had influenced the Russians; but for lack of proper research the full extent of this influence has not been established. However, it is clear that the ceremonial of the Russian court, besides strong Byzantine and ancient Russian elements, displayed a fair number of traditional Tatar features, often combined with others. The Russian vocabularly also gained some Tatar expressions, reflecting important cultural and technical borrowing from the Tatars. Their influence can also be seen in the Russian postal and financial systems, as well as in trades such as metal forging. But it was the army and military organization which owed most to the Tatar model, particularly in the significance of the figure ten in military formations. Many Tatar weapons and tactical methods, especially those of the cavalry, were adopted by the Russians."[44] So in Russia, as in Ming China, Mongol cultural influences lingered long after actual authority had vanished.

If it was true that Mongol influence persisted within states, then it was almost certainly true among states as well, although the topic is almost entirely unexplored by historians. The Mongol empire provided the first framework for and model of pan-Eurasian war and diplomacy, remembered after the empire itself had disappeared. Thus, the campaign of Tīmūr against the Ming makes sense as an attempt by a successor of the Mongols to recapture a formerly subordinate territory. The same context makes sense of the correspondence, framed in terms of equality, among Chu Ti, Tīmūr and Shāhrukh Bahādur; all are of course former Mongols one way or another, Shahrukh a Tīmūrid, Chu Ti in style—and perhaps partly by blood—very much a Mongol.[45] This persistence of a common framework has not been easy for historians of national states to see. The example just given, for example, comes up in a volume devoted to describing an allegedly traditional "Chinese world order." It may be, however, that the really important world order was the model of international relations among khans.[46]

Finally, the importance of economics must not be forgotten. Although the initial Mongol conquests of the thirteenth century did great damage, that was compensated by the growth, over the decades that followed, of pan-Eurasian trade under the *pax Mongolica.* The damaging division of China between north and south was ended, as too was the hostility between the steppe and the forest zone in Russia. For the first time in history, something like regular trade and diplomacy could be carried out over a territory ranging from Eastern Europe to Southeast Asia. Initially such benefits were probably not part of the Mongol plan, but they developed nevertheless, so much so that the later history, for example of the Golden Horde and its successors in Russia, cannot be understood without reference to shifts in overland trade, and their ultimate supersession by new sea and riverine routes that bypassed Inner Asia.

The legacy of Tīmūr, to which Spuler devotes considerable attention, is in certain respects more difficult to evaluate than that of Jingiz and his immediate successors. Tīmūr was no administrator; his conquests, moreover, were extremely destructive. As Spuler sums up; "The effects of Tīmūr's failure to integrate his conquests were felt immediately [on his death, February 18, 1405] The estate which he had left had none of those qualities of permanence which had marked the empire of Jingiz Khān; and his enterprises, seen as a whole, were shown to have been not only hurtful

Tīmūr Lenk, Tamurlane the Great on his throne.

in the extreme but also intrinsically futile. To Western Asia and the civilizations of Islām, as also to Caucasia and oriental Christianity, they brought nothing but destruction and decay, with no such benefits as had accrued from the opening up of world-wide communications a century and a half earlier" (page 68).

Tīmūr Lenk leads his army through the mountains down to the plains of India.

But this very failure to keep the empire united was itself of great importance. Tīmūr never conquered China: his most important achievement had been to bring Persia and most of the Middle East into an empire that was based in Inner Asia, in Transoxiana. But as authority fragmented after Tīmūr's death, the result was that Persia permanently split from Transoxiana, as two new dynasties came into being: in Persia, the Safavids; in Transoxiana, the Shaibanids, who ended the last Timurid dynasty in 1507. This division redrew the political and cultural map of the region in ways whose impact is still felt today.

The Safavids (1501-1736) traced their origins back to the Safaviyya, "a widespread sūfī order centered on Ardabīl on the south-western coastal region of the Caspian Sea, and named after Shaikh Safī al-Dīn Ishāq (1252-1334). "Never," writes R. M. Savory "was the Divine Right of Kings more fully developed than by the Safavid shahs. [Their founder] considered himself to be the living emanation of the godhead, the Shadow of God upon earth, and the representataive of the Hidden Imām by virtue of direct descent from the Seventh Imām of the Twelver Shī'a."[47]

Certainly this was a dramatic departure from previous patterns of rule and legitimation, but perhaps not so great as might be thought. For the fact was that because his rule was based in Transoxiana, even Tīmūr himself had to mix the legitimating power of the Turco-Mongol tradition with many strands drawn from Islam. He sought the blessings of Sufi shaikhs for his campaigns, and his victories were regularly attributed, by pious commentators, "less to his numberless armies than to the will of the religious figures in his retinue." Monuments to Sufi saints were among the most splendid works of Timurid architecture. And on Tīmūr's tombstone, a spurious genealogy traces his descent back to the fourth caliph 'Alī (c. 600-661), the cousin and son-in-law of Muhammad, who is venerated by Shi'ites as the Prophet's true successor.[48] So subsequent developments in Persia were to some extent foreshadowed in Tīmūr's time.

The division between Persia and Transoxiana that emerged after Tīmūr's death, however, proved enduring. In 1510 Bābar, as we have seen a proclaimed Timurid, attempted to reunite Persia and Transoxiana by allying with the Safavids. He succeeded initially in conquering Bukhārā and Samarqand, but in 1512, after a defeat north of Bukhārā was forced to withdraw to Harāt: Persia and Transoxiania went their separate ways (and Bābar went on to establish the Mughal empire in India).

Bābar's defeat had two very important results. First, "the Amu-Dar'ya became, and remained for centuries, the frontier between the two great powers of Safavid Iran and Shaibanid Transoxiana and their successors, and thus between the Shi'ite and Sunni sections of Islam"; at the same time, the defeat made clear that "the strength of the Turkic peoples of Central Asia was no longer sufficient, as it had been several times since the eleventh century, for them to take control of the Iranian plateau." Culturally, this opened the way to ethnic differentiation: the eventual decline of Persian culture and language in Inner Asia and its replacement by Turkic. Politically, it meant the marginalization of the Central Asian territories that had for centuries been the sources of conquest and authority. This was because, as Spuler notes, the states of Transoxiana "could exert an influence outside that region only if they expanded towards the Iranian plateau to become rulers of a significant part of the Muslim world . . . [Tīmūr's successors] failed to invade the heart of the Islamic world, notwithstanding their power in the sixteenth century, and played no part in world history. Henceforward the importance of Central Asia was to be no greater than that of the other countries bordering on the Islamic federation."[49]

Spuler pays considerable attention to the rule in India of both Tīmūr and Bābar. Whether Bābar in fact possessed any but the most remote connection to the Mongols of Jingiz is debatable. As the *Cambridge History of Iran* reminds us, the princes in Transoxiana, "regardless of their respective genealogies, even if they boasted descent from Chingiz Khān himself, were, like their peoples, Turks or Turkicised. It is doubtful, even in the case of the inhabitants of Mughalistān, who called themselves Mongols and were thus designated by other ethic groups, whether by this time they spoke the Mongol language."[50] More important than the issue of ethnicity, however, is the way that the Mughals consolidated the position of Islam in India. This has usually been overshadowed by the arrival of Westerners, signaled by the Portuguese arrival in the subcontintent, and acquisition of Goa in 1510, on the eve of Bābar's advance. The continuing Hindu-Muslim tensions in the subcontinent may suggest, however, that in the long view Bābar is at least as important as Vasco da Gama.

Although Bertold Spuler was an orientalist in the old German sense of the word: a meticulous textual scholar, impressive in linguistic command (fluent in French, English, Russian, Polish, Arabic, Turkish, Persian, and Italian, among others), respectful of chronological exactitude and impatient with speculation and grand but schematic comparisons, his work was nevertheless informed by an awareness of the sorts of broad issues mentioned above. He was, after all, a specialist on the Mongols and on the history of Islam, which he studied not—as is still done today—in a vacuum, isolated from Europe and its historical experience—but rather as important, if usually missing, pieces of European history. Spuler was well aware of the intricate cultural and diplomatic connections between the realms of Islam and Europe. He wrote an early work about European diplomacy with the Ottoman empire in connection with the conclusion of the Russian-Turkish war of 1736-1739.[51] Something of the same interest, not just in dynasties, but also in diplomatic and political relations among states, can be detected in this book as well. Finally, like many Germans of the twentieth century, he looked to the Mongol heritage as an approach to understanding Russia.

Spuler's book is straightforward and his prose is unembellished. Some readers may find it hard to see in it more than a thicket of names and dates. They are mistaken. Understand the Mongols, we said at the outset, and you have a framework for Eurasian history. European specialists regularly recur to the division of Charlemagne's empire in 843; it contained in potentiality both the future shape of Europe and many of its problems. Something similar can be said of the Mongol empires and their more numerous divisions—but of course Eurasia is vastly bigger than Europe. The areas around which the domains of the successors of Jingiz and Tīmūr coalesced, and the lines along which they divided, reflect many of the basic geographic, demographic, cultural, and political contours of the Eurasian continent.[52] And given the flux introduced into that area by the collapse of one great communist empire—the Soviet—and the possible reconstitution of another—the Chinese—those basic contours are even more important to understand today than they were when this book was first published in 1960.

Arthur Waldron
Providence, R. I.
December 1993

Arthur Waldron is author of *The Great Wall of China: From History to Myth* (Cambridge University Press, 1990) and co-author of *The Modernization of Inner Asia* (Armonk, H.Y.: M. E. Sharpe, 1991), among other works. Trained at Harvard, he is currently Professor of Strategy at the U.S. Naval War College and Adjunct Professor of East Asian Studies at Brown University.

NOTES

1. One exception is Thomas T. Allsen, *Mongol Imperialism: the Policies of the Grand Qan Möngke in China, Russia, and the Islamic Lands, 1251-1259* (Berkeley: University of California Press, 1987).
2. Morris Rossabi, "Genghis Khan," in *Encylopedia of Asian History*, ed. Ainslie T. Embree (New York: Scribner's, 1988), vol. i, pp. 496-498.
3. Beatrice Forbes Manz, *The Rise and Rule of Tamerlane* (Cambridge: Cambridge University Press, 1989); "Timur," in *Encyclopedia of Asian History*, vol. iv, pp. 100-102.
4. Arthur N. Waldron, "Karakorum," in *Encyclopedia of Asian History*, vol. ii, pp. 272-73.
5. Rhoads Murphey, Jr. "Samarkand," in *Encyclopedia of Asian History*, vol. iii, p. 374.
6. See Morris Rossabi, *Khubilai Khan: His Life and Times* (Berkeley: University of California Press, 1988).
7. The present volume is part of the series, *The Muslim World: A Historical Survey*, published in Leiden by E. J. Brill. The other volumes are *The Age of the Caliphs* (also by Spuler, 1960), *The Last Great Muslim Empires* (1969), and *Modern Times* (1981).
8. Allsen, *Mongol Imperialism*, p. 7.
9. See John Masson Smith, Jr. "The Mongols and World-Conquest." Paper Presented at the International Congress of Mongolists, Ulaanbaatar, 1992.
10. Allsen, p. 225.
11. On this battle, see John Masson Smith, Jr. " 'Ayn Jālut: Mamlūk Success or Mongol Failure," *Harvard Journal of Asiatic Studies* 42.2 (1984), pp. 307-45.
12. Denis Sinor, ed., *The Cambridge History of Early Inner Asia* (Cambridge: Cambridge University Press, 1990) provides a good introduction to this history.
13. See Smith, "World-Conquest," pp. 5-8 for discussion of this point.
14. Allsen, p. 190.
15. Allsen, pp. 219-220.
16. Allsen, pp. 56-57.
17. Allsen, pp. 70-74.
18. Allsen, pp. 45-50.
19. Allsen, pp. 119-124.
20. Allsen, pp. 144-151; 171.
21. For a review see Arthur N. Waldron, "Nomadism," in *Encyclopedia of Asian History*, vol. iii, pp. 129-131.
22. *Han shu* (Chung-hua shu-chü ed.), 94B.3834, cited in Arthur Waldron, *The Great Wall of China: From History to Myth* (Cambridge: Cambridge University Press, 1990), p. 35. On settled stereotypes of the nomad, see Ruth I. Meserve, "The Inhospitable Land of the Barbarian," *Journal of Asian History* 16.1 (1982), pp. 51-89.
23. A.M. Khazanov, *Nomads and the Outside World* (Cambridge: Cambridge University Press, 1983), pp. 85 ff., provides an excellent discussion of the origins of nomadism.
24. B. Shirendev, *Mongol ardyn khuvsgalyn tuukh (Istoriia Mongol'skoi narodnoi revoliutsii)* (Ulan Bator, 1969), p. 20, quoted in V. V. Graivoronskii, *Ot kochego obraza zhizni k osedlosti (na opyte MNR)* (Moscow: "Nauka," 1979), p. 27.
25. Graivoronskii, *Ot kochego obraza zhizni k osedlosti*, p. 37.
26. See Fredrik Barth, *Nomads of South Persia: The Basseri Tribe of the Khamseh Confederacy* (London: George Allen & Unwin, Ltd., 1961), p. 107 *et passim.*
27. Khazanov, *Nomads and the Outside World*, p. 240.
28. Khazanov, p. 162.
39. Khazanov, *passim.*
30. Khazanov, p. 240.

31. See in particular Thomas J. Barfield, *The Perilous Frontier: Nomadic Empires and China, 221 BC to AD 1757* (Oxford: Blackwell, 1989), *passim.*
32. John Masson Smith, Jr., letter to the editor of the *Times Literary Supplement*, February 5, 1993, p. 15; see also "The Barbarian Invaders" (unpublished manuscript, 1986), and "The Mongols and World-Conquest." Professor Smith is preparing a book on this general topic.
33. Joseph Fletcher, "Turco-Mongolian Monarchic Tradition in the Ottoman Empire," *Harvard Ukrainian Studies* 3-4 (1979-1980): 236-51; Allsen: 218-219 note 4.
34. See Edward L. Dreyer, *Early Ming China: A Political History 1355-1435* (Stanford: Stanford University Press, 1982); also John Dardess, "From Mongol Empire to Yüan Dynasty: Changing Forms of Imperial Rule in Mongolia and Central Asia" *Monumenta Serica* 30 (1972-73), 117-165; *Conquerors and Confucians: Aspects of Political Change in Late Yüan China* (New York: Columbia University Press, 1973); Elizabeth Endicott-West, *Mongolian Rule in China: Local Administration in the Yüan Dynasty* (Cambridge, Mass.: Council on East Asian Studies, Harvard University and the Harvard Yenching Institute, 1989).
35. On the military, see Romeyn Taylor, Yüan origins of the *Wei-so* system" in *Chinese Government in Ming Times: Seven Studies*, Charles O. Hucker (New York: Columbia University Press, 1969), pp. 23-40; Waldron, *Great Wall*, 72-73; for culture more generally, see Henry Serruys, "Remains of Mongol Customs in China during the Early Ming Period," *Monumenta Serica* 16.1-2 (1957), pp. 137-190.
36. See Waldron, *Great Wall*, pp. 74-81.
37. Waldron, p. 73.
38. Charles J. Halperin, *Russia and the Golden Horde: The Mongol Impact on Medieval Russian History* (Bloomington: Indiana University Press, 1985).
39. J. L. I. Fennell, *Ivan the Great of Moscow* (London: Methuen & Co., Ltd., 1961), p. 17.
40. See Fennell, *Ivan the Great*, pp. 316-323.
41. For Ivan III's ending of vassaldom to the Golden Horde, see Fennell, pp. 79-88.
42. Halperin, *Russia and the Golden Horde*, pp. 70-74.
43. Halperin, p. 60.
44. Bertold Spuler, *The Mongols in History*, transl. by Geoffrey Wheeler (New York: Praeger Publishers, 1971), pp. 105-106.
45. Joseph F. Fletcher, "China and Central Asia, 1368-1884" in *The Chinese World Order: Traditional China's Foreign Relations*, ed. John King Fairbank (Cambridge, Mass.: Harvard University Press, 1968), 206-224.
46. The essays in Morris Rossabi, ed., *China among Equals: The Middle Kingdom and its Neighbors, 10th-14th centuries* (Berkeley: University of California Press, 1983) do not make exactly this argument, but they provide a good survey, and one by no means incompatible with it, of some of the actual patterns of Eurasian diplomacy at about this period.
47. R. M. Savory, "The Safavid Administrative System," in *The Cambridge History of Iran*, ed. Peter Jackson and Laurence Lockhart (Cambridge: Cambridge University Press, 1986), vol. vi, p. 352.
48. On this topic, see Beatrice Forbes Manz, "Tamerlane and the Symbolism of Sovereignty," *Iranian Studies* 21.1-2 (1988), pp. 105-122; quote is at p. 117; *idem, The Rise and Rule of Tamerlane*, pp. 14-19.
49. Spuler, *The Mongols in History*, pp. 110-111.
50. H. H. Roemer, "The Successors of Tīmūr," in *The Cambridge History of Iran*, vol. vi, p. 119.
51. *Die europaeische Diplomatie in Konstantinopel bis zum Frieden von Belgrad, 1739* (Berlin, 1935).
52. For a survey of the recent period, see Cyril E. Black *et al.*, *The Modernization of Inner Asia* (Armonk, N.Y.: M. E. Sharpe, 1991).

TRANSLATOR'S PREFACE

Under the general editorship of Professor BERTOLD SPULER of the University of Hamburg a group of specialists is preparing in German a series of "Manuals of Oriental Studies" *(Handbuch der Orientalistik)*. The series is likely to form a most valuable compendium of modern knowledge in this vast field.

The sixth volume of the series is to be a "History of the Islamic Countries" *(Geschichte der Islamischen Länder)*, surveying as a whole the development of the many lands in which the religion and civilization of Islam are, or have been, predominant. Parts I and II of this history have already been published by Messrs. E. J. BRILL of Leiden, Holland; they are *Die Chalifenzeit*: *Entstehung und Zerfall des Islamischen Weltreiches* (1952) and *Die Mongolenzeit* (1953), both from the pen of Prof. Spuler. They have been translated under the titles *The Muslim World: a Historical Survey:* Part I, *The Age of the Caliphs*; Part II, *The Mongol Period*. Part III, *Neuzeit*, has also now appeared (1959).

The translations have been approved by the author, who has added passages and notes which do not appear in the original.

The transliteration systems used are, so far as possible, formal and consistent. This may be useful for reference to articles in the Encyclopaedia of Islam.

Gratitude is due to Messrs. E. J. BRILL's printers for the great trouble they have taken.

F. R. C. BAGLEY

MCGILL UNIVERSITY,
MONTREAL, CANADA
AND DURHAM UNIVERSITY,
ENGLAND.

THE MONGOL EMPIRE

West and north-west of China lies an immense tract of land which holds the sources of the great Siberian rivers but is made up mainly of steppe and partly of desert. The climate at so great a distance from the sea is of the interior continental type with extreme variations of temperature. The north is gashed by the rift of Lake Baikal; the west is ribbed with high mountains which come together in the Altai complex. After the great eastward migratory flood of the Indo-European peoples had subsided, this region became around 200 B.C. the gathering place of opposing forces which were to transform the population picture of Central Asia and determine its fundamental character till to-day. The region was inhabited by two nations living side by side and displaying many common features, but markedly distinct in language: the *Turks* and the *Mongols*. From the beginning of the Christian era, groups belonging to these two nations are encountered with increasing frequency in Chinese historical sources. Their repeated raids for plunder attracted more and more Chinese notice, until at last only the construction of the Great Wall put a stop to their devastations.

The great westward migration of the Huns started in this region; and from the 6th-7th centuries A.D. onwards its Turkish inhabitants, who had come under the cultural influences of both Īrān and China, grew rapidly in political stature. They were able to thrust south-westwards into the land now known after them as Turkistān and create important political entities such as the *Kök Türk* and *Uigur* states, which not only took a considerable part in the affairs of Central Asia but also, through their religious policy and commercial activity, played a quite significant rôle in the history of civilization. In the same period, the first Turks pushed through to the Volga and even into Mesopotamia. The Mongols during this period remained in their homeland and took no part on the stage of world events. They were then frequently designated as *Tatars*, after one of their most powerful component groups, the Tatar tribe, who dwelt in the extreme east: to-day, however, the name has a different meaning (see below p. 50)[1].

The Mongol nation was divided into various tribes. In the extreme

---

[1] Bertold Spuler, *Geschichte Mittelasiens*, in "*Handbuch der Orientalistik*" V/5.

west, between the upper Irtysh and Orkhon rivers north of the Altai mountains, dwelt the *Naiman*. On account of the proximity of the Turkish Uigurs to the south, the Naiman had at an early stage absorbed numerous elements of Central Asian culture, such as the Uigur alphabet and Christianity of the Nestorian rite. In civilization they were the most advanced of the Mongol tribes. Not far behind were the *Keräit*, who adjoined them on the east, along and to the south of the Orkhon; at the middle of the first millennium A.D. the majority of the Keräit had also adopted Nestorian Christianity. North of the Keräit, on the middle and lower Selenga, lived the *Merkit*; and west of the Merkit and north of the Naiman lived the very backward *Oirats*. The Chinese classified the Mongol tribes according to their grade of civilization into "White Tatars" of the southern zone immediately north of the Chinese frontier, "Black Tatars" further to the north, and lastly "Savage Tatars" or forest dwellers who, in contrast with the other nomadic tribes, lived by hunting and were particularly devoted to the *Shamanist* religion. For long to come, *Shamans* (priests) originating from these areas were considered to be more reliable and efficacious than others.

More or less simultaneously with their absorption of Christianity, the Mongols began to go ahead politically and economically. In the early years of the 10th century they flung the Turkish *Kirghiz* back from Mongolia to the Yenisei, and drove the *Khitai* into North China. There the Khitai founded the important *Liao* empire, and as a result, the Mongols came for the first time into close and regular contact with Chinese civilization. At the same time the Naiman moved to the west, devastating Central Asia in repeated campaigns. The Liao empire collapsed in 1125, and a section of the Liao fled westwards from China to the Tārim and Farghānā basins; they there founded a new state, the *Qara-Khitai* kingdom, which lasted 100 years.

With the collapse of the Liao empire, Mongol life apparently reverted to its old rut. Among the various tribes, power remained as previously in the hands of a few prominent clan-groups, who contended or combined with one another in constantly changing coalitions. The questions generally at issue were control of tribal subdivisions, ownership of flocks or simply robbery. No sort of higher concept is discernible in the picture of the age.

On this scene of never-ending strife, a certain *Yesugai* appeared. He was a scion of an ancient noble family of the tribe of *Mangkhol*; but concerning his importance and authority the sources differ. Many describe him as a simple decurion or commander of a ten-man section, while others represent him as an independent prince. No outstanding deed distinguished his life, which was spent in incessant fighting to defend his property. When he died in 1165, he left several sons, the eldest of whom, *Temujin,* was then about ten years old and in accordance with Mongol custom was residing with his future parents-in-law. The misfortune which thus befell the boy compelled him to shift for himself from an early age and find means of securing his patrimony. To vindicate his claims, he was obliged to seek out influential friends.

He was in fact able to win the backing of the prince of the Keräit, *Toghril (To'oril),* for a campaign against the Merkit tribe, who had raided his camp and made off with his wife *Borte.* His victory and recovery of Borte earned him such prestige that he succeeded around the year 1196 in getting himself proclaimed paramount chief of the Mangkhol tribe. At the same time he received the title (linguistically still unexplained) of *Jingiz Khān.* The competent dignitaries of the Mongol tribes, including his influential friend *Jamukha,* concurred in this advancement.

Hitherto Jingiz Khān's efforts had followed the usual course. By dint of his personal exertions he had gathered round him a host of devoted supporters whom he could trust without reserve. His successes permitted him to grant rich rewards and high-ranking offices to his friends, and drew to his side a large proportion of the wavering elements ever present in the steppe. None of these developments overshot the range of normal adjustments within the nomad aristocracy, or had any significance in world history.

But Temujin's dynamic energy reached out for more distant goals. Certain deeds of brigandage, insignificant in themselves, compelled him to take action against his former friend Jamukha. Whether these struggles denote the emergence of two movements, one based on the broad masses supporting Jamukha, and the other aristocratic under Jingiz Khān, as recent research, particularly in Russia, has claimed, is a question which must remain doubtful in the light of the existing sources. It may well be that the upheavals in Mongolia and the overlapping cultural influences resulting from the migrations of the preceding centuries had produced social tensions which found release in the struggles between the various potentates of the steppe. The decisive battle, in which the number of troops taking part is said to have been already considerable, turned out unfavourably for Temujin, who was forced to retire to the headwaters of the Onon. It was only when he succeeded in routing the Tatar tribe — and thereby in doing a favour to the *Kin* dynasty now ruling in North China — that his prestige revived. His ally Toghril obtained the Chinese title

Wang Khān. The other Mongol tribes in the steppe now saw clearly that Temujin was aiming at something higher than his former station and could only be restrained if they formed a league, of which Jamukha was made head. In this perilous situation, Jingiz Khān displayed all the pluck and craft of a hardy nomad leader. He contrived to defeat separately each of the tribes, including the Merkit and the Naiman, and so to attain by force the highest place in Mongolia. His adversaries nevertheless made one more attempt to eliminate him, by a conspiracy in which Wang Khān took part. Temujin, however, got wind of the scheme in good time, and successfully attacked and destroyed Wang Khān and with him the Keräit tribe. Before long the Naiman, Jamukha and the Merkit were also crushed in hard-fought struggles (1204). The survivors of these tribes were partly exterminated and partly incorporated into units of Temujin's army. Jamukha appears to have been captured and put to death shortly afterwards. *Küchlüg*, the leader of the Naiman, who either was or had been a Nestorian Christian, fled westwards to the kingdom of the Qara-Khitai, where he was able to seize power.

This scarcely interrupted series of victories and the almost complete smashing of the hostile tribes raised Jingiz Khān in the course of a decade to the position of absolute sovereign of Mongolia and conferred on him a power over his own people such as no previous Mongol tribal ruler had even remotely attained. He now united all the Mongol tribes under his sceptre and could thus view himself as the exponent of the general will of the nation. His first desire was to give a legal basis to the power which his success had embodied in his person. He used his influence to bring about the holding in 1206 of a great national assembly or *Quryltai*, which appointed him supreme lord of the Mongols and confirmed his title of Jingiz Khān. This act set a seal on the decision of the *Mongols* — as the tribes now collectively called themselves, after the Mangkhol — to conduct their politics henceforward as a single unit. It invested the new ruler with a supernatural aura, by virtue of which his commands seemed not merely to issue from an established wordly authority but also to give voice to divine instructions. Further developments, of course, depended wholly on the will, energy and military success of Jingiz Khān. He alone had the power to give real meaning to his new dignity and thereby realize the aspirations of the Mongol people.

The Mongols doubtless had such aspirations, even if the whole community did not press with equal zeal for their fulfilment. The leading groups, however, knew exactly what they wanted; and as always in semi-nomadic feudal societies, only they mattered. With the typical steppe-dwellers' instinct to acquire land, they longed to subdue the adjacent regions of higher civilization — not so much, of course, with the object of learning anything of the civilizations in question as with an eye to the limitless booty and also to a more luxurious way of life. They no longer felt satisfied with looting expeditions such as their forefathers had carried on for years. They set as their goal the foundation of a powerful far-flung state, of a universal empire, which in their design should embrace the entire (known) world. Such ideas, though peculiar, were not in all respects new. China had long been regarded by its inhabitants as the "Middle Kingdom", the centre of the earth, though they had never in fact striven for world domination; and the centralist political principle of the Chinese empire may have contributed to the rigidly unitary concept of the incipient Mongol empire. Some contribution was no doubt also made by Christian theories of an oecumenical church under a single central leadership, since certain Mongol tribes had for about two centuries been firm adherents of Nestorian Christianity and had thus had access to Christian thought. Insofar as inferences can be drawn when direct evidence of contemporary political ideas is lacking, it would seem that a peculiar metamorphosis of Christian doctrinal theories into political notions had considerable importance in the development of the Mongol concept of world empire.

Nations consumed with missionary ideas — whether these have a purely spiritual or a partly mundane quality — acquire a formidable power of expansion, as shown for instance by the rise of Islām. Once this idea had taken root among the ruling classes of the Mongol nation, there was intense pressure for its fulfilment. The elevation of Jingiz Khān meant that a leader had been appointed to carry out the national will. There can be no doubt that the new Great Khān believed that he carried a divine commission. His whole attitude to neighbouring states, as attested by many different sources, is sufficient proof of this, as are his proud words which the Mongols often repeated: "*One* sun in heaven, *one* Lord on earth". When Jingiz Khān reorganized the national strength of the Mongols and subjected them to hitherto unknown discipline, he saw himself as an instrument of God; and Mongol public opinion was very largely willing to go along with him. There can be no other explanation of the fact that henceforward he did not encounter any opposition worth mentioning among his own people. The Mongol nation thus acquired the strength with which to found an empire unparalleled in extent by any previously seen in world history.

The sense of an immediate God-given mandate did not, of course, suffice to transform the will of heaven into immediate reality. For this it was necessary first to build up a material strength outstripping the resources of the neighbouring states: that is to organize an aggressive army. The soldierly valour of the Mongol tribes had often been proved during the preceeding centuries; it had now to be integrated in a national force. Jingiz Khān set about this task without delay. He divided the whole army into units on the "decade" system, so that every ten men formed a section under their own leader; ten such sections made up a company or "century", and ten of these a battalion or "chiliad". A division of ten thousand men, headed by a general, constituted an independent tactical formation, and the individual soldier was permanently attached to a particular divison. These last units fitted into the topmost structural grouping into "right wing", "left wing" and "centre", which was a permanent feature of the army and had probably not originated solely from some fortuitous order of battle. The newly created army was imbued with a spirit of the sternest discipline. Any breach of duty or act of cowardice was relentlessly punished with death. Jingiz Khān's unfailing confidence in the comrades of his youth, who now held posts of high command as his generals, placed at his disposal a number of right hand men who could be trusted to carry out his orders and directives absolutely. While foreign, probably Chinese, models may have influenced the shaping of the army, the Great Khān's rôle in this respect was a unique and highly personal contribution of his unquestionable genius.

The extraordinary qualities of his character are not only to be seen in his amazing military victories. No less importance must be ascribed to his achievement as lawgiver and indeed as organizer of the Mongol nation. He collected, arranged and expanded the legal notions of his compatriots and produced the *Yasa(q)* or fundamental law of the state, by which Mongol public life was ordered for long after his death[1]. Besides military regulations, the Yasa contained provisions governing civilian life; it emphasized the principle of private property and accordingly punished theft and brigandage with great severity, making death the penalty even for quite petty offences. Family life was also regulated; women enjoyed ample independence and high respect, in complete contrast (generally speaking) with the position accorded to them over the centuries by Islāmic law. Women also distinguished themselves as auxiliaries on military campaigns; they not only took charge of household management and the upbringing of children, but often accompanied the army on its campaigns and looked after the needs of

[1] G. V. Vernadskiĭ (See Bibliography, p. 110).

the fighting men. During battles, the women were kept hidden in wagons at the encampment, but in emergencies they frequently joined in combat. This high status of women explains why female portraits first made their appearance in oriental art during the Mongol period. To maintain the administration, provision was made for a dual taxation system, with a land-tax for agriculturists, graded according to soil values and crop yields, and a turnover tax for traders. Jingiz Khān also set up an official postal service, which transmitted intelligence and instructions from one end of the state to the other with remarkable speed; this too was probably copied from ancient models.

Such was the prestige of Jingiz Khān that his writ quickly prevailed through all the length and breadth of Mongolia; and the Mongol people, with their consciousness of a higher mission, were moulded into a powerful, aggressive body, which was soon to prove itself superior in elemental force to the adjoining empires. Only a few years were needed for Temujin to complete the internal organization of his state and acquire weapons and other equipment through opening trade relations. Then he launched the campaigns which were to result in the foundation of the universal Mongol empire. First he turned eastwards, against the country which by reason of long-standing cultural and commercial relations inevitably exerted most attraction on the Mongols: namely China. Two vigorously conducted expeditions brought him in 1215 before the capital of the Kin dynasty, which finally yielded to his assault. The North China empire then collapsed, and the Mongols began to establish themselves in the northern half of the huge Chinese domain. The South China empire remained for the time being undisturbed.

The rapidity of this victory in the east meant much to the Mongols. It spared their resources for further undertakings and above all gave them confidence in their own strength. An empire such as North China must for all its actual weaknesses have appeared immensely mighty to the steppe-dwellers' eye; and if they had succeeded in overwhelming it with such remarkable speed, their success was a sure sign of the divine intention to entrust the governance of the world to the Mongols. The Chinese attitude towards the foreign conquerors was, on the whole, the same as it had nearly always been throughout their country's long history; they submitted to the authority of the foreigners and brought to bear on them the tremendous force of Chinese civilization to which the latter soon succumbed, but themselves never forgot that the intruders were aliens whose rule was incompatible with the principle of Chinese sovereignty in the Middle Kingdom. Chinese nevertheless joined the Mongol services, particularly at the capital city of *Qara Qorum*, which arose during this period on the Upper Orkhon. A descendant of the fallen Khitai dynasty, *Ye-lü-chu-ts'ai*, became minister to the Khāns and performed a most important function in the building up of the Mongol empire. It may be taken for certain that he did not stand alone, but had around him numerous real or assimilated Chinese who served as his colleagues and subordinates in the administration and as bearers of Chinese civilization and commerce. The inflow of Chinese culture had fruitful effects on the Mongols. Chinese ideas found their way into the Yasa and thus into Mongol usage. Chinese concepts of the art of war, and above all Chinese weapons including gunpowder, were put to use by the Mongols in their subsequent campaigns.

The success in China was thus the starting point for the further victories of the Mongols. Only two years after the conclusion of the Chinese campaign, Jingiz Khān turned his gaze to the west. In that quarter lay the realm of the *Khwārizm-Shāhs*, which at this moment under its ruler *Muḥammad II* had reached the summit of its might (see "*The Age of the Caliphs*", p. 97). Since the voluntary submission of the Uigurs to Jingiz Khān's suzerainty in 1207, the Khwārizmian state had appeared to be at least as formidable an opponent as the North China empire. The course of Mongol-Khwārizmian relations cannot now be determined at all clearly. Certain later oriental sources report that the energetic Caliph of Baghdād, *al-Nāṣir* (1180-1225), when in difficulties with Muḥammad II, addressed himself to the Mongol ruler and urged him to attack the Khwārizm-Shāh in the rear. This account would signify that it was the Caliph himself, nominally at least still the supreme leader of Islām, who albeit unwittingly brought down on Islām the greatest calamity which had befallen it in its history. Against this are reports to the effect that Muḥammad II had long been anxious about his north-eastern neighbours and busy procuring information on their military strength and internal conditions through spies. Conversely, it is possible that the merchants sent by Jingiz Khān not only had the function of establishing commercial relations, but were spies too. In any case Muḥammad II viewed them as such and had all but a few of them despoiled and put to death.

To such treatment of their ruler's representatives the Mongols invariably reacted in one manner only: by immediately making war. Perhaps Muhammad II was unaware of this, because the usage was not yet known in Western Asia at that time. On several subsequent occasions the Islāmic world was to find that such would be the result of perfidy towards

Mongol ambassadors and envoys. After beating back a move by the Khwārizm-Shāh over the Oxus, Jingiz Khān thrust forward into Khurāsān, driving Muḥammad's army before him in a way which must have produced a most startling impression. Hitherto the Khwārizmian rulers of Īrān had been regarded as well-nigh invincible conquerors; now their might began to collapse almost without pause before the cohorts of Jingiz Khān. The new Mongol offensive technique of the surprise cavalry attact cannot have been the sole reason for this, as the numerous Turks in Muḥammad's army were already familiar with it; more probably the Khwārizmians were intimidated by the new siege devices, partly of Chinese origin, which the Mongols used. It would probably also not be incorrect to attribute Muḥammad II's failure very largely to the unreliability of the multinational Khwārizmian forces. The further west the Mongols advanced, the greater was the number of Turks who joined their army — voluntarily or perforce. By the time of the invasion of Khurāsān, Jingiz Khān's forces already consisted overwhelmingly of Turks. The Mongol ruler always made a point of enticing Turks in enemy armies to desert, with an appeal to them against the folly of "fraternal strife". Muḥammad almost certainly had trouble of this sort with his men at the very start of the campaign, while similar stirrings no doubt affected the troops still stationed in the rear; and the experience must have been one of the main reasons why he lost heart.

The headlong flight of their ruler left the great urban centres of Khurāsān — Marv, Bukhārā and Samarqand — in no position to hold out for long. With the retreat of the Khwārizmian army, they could have no hope of relief. After rejecting preliminary calls to surrender (which were a regular feature of Mongol warfare), they were unrelentingly besieged and then, with the help of novel methods — battering rams, catapults, fire-floats and smoking-out — were taken by storm. Their fate was dreadful. A great part of the population was pitilessly butchered, and this calamity ruined the economic and cultural prosperity of Central Asia; never since have its cities been able to recover in full their previous standing as life-centres of Islāmic civilization. It was the policy of the Mongols, however, to spare learned men, artists and technicians, who could be of use in their service, and also women and children, who were enslaved. Some of the men of military age were likewise passed over, but only so that they might be employed as cannon-fodder in subsequent sieges and assaults; they were driven ahead of the Mongol troops and forced into combat with their fellow-countrymen. There was no escape from their grim dilemma; either they made the charge up the walls of the cities, or if they held back, they were ruthlessly mown down.

These frightful methods and Muḥammad II's ceaseless retreat opened the way through northern Persia to Jingiz Khān's generals *Sübödei* and *Jebe*. In the course of a few years they thrust as far as the plateau of Āẕarbāyjān, where alone they continued to meet resistance; though not organized, this was kept up for several years by *Jalāl al-Dīn Mangūbirdī*, a son of Muḥammad II (who had meanwhile died) and a gallant adventurer. He marched through Īrān from the Caucasus to the Indus, fell back into northern India before a Mongol threat of encirclement, reappeared in ʿIrāq and then in Georgia, always at grips with Mongol detachments, and finally, in 1231, was killed by a Kurdish bandit.

The Mongols had meanwhile, in 1223, pushed around the eastern end of the Caucasus into southern Russia. In the battle of the Kalka river they had crushingly defeated an army got together at the last moment by some of the Russian princes, and thereafter they had plundered some of the trading cities of the Crimea. Then, on orders from Jingiz Khān, they had turned back to the east. The areas touched by the conquerors in Western Asia and eastern Europe were thus quite limited, and these areas were not effectively incorporated into the Mongol realm. Northern Persia, however, and especially Khurāsān, remained under strong Mongol influence. In Caucasia and Russia the expedition of 1223 represented no more than an episode, on a par with the frequent incursions by nomadic Turkish peoples which the Russian princes had experienced in recent times, but without any lasting repercussions on the political structure of East Europe.

Jingiz Khān was planning a new eastward onslaught when — probably on August 18, 1227 — he died. The empire which he had founded survived his loss. In the crisis following his death, no enemy stood at hand to overthrow the Mongol yoke. The unity of the empire, however, was not preserved. Jingiz Khān had decreed that it should be divided between his principal wife's four sons, who alone had taken part in state affairs. Ancient Mongol usage held the youngest son to be the chief heir and custodian of the paternal estate; and in conformity with this principle, the Mongolian homeland went to the youngest of the four, who was named *Tolui*. To the other three sons, the shares allotted were as follows: to *Jagatai* the territories north and north-east of the Oxus known to dwellers in the west as Transoxiana, to *Ögedei* the territories lying further east, and to the eldest, *Jochi*, the westernmost territories, i.e. Russia. This apportionment could not at the time be made fully effective, because the empire had not yet attained the amplitude envisaged by Jingiz Khān, who had been contemplating an advance to the western sea — though his notions about the geography of the west were probably somewhat vague. Furthermore, six months before Jingiz Khān's death Jochi also died, and his children consequently became their grandfather's direct heirs.

In decreeing this division of the immense territories of Central Asia — as regards China, he left no definite instructions — Jingiz Khān had not intended that the empire should be split into completely separate independent states, but had desired that one of his four sons should exercise supervision over his brothers as paramount ruler or *"Great Khān"*. In accordance with this desire, the supreme office had to be filled; and it was appropriate that this should be done by election, since nobody had been designated by the immortal founder. At a national assembly *(Quryltai)* held in 1229, the brothers agreed without much difficulty on *Ögedei*. He, however, had inherited none of his father's talents for war; in the accounts which have come down, he appears rather as a calm and not very forceful, but conscientious and astute, ruler. He extended and adorned with fine new edifices the capital city of Qara Qorum, made efforts to introduce fruit and vegetable cultivation into its inhospitable surroundings, organized the supply of food for Mongolia from China and opened up trade relations between his country and India and Western Asia. He was particularly interested in preparations to round off the imperial domain in accordance with his father's design, and thereby permit the endowment of his brothers with their prescribed territorial portions. Continued training in the military art was afforded by the subjugation of the rest of North China, by various lesser operations and also by the chase, which was organized systematically as a semi-military exercise.

In or around the year 1236, massive new armies were set in motion, mainly towards the west. Their principle objective was to subjugate at least the whole of eastern Europe; but an advance further west was included in the overall plan. By this means the sons of Jochi, among whom *Batu*, the second-born, was the most outstanding, were to acquire the heritage fixed for them by Jingiz Khān. The host of Mongol and Turkish troops rolled through the territory north of the Aral and Caspian seas, and fell first upon the kingdom of the *Volga Bulgars*, round the city of *Bulgār* (in Russian *Bolgáry*) on the middle Volga a little south of the present Kazán. This state had for several centuries played an important part in trade and politics as an emporium for goods from Central Asia and from eastern and northern Europe; but it now collapsed at the first blow.

The road to Russia then lay open. In the following year, the city states of Moscow, Múrom and Yarosláv and other principalities of the upper Volga region were overwhelmed. Some of the cities fell after a heroic defence; others offered no resistance to the conquerors, whose cavalry proved extraordinarily effective in these parts. The technical superiority of the newcomers from the east proved to be so great that it was quite impossible for the Russians to hold their ground. Only the forces of nature proved capable of halting the progress of the Mongols. While they were advancing against the city of Great Nóvgorod on Lake Ilmen, which held the key to the Baltic approaches, an early thaw set in. The invaders had been delayed by the resistance of the small town of Torzhók, and now they could no longer get across the Nóvgorod swamps; the mud which had made all the roads impassable even held up their horsemen. They therefore decided instead on a sweep to the south. After cutting diagonally through Russia west of Moscow, they reached Kozélsk. The storming of this fortress-city required more time and preparation than usual; but after its fall, the strangers invested *Kíev*, seat of the Grand Prince and of the Metropolitan Bishop of the old Russia and heart of the ancient state of the "*Rus*". The siege was of short duration, and on December 6, 1240, after the then Grand Prince, *Michael of Chernígov*, had fled, the city fell. In the resultant looting, many valuable artistic relics and architectural monuments were reduced to rubble. The early Russian (or in the Ukrainian view, the early Ukrainian) period of history was thus brought to a close; the political centre of gravity in East Europe shifted from there to a more northerly clime.

To the Mongols this great victory appeared only as a phase in their war venture, which was not meant to be confined to Russia. They accordingly moved forward through Podolia and Volhynia into Galicia, and in midwinter quelled the opposition of the state of Halycz. There the army split into groups, with the object of attacking the border-states of Central Europe simultaneously from several directions. It has been inferred from the course of the campaign — allowance being made for the vagueness of the invaders' geographical knowledge — that they had a grandiose strategic plan to encircle their enemies and crush them at a predetermined point; closer investigation and the inadequacy of the records show this to be pure conjecture, though the precision and immense scale of the movements of these Asiatic legions certainly do suggest overall planning.

One part of the Mongol army pushed through Galicia, beat the Poles at Chmielnik, took Krakow and then followed the Oder down to the recently founded German settlement of Breslau, which was destroyed. It may be true, though there is no authentic proof, that other Mongol detachments simultaneously executed a wide encircling movement through central Poland and Moravia, so as to arrive on the scene when the decisive battle took place on the Walstatt plain near Liegnitz on April 9, 1241. However this may be, Duke *Henry II* of Silesia and his German-Polish troops suffered a severe defeat, in which the Duke himself lost his life. The fact that the Mongols advanced no further to the west, but withdrew south-eastwards through the Silesian foothills and the Moravian Gap, where they besieged the city of Olmütz, can hardly have any other explanation than that their main objective was to bind together the various territories which they had conquered. In the light of their conduct elsewhere, no credit can be given to the theory that Duke Henry's vigorous resistance at Liegnitz deterred the Mongols from invading central Germany. The Mongols had probably by now begun to make use of geographical information supplied by prisoners of war, in accordance with their general practice of inveigling scientists and artists into their service.

The Mongol army groups in the south had meanwhile forced their way by two routes — through the central and the southern Carpathians — across Transylvania into Hungary. Here they took King *Béla IV* by complete surprise and on April 11, 1241, utterly defeated him on the Plain of Mohi. The northern army group continued to advance through Moravia and rejoined those now in Hungary. The whole foreland of Germany thus saw the passage of the victorious invaders. The conduct of the Mongols, however, was not consistent. In Silesia and Moravia, apart from eliminating hostile local forces at the battle of Liegnitz and capturing the city of Olmütz, they had merely plundered and moved on. In Hungary, on the other hand, they began to settle down; they minted in that country the only coins which have been found from the period. Their behaviour suggests that they had chosen the Danube-Tisza plain as well as the middle and lower Volga steppe to be a future dwelling place and grazing ground.

On December 11, 1241, however, at Qara Qorum, the Great Khān died. Thanks to the highly organized postal service, the news became rapidly known; and in all probability it was this event which determined Batu and his generals to retire eastwards with the bulk of their army. One corps moved along the Danube, another made a broad sweep through Croatia and Slavonia; then they pushed through Danubian Bulgaria back into the open country north of the Black Sea and along the Volga, whence Batu planned to observe the issue of the succession to the Great Khānate. He thus let slip from his grasp the conquests which he had made in Hungary. As a result, however, of the Mongol passage through Bulgaria, the king of that country submitted to the suzerainty of the Khāns on the Volga.

At that time, the cultural characteristics of Batu's horde — the *"Golden Horde"*, as it came to be termed — presumably after the Khān's Golden Tent — were still essentially nomadic. He therefore chose the more steppe-like parts of the middle and lower Volga grasslands and the area north-east of the Black Sea as the centre of Mongol settlement in East Europe. Here were to be found suitable grazing grounds for the victorious army's horses and ample room for the Mongol herdsmen who practised nomadism along the course of the Volga. In the neighbourhood of the present village of Selítrennoye, roughly midway between the modern cities of Stalingrád and Ástrakhan, the first capital of the new Mongol realm took shape. This was *Old Sarai*, which like Qara Qorum soon acquired an urban aspect. Here Batu used to spend at least the winter months and had palaces built for himself and his grandees. Before long the city became the scene of the first close contacts between the Mongols of Russia and the Islāmic civilization of Western Asia, as portrayed to us by the missionary and Papal emissary *Giovanni di Plano Carpini*, who passed through in 1245-46. Already the Mongol empire on the Volga — the *Ta(r)taria Aquilonaris* of medieval cosmography — appeared to Carpini as a well established entity. This empire, which had been brought into being by the campaigns of Batu, was to be ruled by him and his successors in accordance with the desire of his grandfather, Jingiz Khān. Its southern frontier was formed by the Caucasus mountains, the principal kingdom in which, Georgia, was obliged to accept a status of vassaldom to the Mongols.

It was not vouchsafed to Batu to extend his dominion any further. Disputes over the succession to the throne of all the Mongols filled the next ten years and forced him to devote his entire energies to Central Asian affairs. Since no arrangements had been made for the succession, the Mongol grandees at Qara Qorum provisionally appointed Ögedei's widow *Töregene* to be regent — another indication of the unique status held by women in Mongol society. Töregene strove with all the means at her disposal to secure for her son *Göyük* the reversion of his father's heritage. This was resisted by Batu, partly because he hoped to assert his own claim as the offspring of Jingiz Khān's eldest son and probably also because he was disinclined, for reasons of religious and cultural policy, to accept the leadership of Göyük. Like Jingiz Khān and Ögedei,

Batu viewed the various oecumenical religions in the Mongol realm with complete indifference. He remained true to the Shamanist faith of his forefathers, who acknowledged one sole God but at the same time viewed the sun and the moon, the earth and the water, as higher beings and offered prayers and sacrifices to them. The religious disputations reported to have been held in the presence of these rulers had not in any way weakened their standpoint. Göyük, however, belonged to a younger generation and represented different tendencies which then seemed about to triumph among the Mongols. Christianity of the Nestorian rite had already (as was earlier mentioned) been well known to the Mongols for several centuries; and with the great outward expansion of their conquering armies, it had acquired a new inner strength and missionary zeal. On the mind of Göyük it had left a deep impression; so much so that, even if he was possibly not himself a Nestorian, he nevertheless showed a very strong predilection for Christians and admitted them to the most favoured positions in his entourage. The choice of Göyük could not fail to signify a victory for Christianity and a setback for the old ideas and customs. Batu, however, was unable to prevent its coming to pass in 1246. The election has been described in detail by Giovanni di Plano Carpini, who was personally present. In the centre of the plain where it was held stood a huge voting tent, in which the eligible noblemen assembled. Round this as far as the eye could see were encamped the hordes of the Mongol nation, who demanded to be entertained with spectacles of every sort and observed with great curiosity the course of the actual voting and the cavalcade of the numerous foreign embassies, which in their eyes gave proof that the Mongol claim to world dominion had been made good. Such also was Göyük's interpretation of the errand of Giovanni di Plano Carpini; he believed that the Pope and King Louis IX of France were anxious to place themselves under his suzerainty. This conviction is clearly expressed in the reply which he handed to the Papal emissary[1].

The choice of Göyük foreshadowed an early outbreak of hostilities with Batu. Both sides were preparing for the recourse to arms and had already begun to move against each other when Göyük died in April 1248. His death put an end to all these difficulties — and also to the hopeful prospects which Christianity, in its Nestorian form, had enjoyed during his reign. The great transformation in the life of the Mongol

---

[1] The letter to the Pope has been preserved in the Vatican archives. It is reproduced in ALBERT MARIA AMMANN, *Kirchenpolitische Wandlungen im Ostbaltikum nach dem Tode Alexander Newskis*, Rome, 1936, after p. 284. ("*Analecta Christiana Orientalia*", CV).

people which had then seemed impending was delayed for a while; and when it eventually did take place under the influence of the highly civilized surroundings into which the conquerors had intruded, it turned out in a way quite different from that which might have been expected when Göyük was elected to the throne.

As the regency was once again entrusted to the deceased Great Khān's widow, *Oghul Gaimysh* by name, Batu thought fit to remain in Central Asia close to the scene of the election. This time the electors showed themselves disposed to pass over Ögedei's descendants and admit the right of succession in the elder line, that is in the posterity of Jochi. Since Batu himself was recognized as the head of that line (although his elder brother *Orda*[1] was still living), he had excellent prospects of becoming Great Khān. On account of his age, however, he declined election and recommended to the electors the descendants of Jingiz Khān's youngest son Tolui, who had hitherto remained in the background. It was finally decided in 1251 to elect *Möngke (Mangū)*, an energetic and courageous prince who stood close to Batu, having taken part in the campaigns in Russia. A plot hatched by another prince who wished to influence the electors' choice in his own favour was promptly unmasked and suppressed. Batu could return to the Volga feeling highly gratified with the outcome of the election.

Thanks to an estimable mother, Möngke had benefited from an excellent upbringing. Though he was not a Christian as she was, his attitude was so tolerant that under his rule all the great religions were able to make headway side by side, and Nestorian Christianity had an opportunity to cultivate even more intensively its vast mission field. At the same time the Muslims and the Buddhists were able to send missionaries of their faiths into Mongolia. Devotees of the ancient Mongol faith meanwhile became fewer and less prominent. At the capital, Qara Qorum, which was being more and more lavishly embellished, churches, mosques and Buddhist temples rose aloft in jealous emulation. A Papal Legate, the North German Franciscan *Wilhelm von Rubruck (de Rubruquis)*, who during this period travelled via Sarai on the Volga to Qara Qorum, has left us a vivid picture of the brisk commercial activity in the city and of the rivalry of the different religious denominations and the Great Khān's interest in their doctrines. Wilhelm von Rubruck was a man of clear vision, who realized that the toleration guaranteed by the Great Khān to priests of every faith was only a sign of religious indifference and that his occasional participation in Christian ceremonies could not be

[1] See genealogical tree on p. 102.

considered evidence of adherence to Christianity; but in accusing the Nestorian priests of superstitious practices or at least of leniency towards such practices, Wilhelm misjudged the situation in which these servants of Christ had to live and work. Occidental standards were of course wholly inapplicable to Central Asian conditions; while in the Occident also, many an ancient superstition then flourished.

The civilization of the Mongols was in Wilhelm von Rubruck's opinion still primeval. The family was patriarchal, the costume simple; honesty and frankness to one another and hospitality to strangers were still the universal rule. The status of the Mongol woman was still one of complete freedom. She could own property and even engage in litigation; she was mistress of the house and instructress of her children. The law punished adultery by the man as well as by the woman with death. Princesses of noble stock could attain great influence. Twice already a sovereign's widow had acted as regent when the throne was vacant. At the same time commerce flourished. An elaborate system of communications had been built up in every direction, and the presence of numerous war-prisoners from the conquered lands had raised the economy to a high level of development. Besides Syrians and Russians, Wilhelm met at the Great Khān's court several Germans, Hungarians and Frenchmen who occupied an esteemed social position as skilled artisans. Envoys from the rulers of almost every land were to be found at Qara Qorum. A strict protocol regulated their access to the sovereign and provided for their accommodation and subsistence. They were allowed complete freedom of intercourse with one another and with the population, and thus had the opportunity to broaden their knowledge of the new civilization which through the influence of the neighbouring peoples was bursting forth in these formerly backward regions. Efficient postal and transportation services ensured not only the rapid transmission of news but also a reasonable degree of comfort for travellers. Qara Qorum had become the centre where all the civilizations of Asia converged and interacted. For the first time in history, continuous and busy traffic linked East Asia to the Near East and so to Western Europe. Knowledge of China, which since the blocking of the ancient silk route through Persia had remained lost to the view of Europe, once more found a way to the West; and the first vague reports of Japan reached the shores of the Mediterranean. For this reason, the establishment of the Mongol empire, in spite of the fearful devastation which it caused, especially during the campaigns of Jingiz Khān, had a positive effect in bringing the nations closer together and gave a stimulus to the civilization of Europe.

Möngke considered that his first political duty was to complete the execution of Jingiz Khān's will, which Ögedei had only been able to do in part. He therefore began preparing expeditions into China and Western Asia. In China, the problem was to consolidate and extend existing conquests. This task the Great Khān reserved for himself. It involved him and his brother *Qubilai* in protracted fighting, which had not come to an end when Möngke died on September 6, 1259, during the siege of a Chinese fortress.

The expedition into Western Asia was entrusted to another of his brothers, *Hūlāgū (Hülegü)*. A large number of troops was placed for this purpose under Hūlāgū's command; and in addition, all other Mongol army commanders were required to assign to him a proportion of their effectives. In this way, the army mobilized for the purpose of subjugating Western Asia reached a strength astonishing for that period; the Russian orientalist WILHELM BARTHOLD has computed it at about 129,000 men. This figure is of course much smaller than those given by many contemporary writers, whose accounts must be judged as no less exaggerated than the fanciful figures cited by authors in ancient times.

The situation in Persia since the first invasion by the Mongols during Jingiz Khān's reign had been somewhat confused. The only province in which the conquerors had maintained their authority on a more or less firm basis was Khurāsān in the north-east. In other parts, petty local dynasties had preserved their power and their independence of the Mongols. The representatives of Mongol authority were at loggerheads among themselves; on several occasions conflicts arose between them which necessitated the recall of individual governors and did not exactly redound to Mongol prestige. In Caucasia also the hand of the Mongol administration at Sarai was lightly felt, doubtless because that mountainous region was too far afield and regular communications could not be maintained.

In these circumstances, Hūlāgū had no easy task before him when he set out from Mongolia in 1255 to conquer his prospective realm. The Mongols did not, however, encounter any organized resistance until they reached the mountains south of the Caspian Sea which shielded the seat of the once formidable and still dreaded sect of the *Assassins* (see "*The Age of the Caliphs*", pp. 86 ff.). The fortress of Alamūt, headquarters of the Assassin organization, offered a desperate resistance to the onslaughts of the Central Asian hordes and only succumbed after a prolonged siege. The leader of the sect, known as "The Old Man of the Mountain" (*"Shaykh al-Jabal"*), was executed forthwith. A celebrated man of learning, *Naṣīr al-Dīn Ṭūsī* (d. 1274), whose religious leanings were Twelver Shīʿite and who had been kept prisoner by the Assassins, recovered his freedom and was to win laurels in Mongol service. He was able to resume all his scientific activities and erect an observatory at the city of Marāghah in north west Persia. The destruction of the citadel of Alamūt was welcomed as a deliverance by the Muslims, who held the Assassins to be no less obnoxious than the Crusaders.

Not much time passed, however, before the Muslims could discern that Hūlāgū had not come with any thought of being their friend. After capturing Alamūt and subduing the petty princes of north west Persia and certain independent chieftains of the Lurs in the Zagros mountains, he marched straight on Baghdād, whose *Caliph* had incurred the displeasure of the invaders by certain ill-advised political moves. The utmost disorder reigned in the capital of the Caliph. The resources of his state, and in particular its available military man-power, were inadequate for any effective resistance. It was nevertheless boldly decided to face a siege of the city. The military situation being such that there could be no doubt as to the fate in store for the Commander of the Faithful, certain groups from the outset counselled negotiation with the Mongols. Among them were the Turkish garrison, who contacted the Turkish troops in Hūlāgū's army and resolved not to fight against brother Turks; and the Caliph's wazīr was also well aware of the futility of fighting. The obtuse ʿAbbāsid prince would not, however, heed any suggestion of compromise and was ready to risk the city's being stormed. There could thus be no escape from disaster. On February 10, 1258, the Mongols assaulted and seized the abode of the Caliph, laid hands on his person, forced him to disclose his secret hoards and then put him to death, reputedly by smothering him in carpets; for the Mongols had an ancient superstition against shedding royal blood.

The capture of Baghdād and the accompanying overthrow of the Caliphate, which in spite of its material impotence still possessed a certain spiritual authority, produced a great upheaval in the social structure of Mesopotamia. The Christians — Nestorian and Jacobite — who were still fairly numerous, especially in the north of the country but also at Baghdād, and likewise the Shīʿites, who lived mainly in the south, were deeply stirred. Hūlāgū himself, who was influenced in favour of the Christians and consequently against the Muslims by his intellectually gifted consort *Doquz Khātūn*, allowed a free hand to all the forces opposed to the hitherto dominant Sunnite group. During the sack of Baghdād, both the Christians and the Shīʿites (for whom Naṣīr al-Dīn Ṭūsī had become spokesman) were largely spared. They were now able to rebuild their churches or mosques and hold public processions. The Shī'ites chose as their senior magistrate a *Naqīb* or Marshal of the Nobles (i.e. descendants of the Prophet), who represented their interests before the authorities.

This attitude on the part of Hūlāgū had profound repercussions all over Western Asia. The Christians of Syria, Palestine and Asia Minor feverishly awaited his coming in the well-grounded hope that it would substantially improve their lot. They contributed directly to the rapid fall of several strongholds in Northern Mesopotamia, only one of which, the fortress of Mayyāfāriqīn, offered vigorous resistance, holding out for two whole years. By 1259 the advance to the Mediterranean was under way. The entry of the Mongols into Damascus was hailed with transports of joy by the Christians of that city, who snapped their fingers at the Muslims with new-found arrogance. Aleppo was taken by storm, and the route to Egypt seemingly lay open before Hūlāgū. Then, during his absence, his troops came up against the *Mamlūks*. The decisive battle took place on September 3, 1260, at *'Ayn Jālūt (Goliath's Well)*, in Palestine. It turned out to the disadvantage of the Central Asian invaders. In bitter fighting, the Mamlūks under *Qotuz*, who were also natives the steppes and experienced in cavalry warfare, put to rout the Mongol force and captured its commander.

This defeat marked the turning point in the tide of Mongol conquest and ensured the continued independence of Egypt. Under its new Sulṭān *Baybars*, who had murdered Qotuz immediately after the battle and now entered Cairo at the head of the victorious troops, the Mamlūk state soon grew to be a powerful counterpoise to the Mongols and bulwark of Islām. To buttress his position, Baybars received at his court a real or reputed scion of the 'Abbāsid house. This prince, after an unsuccessful attempt to recapture Baghdād, was obliged to take refuge at Cairo and there play the rôle of a religious suzerain — which suited Baybars' interests well. Though the claim of the Cairo 'Abbāsids to the Caliphate only won outright recognition from certain princes of northern India and for a time from certain Khāns of the Golden Horde, it lent support to the authority of the Mamlūks until their downfall in 1517. Egypt continued till then to control the destinies of Syria and Palestine; whenever a Nile valley state has been strong enough to pursue a forward foreign policy, it has always treated the Syro-Palestinian region as its outer rampart.

There was a reason why Hūlāgū had not been with his army at the time of the defeat. He was preoccupied with the circumstances attendant upon the death of the Great Khān. Möngke's decease gave rise to grave dissensions. There can be little doubt that he had intended to appoint his brother *Aryq Böge* as his successor; but his other brother *Qubilai*, who was fighting in China as emperor-designate of that country, objected to this arrangement and was prepared to vindicate his own claim with the sword. After having himself proclaimed emperor in China, he made over the command of the troops in that country to a trusted general and advanced in person on Mongolia. Here Aryq Böge had established his position at Qara Qorum. A civil war followed, in the course of which the interior of Mongolia was subjected to an economic blockade and entirely cut off from the outside world. Hūlāgū, on account of his old friendship with his brother Qubilai, assented to these measures. The struggle was thus fairly soon decided in favour of Qubilai. Aryq Böge was obliged to submit and vanished from the political scene. He died in 1266.

As a result of this turn of events, Mongolia became an outlying territory of China: a source of strength to the ruling Mongol or *Yüan* dynasty of that country, but never again a significant factor in world history. (Arabia, the cradle of Islām, had likewise reverted to obscurity after the establishment of the Umayyad Caliphate). The embassies from other parts of Asia, including other Mongol dominions, now made their way to Peking. The manners of the Great Khān and his court became Chinese; the ladies of the royal house were in all but name Chinese princesses. The interests of the Mongol nation were judged by Qubilai from the standpoint of the empire as a whole, and in consequence they were often subordinated to Chinese interests. By Qubilai's order a new Mongol alphabet was devised by a Tibetan monk in place of the Uigur script, which the Mongols had learned in the Uigur territory at the beginning of the 13th century and which was ultimately derived from the ancient Semitic; but in spite of its relative simplicity, the new system of writing, which because of its shape is known as the quadratic script, did not win general acceptance. On the one hand, the old usages were too strong; on the other, it appeared simpler, in case of need, to transcribe the Mongol language into Chinese characters. As a result, Chinese couriers could read Mongol documents, though only imperfectly, without fully understanding their meaning. The true Mongol script continued nonetheless to be the Uigur, which has remained in use till the present day.

The civil war of 1259 also produced an immediate effect on the western parts of the universal Mongol empire. The feud between Qubilai and Aryq Böge had its counterpart in a feud between Hūlāgū and the Khān of the Golden Horde, *Berke*. After the death of Batu in 1256 and a brief intervening reign [1], Berke, brother of Batu, had become sovereign of the Tatar empire in South Russia (see below, p. 47). He was the first Mongol ruler to embrace the Islāmic faith, probably before his accession to the throne. For this reason he had disapproved of the campaign against the Caliph and attempted to mediate; but he could not prevent the contingent which he had sent from his army from participating along with those sent from the other armies in the capture and sack of Baghdād. This was all the more galling to him because Möngke had assigned the Caucasus, hitherto a possession of the Golden Horde, to Hūlāgū's sphere. Berke accordingly bore a deep grievance against his new neighbour to the south, as a result of which he stood by Aryq Böge, whereas Hūlāgū rallied to Qubilai.

When Qubilai won the day and became Great Khān, Berke was thus politically isolated; and to all intents and purposes he cut off contact with the former's capital at Peking. Hūlāgū, on the other hand, continued to foster close relations with the Great Khān. The two Mongol rulers who held sway over the ancient civilized lands of China and Persia thus worked closely together, while the champions of Mongol tradition were ignored or thrust aside. The relations between the Mongols of Persia and Qubilai long remained friendly; and in accepting the title "*Īlkhān*" *(Viceroy)*, the rule of Persia affirmed his subordination to the central authority of the Great Khān in China. In the cultural sphere also, the good relations between the two countries had fruitful effects.

The strained relations between the Golden Horde and the Īlkhān exploded into fierce fighting on the occasion of the civil war between Qubilai and Aryq Böge. Berke, who was a man of exceptional energy, had no intention of abandoning his southern bastion without a struggle. In 1261 he commenced hostilities along the Caucasus. This was the start of an inconclusive war during which Berke won an important battle on the River Terek on January 13, 1263, but did not succeed in dislodging Hūlāgū from the Caucasus.

The situation would not have presented any great danger to the Īlkhān had not Berke resolved on a step unprecedented in the annals of inter-Mongol relations. After the fall of Baghdād in 1258, Berke had sent instructions to his troops fighting in Hūlāgū's army to quit the service of the Īlkhān and proceed to Cairo. In this way, the Khān of the Golden Horde had reinforced the armies of the Egyptian Sulṭān and for the first time combined with a foreign power against brother Mongols. The

[1] Batu's immediate successor was his son *Sartaq*, who is said to have had Christian sympathies.

outcome of the battle of ʿAyn Jālūt, so momentous for the newly established Mamlūk régime (which only dated from 1259), may perhaps have been appreciably influenced thereby.

The entente between the Golden Horde and Egypt was suggested in the main by political considerations; but another determining factor was trade. In structure, moreover, the two states were remarkably alike. Both on the Nile and on the Volga, a ruling class with Turkish characteristics governed a population of a very different nature; and in both states the ruler had embraced Islām. The religious element, which has always carried such weight with the Near Eastern peoples, received particular emphasis when a formal alliance between the two states was concluded in 1261; and as so often in history, it cut across blood ties and turned kindred nations into enemies. In the commercial sphere, the Black Sea coasts now ruled by the Golden Horde were the chief source of the large numbers of slaves imported annually into Egypt — slaves who in military careers had risen to supremacy in that country under the name of *"Mamlūks" ("men who have been bought")*. This trade was only possible so long as the Khān at Sarai, and also the Emperor at Constantinople, raised no objection. The Byzantine Emperor *Michael VIII Palaeologus*, who had just become master of Constantinople after the fall of the alien "Latin" régime, showed little concern about these "heathen" transactions and could not afford to intervene in negotiations between Muslim states. Of greater importance was the attitude of Berke towards the question. By collaborating politically with Egypt and by supplementing the alliance of 1261 with a commercial treaty to which the Byzantines adhered, he ensured the continuance of slave-exports from the Black Sea and therewith of Mamlūk domination on the Nile. At the same time, the fighting in the Caucasus made it impossible for Hūlāgū to undertake more than a few weak incursions into Syria. A number of factors thus drew the two states togeher. In view of the origin of the Mamlūks, it is not surprising that many customs and institutions, including perhaps the military system, which are known to have existed on the Volga, should be found to have existed also on the Nile [1].

In another respect also, Berke's entente with the Mamlūk Sulṭān Baybars I represented a breach with former Mongol traditions. Hitherto, a Mongol state had never concluded an alliance with a non-Mongol state except on the basis of the latter's formal or informal subordination. The rulers of Georgia or Armenia, for example, or the various princes of Russia,

[1] A. N. Poliak, *Le caractère colonial de l'état mamelouk dans ses rapports avec la Horde d'Or*, in the "*Revue des Etudes Islamiques*", *IX* (1935), pp. 231-248.

were treated as feudal vassals; and the Emperors of Byzantium and Trebizond could also be regarded as such, at any rate from the Mongol viewpoint. In regard to Egypt, however, no such claim could be sustained. Berke did not even object to accepting the status of a vassal of the ʿAbbāsid Caliph in Cairo — a step of considerable ideological, even if of little practical, significance. In deciding upon it, he renounced in the spirit if not in the letter his membership in the universal community of the Mongol states, which were still presumed to constitute a single empire acknowledging the suzerainty of the Great Khān at Peking. This breach was another important consequence of the civil war which had followed Möngke's death. Qubilai had defeated his brother Aryq Böge and banished him from the political scene; but the Golden Horde could not now be likewise eliminated. One indication of the new state of affairs was the disappearance of the Great Khān's name from the coins of the Golden Horde; this began around 1260 and was particularly significant because coins in those days, like postage stamps today, were known everywhere to be symbols of legal sovereignty.

The new trend of events after 1258 was not merely the outcome of geographical influences, political power-shifts or religious and cultural stresses. It was paralleled by a transformation in the structure of the Mongol nation, which reflected all the above-mentioned phenomena and also contributed in itself to the break-up of the unitary Mongol empire. In expanding all over central, eastern and western Asia, the Mongols had thrust their way into utterly dissimilar geographical regions and into the midst of peoples with the most varied religions and cultures. It has been emphasized above that during the civil war of 1260 the Mongols occupying the homelands of ancient civilized nations, that is of the Persians and Chinese, acted differently from those living in the more steppe-like regions of Transoxiana and the Volga basin. Furthermore, the two last-mentioned regions were both already inhabited mainly by peoples of Turkish speech, or with Turkish affinities like the Volga Bulgars (though numerous other splinter groups were also present). The culture of these peoples was relatively similar to that of the Mongols; and accordingly a fusion between the two elements came easily to pass, the more so as large numbers of Turkish warriors had poured into Central Asia and East Europe along with the Mongols. In these regions, assimilation between the newcomers and the natives took place to an extent which soon turned the Golden Horde and Transoxianan realms into comparatively homogeneous territories; whereas in Persia and China the Mongols continued to form a mere ruling caste, superimposed on the country but differentiated from the natives by language, and in Persia during the next few decades also by religion.

All these phenomena are clearly discernible in the dissensions of 1260. Their subsequent effects were far-reaching. Transoxiana lay like a wedge interposed between the friendly states of China and Persia; and the Golden Horde was henceforward to all intents and purposes outside the Mongol community. Such being the situation, it becomes necessary to follow the destinies of each individual state separately. The state in China was the hub of the Great Khān's empire; but its evolution more and more assumed a specifically Chinese trend and must be followed within the framework of Chinese historical studies.

THE ĪLKHĀNS IN PERSIA

Hūlāgū, the master of Baghdād, did not enjoy many more years of life in which to organize his conquests. As a result of the comparatively long duration of the Mongol rule in Khurāsān, that province had become a stronghold of Mongol influence, which was consolidated by the establishment of Mongol and Turkish colonies. A second centre now took shape in Āẕarbāyjān. There too the inhabitants had for centuries consisted partly of Turkish tribes, which had thrust through the surrounding Persian population and since the 9th century had provided welcome military reinforcements for the Caliphs of Baghdād. More than half of Hūlāgū's army consisted of Turks, and the area had an attraction for them. The Mughān steppe, which lies north of Tabrīz and offers excellent pasturage, was settled by one large group of the invaders. The two cities of *Tabrīz* and *Marāghah,* where the Khān resided, became the capitals of the new realm and hence the headquarters of trade and business. However slight an interest the Īlkhāns may have taken in learning for its own sake, they were far-sighted enough to make use of Perso-Arab science for their own ends and encourage it so far as they could, or at least not to place obstacles in its way.

The location of the capital meant much to the Christian population of Northern Mesopotamia, who now had their protector dwelling close at hand. The Nestorians could naturally expect special benefits, since a large proportion of the newcomers from Central Asia were coreligionists and the Īlkhān's consort, Doquz Khātūn, professed their faith. The Īlkhān himself not infrequently took part in Christian festivals and attended masses; he authorized the building of a court chapel, made provision for church endowments and showed preference for Christians over

Muslims. The other Christian sects — Syrian (or Jacobite) and Armenian Monophysites and to some extent also the Orthodox Georgians — likewise enjoyed the ruler's favour. Their dioceses multiplied, their influence mounted and they recovered the right to parade in public and repair or enlarge their churches and monasteries, which strict Islāmic practice forbade. Hūlāgū did not, indeed, himself embrace the Nestorian faith; he inclined rather to a quite different creed, which had failed to take root in Western Asia but had become familiar to the Mongols from China, namely Buddhism. Although there is no definite evidence that the Īlkhān was a formal Buddhist, he was at any rate well disposed towards that religion. Not a few Buddhist priests (*Bhikshus*), whom the Mongols called *Bakhshys*, resided at his court. Before long, however, Hūlāgū, who in the authentic Mongol tradition was a heavy drinker, departed this life; and his death on February 8th, 1265, was followed shortly afterwards by that of his wife Doquz Khātūn. His son *Abāqā* became the new ruler. From the outset of his reign, Abāqā was confronted with grave external problems, which made it impossible for him to risk new departures in internal policy. A fresh attack in the Caucasus was promptly launched by Berke. The Īlkhāns' troops entrenched themselves behind wooden stockades along the south bank of the Kur river. Having no hope of making a break-through there, Berke moved upstream and after successfully crossing the river further to the west, above the old Georgian capital Mtskheth, began advancing southwards through the Little Caucasus. During this campaign — probably in January 1267 — Berke died. His venture then collapsed, and Abāqā could again breathe freely; for new dangers had already begun to pile up against the Īlkhānid realm in the east and south-west.

The geographical factors which have affected the evolution of Persia throughout its history once more came into play. The natural homeland of the Persian nation was to a great extent protected by its rim of formidable mountains — the Caucasus in the north-west, the Zagros in the west and south-west, and the Pamīr plateau and the Hindū Kush with their outliers in the east. Only to the north-east, in the Oxus-Jaxartes region, did the country lie open; and it was here that new perils now threatened. The Golden Horde and Transoxiana had concluded an alliance with a view to a simultaneous attack on the Īlkhāns. Fortunately for Abāqā, this never came off. The fighting in the Caucasus had already ceased by the time that the Transoxianan ruler began his offensive against Khurāsān in 1268. The youthful and energetic Īlkhān was consequently able to drive out the invaders and ward off the danger from the north-east before a new threat loomed in another quarter of the horizon.

One of the main concerns of rulers of Persia since ancient times has been to secure control not only of Mesopotamia, but also of Syria and therewith of an access to the Mediterranean. To gain possession of Syria, it was necessary to eliminate Egypt; and plans were accordingly made for expeditions along the line of the Euphrates. The earlier attempt of Hūlāgū to attain this objective had failed with the defeat at ʿAyn Jālūt; and now, as then, the Mamlūks had a firm foothold in Syria and posed, through their possession of Aleppo and Damascus, a standing threat to the western areas of the Īlkhānid realm. Baybars I was not the man to let slip the favourable opportunity presented to Egypt. He launched one attack after another from Syria against Mesopotamia, but could achieve nothing more than to keep the frontier districts in a state of chronic unrest. Baybars at the same time moved against the kingdom of Little Armenia in Cilicia, which had worked closely with the Mongols ever since their first irruptions from Central Asia; he inflicted severe and repeated devastations on the kingdom, but on account of the support which it received from the Īlkhāns, could not put an end to its political existence. The Saljūq Sultānate of Rūm in Asia Minor (see "*The Age of the Caliphs*", p. 95) had been obliged by military defeat to submit to the Mongols as early as 1243; and with Syria barred, it gave them an indirect access to the Mediterranean. Baybars was thus bound to aim at counteracting the dominant Mongol influence in the country, especially as the followers of Islām in Asia Minor had suffered hardships at the hands of the anti-Muslim Īlkhān. Internal dissensions between the local Turkish principalities facilitated an invasion in 1277 by the Mamlūk Sulṭān, who penetrated to the city of Malatya (Melitene), drove out the Mongol "High Commissioner" *(Parvāneh)*, rallied the Muslim forces which were his natural allies and destroyed Christian churches. The energetic resistance offered by the still numerous Orthodox and Armenian Christians, the help sent by Abāqā and finally the death of Baybars early in the campaign prevented any conclusive result; and the situation in the Near East reverted to its former pattern. However uncongenial the Mongol régime may have been to the Persians at this time, geographical factors obliged it to defend their country against attack in Caucasia and on the Oxus, on the Euphrates and in Asia Minor, and thus confronted the Īlkhāns with external responsibilities similar to those which have devolved on every national Persian dynasty.

The interplay of forces in which Abāqā's government was involved went beyond the limits of Western Asia or the Near East. An account has already been given of the coalition formed by the Khān of the Golden Horde, the ruler of Transoxiana and the Mamlūk Sulṭān with a view to joint action against the Īlkhān as their common enemy. One result of the collaboration between Sarai and Cairo was that the Golden Horde came into contact with other states which were politically associated with Egypt. Among these were the Sicilian kingdom of the Hohenstaufen and through it Catalonia, which had dynastic ties with Sicily. In the setting of the contemporary politics of the Italian states, the Hohenstaufen were hostile to the Pope and the French King, who worked closely together in the East. The surviving Crusader states on the Syrian coast — Tripoli and Acre — depended on Papal and French backing. These states were a thorn in the eye of the Mamlūk Sulṭān. Being the enemies of Egypt, the Crusaders and with them their patron, France, and the Roman Curia became the natural friends of the Īlkhāns. Papal and French envoys made frequent appearances in the Īlkhānid dominions during this period. They did not, however, succeed in bringing about any direct political collaboration. A plan for a combined Franco-Īlkhānid attack on Northern Syria in 1269 miscarried; the necessary surprise could not be achieved on account of defective liaison. They nevertheless brought the Īlkhānid realm and its capital Tabrīz into closer touch with Europe and promoted European knowledge of this Near Eastern state. They also took advantage of the general situation to engage in missionary activity, less perhaps among the Mongols themselves than among the indigenous Christians, some of whom were temporarily won over to union with Rome. It even appears that monastic settlements were formed in Mesopotamia and Caucasia at this time.

Looser bonds were established with the Italian maritime republics of Genoa and Venice, which in the orient at least avoided political entanglement as far as possible and thus had access to Cairo and Tabrīz alike, as well as to the Crimea (which belonged to the Golden Horde). Clashes between the two republics were not uncommon, and the successive wars of the Straits which they fought for commercial supremacy in the Near East excluded any possibility of concerted action on their part. At Tabrīz, Venice succeeded in gaining the upper hand, partly through strenuous exertions and liberal dispensations of gifts, but mainly because her enemy Genoa had acquired the strongest influence at Sarai and after founding settlements in the Crimea, first at Kaffa and then at other points, had become closely aligned with the Golden Horde. At all events, the Italian trade in the Near East was to some extent bound up with the political situation on the Mediterranean coasts.

These cross-currents were of particular importance to the newly reconstituted Byzantine empire. In Asia Minor, the Īlkhāns had on the whole won the day; besides making good their hold over the Saljūqs of Rūm, they had been able to reduce the Emperor of Trebizond to virtual vassalage. On the other hand, economic considerations and the possession of the Straits caused Michael VIII of Constantinople to be deeply interested in the export trade from southern Russia to Egypt and vice versa. He accordingly could not adopt an unfriendly attitude towards those two states. When the power of the Īlkhāns was at its height, he did indeed feel obliged to seek a rapprochement with them, and he then attempted to impede the traffic between Cairo and Sarai; but a raid by Berke forced him to give up this policy. His position midway between the two powers was clearly illustrated in his gifts of a natural daughter in marriage to Abāqā and of a niece to the then master of the Golden Horde, Nokhai. This statesmanlike founder of the dynasty of the Palaeologi successfully overcame all the difficulties of his position and piloted his state virtually without damage between the opposing reefs.

The external policy followed by Abāqā reflected in the main the internal structure of his realm. The motives of *Louis IX of France (Saint Louis)* and of the Pope in favouring such close cooperation with the Īlkhāns had nothing to do with the political tensions in the Mediterranean, in which the rulers of Tabrīz could hardly intervene when they were not in possession of Syria. The Roman Curia viewed the Īlkhāns primarily as the inexorable enemies of the Mamlūks, who in the later period of the Crusades were the principal adversaries of Christian statehood in the East — that is of the Crusader states and certain native Christian remnants. Western Christianity's hopes of eventually mastering the Crescent depended mainly on the possibility of help from the Īlkhāns in the struggle against Egypt. This idea is eloquently expressed in several contemporary Western European writings and also in the "*Flos Historiarum Terrae Orientis*", an account of the times written by *Haytonus*, a prince of Little Armenia. These works also show how extravagant, for the most part, were the ideas of the Curia. On the strength of such largely misleading reports, the Popes cherished for years the belief that they would be able to win over the Īlkhāns to Christianity and so make a reality of the dream of "Prester John". Since the first arrival of news about the Mongols, *Gregory IX* and *Innocent IV* had counted on the legions of this fabulous king and looked upon the destruction of Islām as an attainable goal. After the tide of Mongol conquest had ebbed without producing the anticipated effect and it had become apparent that the Mongols were not Christians, people in the West did not altogether abandon this hope. On the contrary, the grand design was still, so to speak, to transform the Īlkhāns into "Prester Johns". Indefatigable efforts were made to win over the Mongol rulers, but without success.

Although from a modern viewpoint this attitude may seem somewhat unwarranted, the circumstances of the time should not be overlooked. The Mongols, except for those who held fast to their ancient Shamanist faith, had been a largely Christian nation, even if the Nestorian creed which they followed did not conform with the tenets of the Western Catholic Church. When the Īlkhān's forces occupied Mesopotamia and invaded Syria, they behaved as friends of the Christians and opponents of the Muslims; and the fact that they encountered fairly compact Christian communities in these homelands of the Nestorian and Jacobite churches made Christianity an influential factor at the Īlkhān's court. Beside Hūlāgū's consort Doquz Khātūn, several other princesses were Nestorian Christians; and as has been seen, one of Abāqā's wives was a Byzantine princess, who maintained her Orthodox faith at Tabrīz. Moreover, two Īlkhāns were Christians in their youth. There was thus considerable apparent justification for the belief that Christianity, albeit of the Nestorian persuasion, would be victorious; and it was hoped in Rome that the Nestorian church could be persuaded to accept Uniat status.

A further ground for this optimism in the West was the evident absence of any inclination on the part of the Īlkhāns to embrace the Islāmic faith of the overwhelming majority of their subjects. Admittedly Islām in Persia and Mesopotamia presented just as disunited a front as Christianity. The Sunnah and the Shī'ah stood face to face in irreconcilable hostility; and the Shī'ites had no scruples about taking advantage of the sack of Baghdād and other occasions to pay off old scores with the Sunnites, build up an organization of their own and intensify their proselytizing activity among the then predominantly Sunnite inhabitants. The attitude of the Īlkhāns did not mean, however, that they had remained true to Shamanism or indifferent to religious questions, as in the days when the Great Khāns ruled at Qara Qorum. They inclined, as has been seen, to Buddhism. Abāqā, during his reign, was a convinced Buddhist. He sought, moreover, to promote this religion among the grandees of his court and among his people generally, and is said to have erected Buddhist temples in numerous Persian towns and even villages. The only reports which have come down to us about these proceedings of the Īlkhān are of Christian and Muslim origin; and they undoubtedly distort the facts. At the most they quote a few malicious anecdotes about the rôle of Buddhism without giving any real picture of the contemporary situation, evidence of which can only be pieced together by critically scrutinizing the sources and inferring probable conclusions. At all events, the position of Buddhism in the realm of the Īlkhāns was so isolated that there could be no prospect of forcing it on the population. Abāqā consequently held fast to the principle of toleration maintained by his ancestors and enjoined by Jingiz Khān in the Yasa. The free practice of all religions was permitted and exemption from taxes was granted to all religious dignitaries with the exception of rabbis, who in Western and Central Asia were specifically subjected to taxation. In thus upholding religious liberty, Abāqā did not act in any spirit of enlightened despotism; he saw in the light of current conditions that such liberty was a necessary expedient of internal administration. To the Islāmic eye, Buddhists appeared as particularly evil unbelievers and idolaters; and Abāqā's religious policies met with sharp resistance from the Muslims, who naturally enough were apprehensive of encroachments in a sphere which meant so much to them. Abāqā reciprocated by harassing Islām where possible. He could most easily do so by supporting the still numerous Christian communities and guaranteeing them freedom of missionary activity. For the Jacobites and Nestorians in Mesopotamia this period was a last golden age; their churches rose anew, their missions spread and Syriac literature bore its last and mature fruit, represented above all by the encyclopaedic learning of the Jacobite Bishop *Gregory Bar Hebraeus* (d. 1286). The Nestorians, too, produced some creditable literary works. Their church's cooperation with the government was so close that when their Patriarch died in 1281 they elected to the office a 35 year old priest of Uigur (Öngüt) nationality, who took the titular name *Yabhalāhā III*: though far from proficient in either ecclesiastical Syriac or governmental Arabic, he won immediate access to the court on the strength of his origin and received many proofs of Abāqā's favour. He made good use of his position in the interest of his church, whose prestige and influence now reached their zenith.

A régime which thus seemed fundamentally well disposed towards Christians and whose motives of internal policy could not be detected was bound to kindle the brightest hopes in Western Europe. Its evolution was followed with keen interest by the various European powers. Their trade with Persia, much of which passed through the favourably situated kingdom of 'Little Armenia, was flourishing, and remarkable growth was shown by the trading establishments of the Italians at Tabrīz. The city also served as an emporium for goods from Central Asia and the Far East. Chinese junks sailed all the way to the Persian Gulf to bring merchandise from the Great Khān's dominions, and caravans kept up an overland traffic with the Middle Kingdom through Transoxiana — so far as political conditions allowed. Since the Īlkhāns and the Great Khān Qubilai continued to be on the friendliest political terms, both governments gave special attention to their mutual commerce. In all probability it was the gifts exchanged between the two courts which provided the stimulus now experienced by many of the arts; and a further impulse may have been given by the Chinese princesses who made the long journey to become brides of princes at the Persian court[1], and by their large accompanying retinues. The Great Khān was permanently represented at Tabrīz by a High Commissioner, who as a political counsellor played a role of some importance behind the scenes and as deputy of the suzerain had a constitutional function to perform at every accession of a new Īlkhān. There are also reports of trade relations with India.

The tolerant attitude to all religions and the broad-minded view of foreign commerce which the Īlkhāns thus maintained were paralleled in their internal administrative and economic policies. They not only took far-reaching steps to encourage industry and agriculture — another field in which detailed contemporary accounts are scarce; they also worked out a system of provincial administration for their realm. The main feature of this was the treatment granted by the conquerors to states which had bowed to their demands without offering armed resistance. As already noted, it was always a Mongol practice to demand submission from the ruler of a territory before making war against him. While the leading sovereigns of the Near East had chosen to fight and succumbed, numerous lesser rulers had preferred the alternative of voluntary submission. They did not fare ill. For climatic and other reasons, the Mongols had not been attracted to southern Persia; and several dynasties in that region thus preserved their internal autonomy. The most important were the rulers of Fārs with their seat at Shīrāz, where the poet and moralist *Saʿdī* (d. 1291) composed his works; the descendants of *Burāq Ḥājib*, a wazīr of the Qara Khitai, at Kirmān (1222-1303); and the islands in the Persian Gulf with Hurmuz as their hub. These states and a number of petty principalities in the Zagros mountains and Māzandarān, together with Little Armenia and the Georgian principalities, had merely to pay tribute to the Mongols in

[1] Such as the princess whom *Marco Polo* escorted from China to Persia via Hurmuz in 1292-4.

money and kind. They contrived ingeniously to adapt their policies to the general line set by the Mongol government and had to supply more or less ample contingents of soldiers when the latter was at war. Troops from Georgia stood particularly high in the esteem of the Mongols, who showed a certain predilection for the Georgians on account of their military prowess and also of their importance as guardians of the Caucasian frontier. In return, these small states were allowed broad independence in their domestic and financial affairs; they could even, as a rule, decide their own mutual conflicts without Mongol intervention. On the other hand, it sometimes happened — in Fārs, for instance, in 1284 — that a local princess was married to a Mongol prince who acquired the right of succession and thus brought the territory into the direct possession of the Īlkhāns. The only local dynasty which consistently strove to throw off the Īlkhānid yoke was that of the *Kurt* (or *Kart*) princes of Harāt, who enjoyed considerable political influence and a great reputation for valour. Their position was strengthened by the proximity of Transoxiana, with whose rulers they could ally themselves against Tabrīz. Several difficult and long drawn out campaigns, in which heavy fighting took place and rival pretenders were installed on the throne, had to be undertaken before the unruly province could be subdued. An expedition sent during this period to subdue Gīlān did not, on the other hand, achieve success; in the humidity and heat of the southern Caspian shore, the Īlkhān's troops could no more gain ground than those of the ʿAbbāsid Caliphs in an earlier age.

Considering how difficult were the external circumstances in which Abāqā had to set about the task of consolidating the internal structure of his realm, he must be judged unhesitatingly to have been a statesman of high calibre. In spite of all the antagonisms evoked by his religious policy, he welded the realm which he had inherited from his father into an effective unit. With increasing age, however, he became increasingly addicted to drink, from the effects of which he expired in delirium on April 1, 1282.

His death was a great loss to the régime, which was deprived of the strong hand needed to guide its policies. Moreover, the problem of the succession had not been solved. The throne was seized by the late Īlkhān's brother *Takūdār*, a weak, rather spiritually minded man, who apparently from sincere conviction had found his way to Islām. He immediately made known his conversion and took the name *Aḥmad*. The new ruler was astute enough to seek political advantage from his change of religion by contacting the Mamlūks and proposing an alliance. The negotiations, however, dragged on inconclusively, as the Egyptians demanded guarantees. They were doubtless aware that the leading class of the Persian Mongols had no intention of imitating their ruler's change of religion. Moreover, Abāqā's son *Arghūn* had from the start laid claim to the throne and enjoyed strong support as representative of the Buddhist party. Aḥmad's reign was thus mainly occupied with internal fighting, which after two years resulted in his overthrow and death in 1284.

The victorious Arghūn, an ardent champion of Buddhism, then ascended to the throne; and a time of hardship set in for Islām, as the Buddhist reaction made conditions far more oppressive than they were under Abāqā. Arghūn himself was a man of scant ability. He lacked, in particular, any understanding whatever of the financial capacity of his realm; he desired to extract fabulous revenues from his subjects, and entrusted the tax administration to a Jewish physician who had gained a name for himself in Mesopotamia as a "tough" official through his success in raising vast sums by extortionate methods. This minister, who received the title *Saʿd al-Dawlah,* won a high place in Arghūn's esteem. He oppressed the provinces to the extreme and found places for his relatives as governors or administrators almost everywhere. Arghūn, who felt the utmost distrust of his Muslim subjects, cut himself more and more off from the world, leaving the field free for Saʿd al-Dawlah and his henchmen. The result was that several revolts and tumults broke out: in some cities the local Jews were victims of the popular fury which the minister's policies had stirred up. As a counterweight to the Muslims, the government favoured both Jews and Christians.

It was fortunate for the régime that during Arghūn's reign only two unimportant clashes with the Golden Horde occurred and that the Egyptian and Transoxianan frontiers were mainly quiet. It was thus possible to suppress a local uprising in the east of the territory and another in Georgia without much trouble. The general unrest, however, could no longer be quelled. During a popular outbreak against the Jews at Shīrāz, Arghūn died on March 9, 1291, from the effects of a long-life potion prescribed for him by a Buddhist priest. While yet he lay on his deathbed, his minister Saʿd al-Dawlah was arrested and executed.

The grandees could not at first agree on a successor; and it was only after much vacillation that *Gaykhātū,* a brother of the deceased, was accepted. He had hitherto served as High Commissioner in Asia Minor, and now entered the capital as the leading candidate. The choice must be judged unfortunate, because Gaykhātū was even more incompetent than his brother. His irresolution was such that he had not the heart to deal harshly with rebels or criminals; for he hated to cause any man to be put to death. In an attempt to remedy the deplorable financial situation which had arisen during Arghūn's reign, he followed the Chinese precedent and introduced paper money. He had currency notes manufactured with denominations inscribed in the Chinese, Persian and Mongol scripts and placed them in circulation as compulsory legal tender[1]. Nobody in Persia, however, would accept this unfamiliar money. The markets emptied, food supplies vanished from the cities, and the countryside soon became infested with bands of robbers. All public life came to a standstill. So great was the disorganization that after six months the whole project had to be abandoned. In the north-eastern province of Khurāsān where the young prince *Ghazān*, eldest son of Arghūn, was governor, it had not even been attempted. The finances were now, of course, completely ruined; and new clashes in the Caucasus dealt a further blow to Gaykhātū's government. It is not to be wondered at that by 1295 a rebellion had flared up, representing at once a protest against the breakdown of authority and a shift in public opinion. During the previous decade, Islām had spread widely among the Mongols and even into the ruling family: a number of princes were sympathetically inclined to it. The new and the old tendencies were in conflict with each other, but they combined against Gaykhātū, who was overthrown in March 1295 and forthwith put to death. His distant relative *Bāidū* who headed the old Buddhist element, could not hold out for long. After a few months he succumbed; and on November 9, 1295, at Tabrīz, Ghazān ascended the throne at the age of about 24.

This event was a turning point in the history of the Mongol state in Īrān; for immediately after his accession Ghazān formally embraced Islām, and all subsequent rulers of Persia have remained true to that faith. In becoming a Muslim, however, Ghazān could not avoid a further choice; he had to decide between the two prevalent versions of Islām. He preferred the Sunnite doctrine, and therewith the system to which the majority of his subjects adhered. In spite of this, he did not treat the Shīʿites with the fanaticism which strictly Sunnite rulers have displayed so often in Islāmic history; he assured them of toleration and in many ways maintained something of the old Mongol attitude of live and let live. It would probably not be wrong to attribute this policy to sympathies which he doubtless felt for the Shīʿah notwithstanding his official adherence to the Sunnah. He actively supported various Shīʿite institutions and visited the Shīʿite sanctuary at Karbalāʾ. With Ghazān's

[1] KARL JAHN, *Das iranische Papiergeld*, in *Archiv Orientální*, X (Prague 1935), pp. 308-40.

conversion to Islām, the position of Buddhism in the community became untenable. A large proportion of the Mongols had already embraced Islām, and others now followed; so that few if any hands were raised in support of the Buddhist cause. The Buddhist temples were transformed into mosques, former Muslim properties were restored to their original owners, and the Buddhist priests, of whom only a few remained in the country, were divested of their privileges. For the Christians also, the consequences were hard. They had to atone for their recent liberties by suffering persecutions at the hands of their surrounding Muslim compatriots. Such widespread disorders took place that Ghazān thought fit to intervene and prohibited further molestation. An end, however, had come to the once great influence enjoyed at the court by the Nestorian Patriarch Yabhalāhā III, who was actually confined to prison for a short while. He was able, nevertheless, to obviate the worst perils threatening his church; but the importance of Nestorianism was now on the wane, even in the land of its birth. Its members either went over to Islām, or withdrew into the inhospitable mountains above the upper Tigris where the Nestorian Church has held out to the present day. The Mongols themselves nearly all turned away from the Christian faith during the ensuing decades. On embracing Islām, they became of one faith with the numerous Turks of Īrān, who had long been solidly Muslim; and when the two peoples thus ceased to be kept apart by religion, they fused into a new amalgam, whose everyday tongue was Turkish. At the beginning of the 14th century, the various Turkish tribes which, together with later arrivals, have formed the backbone of the present Turkish-speaking element in the population of Persia, began to take definite shape. The province of Āẕarbāyjān, which as the centre of Īlkhānid power became the main focus of Turco-Mongol colonization, has remained solidly Turkish-speaking ever since, the Mongol speech having soon given way to the Turkish. Any future reference to a "Mongol" state in Persia must accordingly be treated with reservation.

In the Orient, religious developments have always had far-reaching political implications; and the present instance was no exception. Ghazān might possibly not have decided on so drastic a switch had it not been for the death in 1294 of the venerable head of the universal Mongol empire, the Great Khān Qubilai, to whom the Īlkhāns had always felt firmly attached. Deprived of Qubilai, the Mongol system lost all cohesion. His grandson who succeeded him in China possessed no great political talent or energy, and the last effective link between the Mongol rulers was severed. The names of the Great Khāns ceased to appear on Persian coins; no High Commissioner from China was henceforth stationed at Tabrīz; the rulers of Īrān set aside the title "Īlkhān" ("Viceroy") and called themselves simply "*Khān*"; and religious policies were no longer shaped according to the desire of a Buddhist suzerain. Ambassadors were indeed still exchanged, and the sovereigns of Persia continued to hold apanages in China; but these were the sole remaining links.

Relations with Western Europe were only gradually affected by Ghazān's conversion. The Khān himself took care to ensure that Western missionary activities would not suffer and allowed dignitaries of the Nestorian church to keep up contact with the West. His success in concealing his real purposes was such that Haytonus (*Hethum*; see above, (p. 29), in his work published around 1300, could still portray Ghazān as the great champion against Muslim Egypt and express confidence that this "friend of Christianity" would liberate Jerusalem and restore it to the Christians. The authors of an inscription in a church at Rome had the same idea.

Besides setting his country on a new course in the international sphere, the young ruler of Persia displayed intense energy in the field of internal reform. His first task was to restore the national economy which had been so gravely impaired during the reigns of Arghūn and Gaykhātū and the recent civil wars. With this in view, Ghazān chose a number of advisers, the most notable of whom were the wazīrs *ʿAlī Shāh* and *Rashīd al-Dīn Faẓl Allāh*, the latter an ex-physician possibly of Jewish descent. Together with their master, they compiled a code of laws governing almost every sector of public life. The financial system was completely reorganized, with new regulations for revenue collection and official expenditure. The taxes due by every province in cash and kind were reassessed and in certain cases, where the area was exhausted, deferred for several years. In this connection, district boundaries were redrawn and new rules laid down for district administration. In the field of jurisprudence, a transition had to be arranged from the old Mongol Yasa to the *Sharīʿah* or law of Islām. Special attention was paid to highway maintenance; and Ghazān reestablished the postal service and took steps to ensure the rapid passage of official emissaries, whose former abuses in requisitioning food supplies and other commodities en route were strictly forbidden. The public welfare services, including the pious foundations *(waqfs)*, which in Islāmic countries perform welfare functions, were also reformed, and provision was made for support of the aged and infirm, relief of destitutes and even care of animals. If the reports are correct, Ghazān took very little interest in army matters, which he apparently considered less important. His reign, however' saw a number of campaigns in Syria (1299-1303) and also revolts in Georgia, which were suppressed. When the Golden Horde, whose ruler had just surmounted a serious internal crisis, came forward with demands for the cession of Caucasia, Ghazān rejected them and had to make military preparations against an attack from the north. His reign was thus filled with unremitting activity; but he was not permitted to finish his task. On May 30, 1304, this most gifted of the Mongol princes who ruled Īrān after Hūlāgū's conquest died at the age of only 31 years.

His brother and successor *Uljaytū (Öljeitü)*, who now took the Perso-Islāmic name ***Khudābandeh*** and in his youth had been a Christian, was of a different type, though not lacking in energy. He let home affairs drift, with the result that few if any of Ghazān's reforms endured for long. The old malpractices soon reappeared in the administration, though thanks to the continuance in office of Ghazān's ministers the worst abuses were held in check. As a military leader, however, Uljaytū exhibited somewhat more vigour than his predecessor. He repelled several incursions in Caucasia and Syria, and promptly and skilfully crushed a most dangerous rebellion backed by Transoxiana at Harāt. Only his attempt to conquer Māzandarān proved abortive, on account of the hot, damp climate.

Uljaitū, like Ghazān before him, had a taste for learning and the arts. Though none of the Mongol rulers played any creative part in these fields, the two brothers rendered great services through their active encouragement and support. The branch of learning which claimed their special attention was history, as it served to exalt their own deeds and those of the Mongol dynasty. Persian literature owes to their patronage a number of valuable works, including the chronicles of their minister Rashīd al-Dīn who has just been mentioned. In this outstanding compilation, remarkably accurate use is made of old Mongol records, and many interesting and pertinent facts are added about the Western world. In all probability Rashīd al-Dīn had assistants who were the authors of important parts of the work. For the detailed knowledge which we possess of this period of Persian history, we have to thank the interest taken by these Mongol rulers. The decision, made in 1307, to lay out a new capital called *Sulṭānīyeh* near Qazvīn, brought encouragement to many artists and gave occasion for the crowning achievements of the Īlkhānid style of architecture in Persia, with its distinctive octagonal towers.

Persia was not destined, however, to find internal political peace under Uljaytū. The new ruler, who had become a Sunnite along with his brother, first pushed through an amalgamation of two of the Sunnite schools of Islāmic law, and then, in 1310 or thereabouts, transferred his allegiance to the Shī'ah. By that time the Shī'ites had already grown numerous in Persia and Mesopotamia; and they were now soon to consolidate their position for good. Attempts by Buddhist monks to win back Uljaytū to their faith were unsuccessful and led to their final expulsion from the country. The ruler's adoption of Shī'ism could not fail to provoke new disorders, as it upset the recently established balance between the religious communities and also gravely affected relations with Egypt, which were strained in any case. So severe was the persecution which Uljaytū inflicted on the Sunnites — though it temporarily alleviated the position of the Christians — that civil strife seemed bound to break out, when the Khān died on December 9, 1316.

All these developments had a chilling effect on Persia's relations with Western Europe. Early in his reign Uljaytū sent ambassadors to the Pope and the Kings of France and England with letters[1] containing a sort of blueprint for the solution of world problems; but the replies which these sovereigns gave were very reserved. In the changed circumstances there was no longer any thought of real cooperation. The natural result of this situation was that people in Western Europe lost interest in the Mongol kingdom of Persia: references to Īrān vanished gradually from literary works, and missionary efforts underwent a sharp decline, having shifted to Golden Horde territory. Only the Italian trading agencies still carried on for some time longer.

Uljaytū's death placed the dynasty in a critical position, because his son, *Abū Sa'īd* — the first Mongol ruler of Persia to bear an Islāmic name and no other — was a minor child. The stage was clear for the appearance of new leaders whose first step was to eliminate, and in 1318 execute, the conscientious minister Rashīd al-Dīn. His place was taken by an army general named *Chūbān* (*Çoban*), of the Suldūz tribe, who steadily increased his power and reinstated the Sunnite form of Islām, which Abū Sa'īd and the court adopted. With the other minister, 'Alī Shāh, Chūbān had no quarrel; and when the former died a natural death in 1324, the chroniclers did not overlook the fact that he was the only minister of the Persian Mongols who had yet done so. Chūbān's eventual fall was caused by a singular chain of unfortunate circumstances. He had given his daughter in marriage to an influential Amīr generally known as "*Big*" (perhaps "*the Elder*") *Ḥasan*; but Abū Sa'īd formed a desire to make her his own wife — another seeming indication that the Mongol women still went unveiled and that Near Eastern and Islāmic

[1] Some are still preserved.

influences were only gradually making themselves felt. Chūbān endeavoured to stave off this marriage, probably for fear that the wrath of the grandees would fall on his own head if Ḥasan were offended. This opened the door for a welter of intrigues at the court. When a son of the general was caught inside the ruler's ḥarem, the latter gave a signal for the Chūbān family to be tracked down and exterminated. Besides Chūbān himself, several of his sons perished in 1327. Abū Saʿīd could now at last possess himself of "Big" Ḥasan's wife.

To such conduct by their young ruler, the nobles reacted with a conspiracy headed by the aggrieved husband, and a number of armed clashes followed. The consequences would have been more serious had not Egypt and Persia concluded in 1323, after years of inconclusive fighting, a peace settlement which maintained the territorial status quo in Syria and proved to be durable. The chaos in Persia could thus develop at its own pace, until on November 30, 1335, while campaigning against the Golden Horde forces in the Caucasus, Abū Saʿīd suddenly died without legitimate issue. Not improbably he had been poisoned for reasons of jealousy by the same daughter of Chūbān around whom all the quarrels of recent years had turned. In the face of the danger threatening from the north, the factions came to terms and chose a distant relative of the deceased to be the new ruler; but no sooner had the Golden Horde aggression been repelled than their intransigent squabbling burst out afresh, and the new Khān was overthrown after six months' reign. Two main parties arose, one grouped round "Big" Ḥasan and the other round Chūbān's son "*Little Ḥasan*", so called to distinguish him from his namesake. Each as it pleased installed and deposed puppet Khāns, many of whom perished in the never-ending strife. For one brief spell of a few months, the nominal sovereign was a woman. Eventually, in 1344, "Little" Ḥasan was murdered by one of his wives whom he had surprised in the act of adultery, while "Big" Ḥasan was obliged to retire to Mesopotamia. From Khurāsān and Transoxiana, army groups intervened in the fighting. In the course of this troubled period, the outlying territories either cut their ties with Persia, as did Little Armenia and Georgia, or disintegrated, as the Saljūq Sultanate in Asia Minor had done somewhat earlier, in 1317. The rulers of Harāt continued to go their own way. The torn and plundered land of Īrān, which for several years past had suffered further cruel ravages from the Black Death, now lay exposed to an invasion from the north. *Jāni Beg*, Khān of the Golden Horde since 1342, thrust through the Caucasus in 1357 and entered Tabrīz, whose inhabitants welcomed him as a liberator. After defeating the local potentates then in control of Āẕarbāyjān (for the last Īlkhānid sovereign had been driven from the scene during the preceding years) he set up his son *Berdi Beg* as his viceroy in the province. The latter, however, on his father's death in 1359, rushed back to Sarai to get possession of the throne, and Golden Horde rule in Āẕarbāyjān then collapsed; for the northern kingdom now also became an arena of ferocious civil wars.

The Mongol dominion in Persia thus fell utterly to pieces. Those of the former vassal states which survived the Mongol downfall, such as the Kurt principality at Harāt, bestirred themselves to extend their power; and several new states also came into being. Of these, one or two need brief consideration, notably that of the *Muẓaffarids* in Kirmān and Fārs. Descendants of an Arab family established in Khurāsān, they had served the Īlkhāns since 1286/7 in various administrative capacities in south-eastern Persia. One of them, *Mubāriz al-Dīn Muḥammad*, obtained possession of Yazd in 1318/9 and later subdued Sīstān. During the break-up of the Īlkhānid regime he added Shīrāz, which became his seat of government and base for continued expansion into north-western Persia. For a time he recognized the suzerainty of Mamlūk Egypt. Before long, however, he came up against the Golden Horde at Tabrīz (see below, p. 54), and in 1358 was the victim of a plot laid by his own son, *Shāh Shujā'*, in whose custody he died in 1364. During the latter's reign, the Muẓaffarid régime reached the zenith of its glory. This it owed not so much to the continual fighting — mainly with the Jalā'irids of Baghdād (see below, p. 42) — in which its Amīr was involved, as to the lustre shed by the presence at his court of the greatest Persian lyric poet, *Ḥāfiẓ* of Shīrāz (d. 1389-90). The works of Ḥāfiẓ, which have given so much delight to the world — to Western Europe not least through GOETHE's "West-östlicher Diwan" — are now considered to reflect the political fortunes of the poet's patron more extensively than was once believed [1]. Muẓaffarid sovereignty did not long survive the death of Shāh Shujā' in 1384. Weakened by civil wars among rival brothers of the ruling family, the realm was engulfed in 1393 by the new Mongol flood under Tīmūr (see below, p. 65 f.). A state which emerged at the other end of Persia, in Khūrāsān, deserves notice not because it gathered any significant strength, but because of its peculiar origin as a bandit state. This was the realm of the so-called *Sarbadārs* (meaning

---

[1] See QĀSIM GHANĪ, *Baḥs dar āṣār va afkār va aḥvāl-i Ḥāfiẓ* (Ḥāfiẓ, his works, thoughts and life), 2 vols. to date, Tehrān 1942-3; ROGER LESCOT in the *Bulletin d'Etudes Orientales de l'Institut Français de Damas*, Vol. X. (Beirut 1944) p. 57-100; cf. also the general study by HANS ROBERT ROEMER, *Probleme der Hafizforschung und der Stand ihrer Lösung*, in the *Abhandlungen der Klasse der Literatur der Akademie der Wissenschaft und der Literatur* (Mainz), Year 1951, No. 3, p. 97-115.

roughly "*Gallows Birds*"), extreme Shīʿites who had their headquarters at Sabzavār, and at the height of their power under *Wajīh al-Dīn Masʿūd* (1337/8-1344) controlled Nīshāpūr and Gurgān and the countryside as far as Damghān and Turshīz. Their subsequent politics followed lines typical of the period (see below, p. 62); one military leader ousted another or his heirs and held short-lived sway until the next coup d'état, while ambitious "Atabegs" and a fanatical Shīʿite darvīsh sect added to the local confusion. Uninterrupted internal and external fighting led to the break-up of this state, which disappeared from history when its territories voluntarily submitted to Tīmūr in 1379 or 1381.

In Mesopotamia, the rule of the Īlkhāns was superseded by that of a dynasty considerably more important and powerful than the Muẓaffarids or the Sarbadār chiefs. The founder was Ḥasan the Great or "Big" Ḥasan, the same Amīr who has already been seen at Tabrīz (see above, p. 39 f.); and he and his descendants are known as *Jalāʾirids* (after a Mongol prince to whom they traced their ancestry), or sometimes as *Īlkānids*. After the death of Abū Saʿīd he had at first maintained his position at the capital, but later was forced by the successes of "Little" Ḥasan to withdraw to Baghdād. From 1340 till his death in 1356 he kept a firm grip on that city, fighting all manner of wars at the head of the Jalāʾirid Mongol tribe. His son *Uways* joined with the Muẓaffarids in checking the Golden Horde's advance in Āẕarbāyjān and secured possession of that province as well as Mawṣil (Mosul) and later also Shīrvān. He was again successful in defeating attempts by the Mamlūks of Egypt to intervene in the affairs of Mesopotamia — attempts which were doubly menacing because the Muẓaffarids became temporarily vassals of Cairo. Mesopotamia enjoyed a happy period of comparative prosperity under the just rule and wise economic stewardship of Uways[1]. His prestige had risen high by the time of his death at the age of little over 30, which occurred in 1374 when he was campaigning against a dynasty of local successors to the Īlkhāns at Astarābād. After the death of Uways's son *Ḥusayn*, the Jalāʾirid realm split into two parts and soon was further subdivided. It thus fell an easy prey to Tīmūr, before whose invading legions the last Jalāʾirid ruler of Baghdād, *Aḥmad*, fled first to Egypt, then Syria and at last to Asia Minor. Eventually, after Tīmūr's death, he recovered Baghdād, but only a few years later, in 1410, met a violent end together with his sons at the hands of the "Black Sheep" Turcomans or Türkmens (see below, p. 74).

---

[1] Uways was also the patron of the great Persian satirist *ʿUbayd-i Zakānī* (d.c. 1371).

THE MONGOLS IN CENTRAL ASIA

The territories between the Oxus and Mongolia, with populations which had for centuries been predominantly Turkish, held a key position in the universal Mongol empire from the time of its inception under Jingiz Khān. To the first generation of Mongol conquerors, in the days before Persia was effectively subjugated, they represented a frontier zone and accordingly possessed great importance as the base where a future conquering expedition would be mobilized. Special arrangements were therefore made for their administration. Jingiz Khān had assigned these countries to his son Jagatai (whose name afterwards came into widespread use to designate the inhabitants of the region); but he had not drawn any line between Jagatai's sector and that which was to go to Ögedei. Since both brothers exercised jurisdiction in the area, occasional unpleasantnesses resulted; but the Muslim merchant *Maḥmūd Yalavach* (i.e. "*the Envoy*"), whom Ögedei had appointed governor of Transoxiana with headquarters at Khōqand (Farghānā), skilfully took in hand the reconstruction of that territory, which had been cruelly devastated by the Mongol tempest. Notwithstanding a rebellion by the townsfolk and peasants of Bukhārā in 1238-9, he succeeded in fostering an impressive new upgrowth of civilization. When Jagatai ordered the governor's dismissal, the Great Khān caused him to be replaced by his son *Mas'ūd Beg,* who conscientiously carried on his father's policies. Mas'ūd Beg's province extended from Besh Balygh to Samarqand and Bukhārā, but he resided by preference at the last-named city, where he was active in building public edifices. His astute handling of affairs brought Transoxiana unscathed through the stormy period between the death of Ögedei and the accession of Möngke (1241-1251). During the latter's reign, his position as governor was further consolidated, and Turkistān, Khwārizm and the Uigur country were added to his administrative sphere. With the virtual elimination of the authority of both Jagatai's and Ögedei's hordes in 1252, following the so-called "Prince's Plot" (see above, p. 16), Mas'ūd's influence correspondingly increased. He was the real ruler of Transoxiana.

The rapid recovery of the area north of the Oxus was halted by the Mongol civil war. When Aryq Böge began to feel the pinch caused by the stoppage of food deliveries to Mongolia from China (see above, p. 21), he dispatched to the west a prince of the line of Jagatai, *Algu* by name, with the task of procuring the necessary supplies from Turkistān. On arriving in Turkistān, however, Algu ignored this assignment and proceeded to grab Khwārizm from the Golden Horde, regardless of the political partnership between Berke and Aryq Böge. Hostilities then broke out between Algu and the ruler of Mongolia. The latter's forces, already hard pressed on other fronts, were beaten, and Aryq Böge had to abandon Turkistān and Transoxiana to his former emissary. Algu married *Ergene (Orgyna?) Khātūn,* widow of Jagatai's grandson and a woman of strong character. With the help of the financial resources made available by Mas'ūd Beg, he maintained his position till he died in 1266 and further enlarged his domain at Berke's expense by capturing Otrār on the Syr Daryā (Jaxartes).

The death of Algu gave rise to prolonged disorders. Several princes of the house of Jagatai contended for the throne until eventually a grandson of Ögedei named *Qaidu* won the day. A *Quryltai* which he summoned in 1269 approved measures to restore internal order and protect the towns and cultivated lands against the nomads. As the Īlkhān's troops had recently crossed the Oxus and destroyed Bukhārā, such action was urgently needed. While descendants of Jagatai continued to be installed as titular sovereigns, the real power remained with Qaidu. Though no reports exist of any frontier delimitation in the broad expanses of Central Asia and the real state of relations with the Golden Horde cannot be ascertained, it seems clear that Berke and his successors, being deadlocked in the Caucasus, agreed with Qaidu to combine against their common foe, the Īlkhān, and left the question of the seizure of Khwārizm and Otrār by the former Transoxianan ruler in suspense.

The practical fulfilment of this alliance was no easy task, because the Īlkhāns offered increasingly effective resistance to incursions from across the Oxus; and the political standing of Transoxiana accordingly declined. Although Mas'ūd Beg's three sons, who one after the other were appointed to the governorship of Bukhārā, were capable administrators and did much to strengthen the state fabric, a gradual economic and cultural decline set in. Its immediate cause was the devastation suffered during the numerous inter-Mongol conflicts of the preceding decades. Over and above this, the effect of changes in the population structure resulting from the Mongol cataclysm were now becoming apparent. On the one hand the indigenous Turkish element had been reinforced by immigration from the east, including that of the Mongols themselves who, as in other lands under their rule, soon merged with the Turks into a single language group. This population shift, which eventually made Transoxiana an almost wholly Turkish land, was bound to affect the general character of its civilization because the local Turks were no longer ready to adopt

Persian culture, and indeed for the most part showed some antipathy towards it. While in Īrān itself the Persian element emerged culturally victorious, in Transoxiana, where Turks in even greater numbers had been pouring in for centuries, it was either destroyed by the Mongols or assimilated. The only exceptions were certain small residual groups, which survive as the so-called *Tājīks* and *Sarts* of modern Turkistān.

In the early years of the 14th century, Transoxiana was convulsed by fierce civil warfare, with only a brief intermission brought about by the attempt of one of the Khāns of Turkistān to arrange peace on the basis of a compact between all the Mongol states. In the course of these struggles, Jagatai's descendants succeeded in recapturing the sovereignty of Transoxiana and Turkistān and in virtually driving Ögedei's descendants from the political scene. Peace was restored in 1309, but the damage caused by the fighting had been so great that many districts became depopulated and only ruins attested the former importance of the cities. Though the reigning Khāns transferred their residence to the south of Transoxiana, they did not wholly give up their nomadic way of life. One of them, *Tarmashīrīn*, who reigned from 1326 to 1334, deserves special note because of his conversion to Islām; a few unimportant Khāns before him had been Muslims, but it was he who headed the subsequently unbroken series of Muslim sovereigns in this country. The religion founded by Muḥammad thus won over the three western Mongol courts; and in spite of their political antagonisms, it stamped each of these states with certain identical features characteristic of the civilization of the Near East. This common cultural background and the never wholly interrupted flow of commerce tended to equate the civilization of all the western Mongol realms at approximately the same level.

In the Jagatai realm, however, the state of feeling between the conservative elements who clung to the Yasa and the more strictly Muslim groups was such that hostilities between them flared up. The outcome was that the eastern half of the territory seceded in 1346-7 and that Transoxiana became independent. Details of this episode are not known, the available sources being extremely meagre. At all events, the control of Transoxiana soon passed into the hands of Turkish Amīrs or Begs who by now were wholeheartedly in favour of Muslim civilization and no longer in this area had any use for the old Mongol ways. They did, however, keep in office Khāns of the lines of Jagatai and Ögedei with a status comparable to that of the ʿAbbāsid Caliphs at Cairo. In the eastern Jagatai country, on the other hand, the Khāns, who had their seat near

Almalygh, were able to destroy the power of the Begs. The split in the Jagatai realm was thus complete and final [1].

A generation later, these territories were to be reorganized by Tīmūr. Before this is considered, however, the other adversaries of the Īlkhānid realm in Persia must receive attention.

[1] For more details, see "*Handbuch der Orientalistik*", ed. by B. Spuler, vol. "Turkologie (Geschichte)".

Ögödei Kha'an

THE GOLDEN HORDE

An account has already been given (see above, p. 22) of the circumstances in which *Berke,* Khān of the Golden Horde from 1257 to 1267, broke away from the universal Mongol empire, proving thereby that the Caucasus formed an international barrier not to be straddled by any unitary political edifice. The struggle for Caucasia kept Berke occupied throughout his reign. With his death the position changed. Necessary though it might be to secure the southern frontier, a more urgent task was to organize the East European sphere of influence on which this Volga-based state was economically dependent. Once the Russian states had submitted to Mongol authority, they had been left on the whole to their own devices, so long as they paid their tributes. An expedition led by the prince *Nokhai* in 1259 had pushed as far as Galicia but had not produced any lasting change in the situation. The Russians thus enjoyed the necessary respite in which to make a considerable recovery from the Mongol terror and recast their national life within the frame of the new order. Their efforts achieved success, for several reasons. In the first place, the Mongols continued to leave the native principalities alone and intact, though individual princes were often deposed for lagging in their tribute payments, fighting among themselves or other offences. Another no less important reason was that the Khāns at Sarai did not interfere with the religious life of their subjects and vassals, and that the Orthodox Church accordingly maintained its position. Orthodox Christianity formed by far the strongest bond of union between the contemporary Russians, split up as they were into many small states, and the Metropolitan of Kíev was the standard-bearer of Russian unity through all the vicissitudes of this period. He remained scrupulously loyal to the Khāns out of gratitude for their tolerance and for their grant to the Church of manifold privileges and rights of protection and inviolability; but at the same time he took all possible care of the interests of his own people. In the then existing circumstances, the church alone was capable of keeping alive the traditions of common statehood and nationhood and of preserving those possessions which would one day make possible the renaissance of Russia. In order to do so, the church had to hold fast and resist outside influences. This explains the rigidity which in past centuries was so often displayed by the Orthodox church and which still seems to Western eyes to be characteristic of it today. Only by tenacious adherence to principles once adopted could the faith, and with it the nation, survive the centuries of foreign domination in Russia.

Far from shunning the political stage, the Metropolitans of All Russia were fully aware that they symbolized the idea of Russian statehood, and they therefore followed political developments with close attention. When the old Russian state fell to pieces after the destruction of Kíev, they moved elsewhere and finally, around 1300, made their seat at *Moscow*. They chose a point where a new state whose future appeared promising had begun to crystallize.

It was not by mere chance that the political centre of gravity underwent this shift. The Mongol invasion had put a stop to the southward and south-eastward expansion of the Russian people, which had been making steady, if slow, progress during the 11th and 12th centuries. Since the areas concerned had passed into the possession of the conquerors, the Russians had to look elsewhere; and they found a new outlet in the vast plain lying to the north and north-east. Not only did Moscow now replace Kíev as the centre of gravity of East Europe; but the Russian colonization movement to the north and east — a movement of the utmost historical importance, comparable with the eastward migration of the medieval Germans — was also a direct result of Batu's conquests.

For the time being, all that mattered to the Mongols was to exploit the Russian princes financially. No other motive underlay the system which they set up in the country. They exercised their control through appointing *"Baskaks" (Basqaqs,* i.e. *tax officials)*, whose function was to ensure the punctual payment of dues, to apply force against recalcitrants, occasionally to suppress disturbances and to safeguard Mongol interests in the event of hostilities between any of the princes. During the 13th century these officials enjoyed considerable independence, as the main interests of the state continued to lie in the south. Not only Caucasia, but also Bulgaria and Thrace, were involved. The Bulgarian Tsar had submitted to Mongol suzerainty, as already mentioned, in or around 1242. Around 1260 and thereafter, the Mongols of Russia intervened in the struggles between Bulgaria and Constantinople with the object of putting pressure on the Byzantine emperor Michael VIII, and then reached agreement with the latter on joint action to counteract Serbian pressures and quell certain national movements, directed against any foreign control, which had appeared in Bulgaria. Good relations with Constantinople also contributed towards the encirclement of the Īlkhān's possessions in Asia Minor. On one occasion, a Saljūq Sulṭān of

Rūm actually fled to the Tatar court at Sarai. By making use of this fugitive, the Khān hoped to acquire influence at Konya (Iconium) and probably thus to link up with the Mamlūks in Syria, thereby barring the Īlkhāns from access to the Mediterranean and contact with Western Europe. Such plans, however, were vain, because the exiled Sulṭān could not be restored to his throne.

The alliance with Transoxiana concluded by Berke's successor, *Möngke Tīmūr* (1267-1280), was also aimed against the Īlkhāns; but since the Transoxianan offensive in Khurāsān and the Egyptian offensive against the Franks in Syria both came too late, this combination to overthrow the Īlkhānid régime in Persia failed. Relations with Egypt, however, remained particularly close, because in this case the political friendship was accompanied by an active commercial association and cultural intimacy. From Egypt came the commodities of civilization, fine textiles, choice fruits, rare perfumes, even exotic animals, and suchlike, which the Khān's embassies often brought back as gifts for their sovereign and his entourage. The Volga basin and the Black Sea coasts supplied Egypt with slaves *(mamlūks)* and so with her soldiers, and received from the Nile valley artists and theologians, whose activities had important effects on the future evolution of the Mongols in Russia. Berke, being a Muslim, encouraged them to the best of his ability. As might be expected, the meagre available sources suggest that Egyptian and Syrian influences as well as Central Asian influences from Bukhārā and Samarqand were at work in the fields of theology and medicine. In the field of art, the Egyptian influence can be more clearly traced in the surviving monuments. Wall-paintings, mosaics and ritual objects such as mosque-lamps and tombstones, show an ever more conspicuous imprint of Egyptian styles as the years went by, and also increasingly reflect Syrian and Anatolian features. The civilization taking shape on the Volga thus acquired a distinctly Mediterranean-Islāmic aspect, whereas the court at Tabrīz became specifically Persian. Egyptian architects and artisans built edifices in the Crimea and also at the successive capitals, *Old* and *New Sarai*. In these two cities a remarkable civilization developed. Solidly built houses arose with mosaics, wall-paintings, porticos and a system of central heating through tiled floors (as in the Roman *tepidaria*) with hardwood tiles. At New Sarai, dams were constructed to provide water for the canals and hydraulic power for the workshops, some of which were almost on the scale of factories. The most important products were glass and pottery. Excavations have brought to light astonishing engineering works, huge palaces and caravansarais and extensive graveyards. In the rubble dumps and cemeteries all sorts of ceremonial accessories have been unearthed, some of them imported from abroad, others manufactured on the Volga bank itself [1].

Islāmic culture thus fixed its grip on the Volga Mongols; and even though Berke's successors were not Muslims, they did not hinder the spread of the Prophet's teaching. Nestorian Christianity had lost all influence after Berke's conversion, and Buddhism had never had any influence in these parts. The Golden Horde empire accordingly remained untroubled by religious conflicts like those which were such a feature of the Īlkhānid realm, and the absorption of the Mongols into the Islāmic communion proceeded smoothly. Their ancestral Shamanist faith survived longer here than in Īrān, but offered less resistance to Islām than did other world religions (such as Christianity and Buddhism in Persia) before being finally extinguished.

Here as in Persia, acceptance of Islām facilitated the amalgamation of the Turks and Mongols. The available evidence, and the present-day physical characteristics of the Volga Tatars, indicate that the Mongol element was from the outset proportionately weaker than in Persia and still more so than in Central Asia. In records and on coins the Mongol language gave way to the Turkish at an earlier date than in the latter countries, though for quite a long time Eastern Turkish (Uigur) was used along with Persian as a vehicle of culture. The process by which the intrusive Mongol ruling class and the Turkish tribes whom they brought with them combined with the pre-existing Turkish inhabitants of the Qypchaq plain to form the modern "*Tatar*" nation thus took relatively little time. At an early stage certain heterogenous elements were assimilated, including the Volga Bulgars (whose speech differed considerably from the other Turkish languages) and numerous members of the Volga Finnish tribes. These elements soon began to affect the physical type of the rising Tatar nation.

Relations with Western Europe meant as much to the Golden Horde empire in the 13th century as they did to Persia. The promoters of these relations, however, were for the most part not missionaries or Papal emissaries but Genoese merchants. As early as 1267, the Genoese gained a preponderant influence at Sarai. They contrived with virtually complete success to frustrate Venetian attempts to found trading posts, and turned the south-east coast of the Crimea into an almost exclusively Genoese preserve. Genoese "factories" arose in rapid succession with their headquarters at Kaffa (the present Feodosia), where a Genoese consul held

[1] F. V. Ballod (Balodis) (Bibliography, p. 112).

office and exercised an autonomous jurisdiction alongside the Tatar authorities of the Crimea. For several decades their mutual relations were good, until in 1308 a violent but short-lived crisis blew up which resulted in the burning and temporary occupation of Kaffa by the Tatars. The trade with the Genoese was at least as important to Sarai as that with Egypt. The imports included Flemish tissues, fine porcelain, silverware and jewelry, while the exports consisted mainly of furs, fish and grain, which were shipped to Constantinople, Egypt and Italy and thence to the rest of Europe. The land routes to the west through northern Rumania (Moldavia) and Polish Galicia played only a minor part in this early phase.

The expansion of Genoese influence was made easier by the outbreak of civil strife within the Horde. The one-eyed prince *Nokhai* (who owed his deformity to an arrowshot) earned such abundant distinction as army commander in Galicia in 1259 and 1286 and Caucasia in 1261-3 that he was able to group the Tatar tribes of the steppe lying north and north-east of the Black Sea into a virtually independent dominion of his own. At Sarai itself he usurped almost all real power from several successive Khāns, one of whom abdicated rather than play the rôle of a puppet. After securing a measure of protection for his rear through a marriage alliance with the Byzantine emperor's daughter, Nokhai was also in a position to strike northwards from his base in the south into Russia. In short he became an all-powerful "mayor of the palace". The young Khān *Tokhtu (Tuqta'a)* who came to the throne in 1291 would have none of this. He disencumbered himself of his brothers whom Nokhai had interposed as conjoint sovereigns, and fought a long and bitter war which ended in the defeat of Nokhai's forces. The general himself was killed in action by a Russian private soldier late in 1299. These protracted struggles sapped the strength of the state. Since Nokhai never actually attained the throne, his machinations had a centrifugal effect. The degree of his ascendancy can be gauged by the fact that the Tatar tribes which had supported him henceforward called themselves "*Nogais*" and that a remnant still surviving in the North Caucasus has kept the name till today.

For several decades past, no powerful offensive had been launched in the Caucasus; but hardly had Tokhtu triumphed in the civil war when he sent a massive delegation to Tabrīz with a categorical demand for the retrocession of Caucasia. The Khān felt all the more confident of his prospects because the ruler of Georgia had rallied to his cause. Ghazān, however, was not intimidated; he made it clearly understood that Persia would never surrender her mountain line except to superior force. In the event, Tokhtu's military moves beyond the Terek river miscarried completely. He therefore had no choice but to concentrate his future attention on Russia. By this time, Russo-Tatar relations had reached a critical phase, with Russian princes flouting Tatar officials, Russian robbers roaming in organized bands for plunder and the tax revenues slipping from the hands of the Baskaks, who no longer possessed the power to enforce their sovereign's requisitions. Gradually the idea gained ground at Sarai that the management of the revenue system might be left to the Russians themselves. The loyal and at times submissive attitude of the princes of Moscow led the Khāns on the Volga little by little to entrust these latter with the collection of the taxes and tributes. For their part the Muscovite princes, who were men of amazing diplomatic agility, knew full well how to discharge this responsibility to the satisfaction of their suzerains. Their position enabled them in due course to reduce the other Russian princes to a more or less subordinate status, and to assume the hereditary title of Grand Prince, which the Khāns confirmed. No steps to check this process were taken by the Tatar rulers, who for the time being were oblivious of any danger from their Muscovite vassals.

The prestige of the Golden Horde dynasty, which had recovered perceptibly with Tokhtu's successful handling of the crisis caused by Nokhai's ambitions, reached a new peak during the reign of his nephew *Özbeg*, who succeeded him in 1313 after overcoming various rivals. Having embraced Islām despite the initial opposition of certain aristocratic circles, it was he who in this particular Mongol state headed the subsequently unbroken line of Muslim Khāns. His action was a decisive step in the long process whereby the Tatar nation came into being. The triumph of Islām among the Qypchaq Mongols had effects which were the reverse of those brought about by its triumph among the Mongols of Persia; for whereas the latter identified themselves religiously with their subjects, the former set up between their subjects and themselves a definite religious barrier. It has sometimes been suggested that the Khāns might have replaced the original dynasty of Rurik and become the Tsars of Russia if they had only accepted Christianity and thus identified themselves with the Russian nation. By choosing not to do this but to guide their own nation to Islām, they precluded any possibility of its russification. There are good grounds for accepting the theory that the religious cleavage was the only obstacle which prevented the complete disappearance of the Tatars as a nation through assimilation with the Russians. In this sense Özbeg can be described as the real founder of the

Tatar nation; and one of the Turkish peoples of Central Asia, the Özbegs (Uzbeks), still calls itself by his name today.

In his conduct of foreign affairs, Özbeg faced a changing situation. The Bulgarian kingdom, in whose affairs Tokhtu like his predecessors had actively intervened, now slipped from the control of Sarai, and Constantinople also began to extricate itself from all obligations to the Golden Horde. The cessation of hostilities in Syria and the conclusion of the Perso-Egyptian peace treaty in 1323, and even more the break-up of the Īlkhānid empire in 1335 and subsequent years, deprived the Cairo-Sarai axis of all significance. On the other hand, the Western Christians transferred their missionary activities from Persia, where their prospects had become hopeless, to "Northern Tartary" as the Volga empire was then called. The Pope, *John XXII*, definitely believed that even though Özbeg could not be won to Christianity, he could be persuaded to uphold toleration and to authorize the establishment of mission posts. The Pope also felt confident of having behind him an influential body of support for Christianity, in the persons of certain princesses at the court and of the heir apparent, *Tīni Beg*. The vision of a Christian Tatar state, at Sarai instead of Sulṭānīyeh, once more seemed near to reality. A number of missionaries and emissaries accordingly proceeded in 1338 to the Volga, stopping on their way at the Genoese settlements in the Crimea, which had already been equipped by the Popes with their own "Latin" hierarchy. A "Latin" bishopric was now established at Sarai alongside the Orthodox bishopric which had been founded as early as 1261 to cater for the growing Russian community.

Meanwhile, the situation in Russia had again become critical. The never-ending struggles between the princes for the favour of the Khān and therewith for the grant of the Grand Princely title demanded extraordinary vigilance by the court at Sarai. After long hesitation Özbeg definitely conferred the Grand Princedom in 1328 on the Muscovite prince *Iván I, Kalitá*, who was considered particularly reliable because he had married a Tatar princess and because like his predecessors he had rendered meritorious service as collector of the Russian princes' tributes. With this arrangement, the Russian problem was provisionally solved.

Under Özbeg's rule, the cultural life of the Golden Horde reached its zenith. Most of the buildings and engineering works unearthed by archeology are thought to have been constructed during his reign, though the scantiness of the written sources and the absence of dates on the excavated remains make it impossible to substantiate this assumption. It is nevertheless clear that by embracing Islām, the Khān and the nobles led the people as a whole to adopt the Muslim way of life and the Sharī'ah as their law in place of the Yasa. Egyptian and Syrian artists, artisans and men of learning could now set to work with unconstrained assurance. The influences from Asia Minor also became steadily stronger, especially in the Crimea; the Turkish origin of the inhabitants of both countries promoted their cultural, linguistic and spiritual assimilation.

The interests of the Golden Horde did not, however, run altogether parallel with those of the rising Ottoman state. The expansion of the latter revolutionized the diplomatic position of Sarai.

In the year 1354, the Ottoman Turks succeeded in crossing the Dardanelles and establishing a foothold on the European shore. The shipping traffic through the Straits accordingly ceased to be under the sole jurisdiction of the weak Byzantine emperor, who had neither the strength nor the desire to obstruct the trade between the Crimea and Cairo and was perhaps still bound by a commercial treaty renewed in 1281. With the Ottoman Turks in control of the Dardanelles, there could be no possibility of further strengthening relations with Egypt, which in any case were already becoming rather less close. The Golden Horde thus came to be excluded from the Mediterranean and from the drama of world politics, in so far as this was played on its shores. The new situation was not unlike that of the Russian empire in later centuries. Geographical factors now turned the Golden Horde empire into a purely East European state, with a future rôle confined to the political arena of that region.

The Khān *Jāni Beg* (1342-1357), who assured the final victory of Islām by overthrowing his pro-Christian brother *Tīni Beg* after the latter's accession in 1341, was by no means disposed to accept without challenge the loss of all access to the south. A new invasion of the Caucasus had already been attempted by Özbeg in 1335; and Jāni Beg now took advantage of the utter anarchy in Persia to launch a large-scale offensive, which this time was crowned with success. After a rapid and well led advance, the Khān marched into Tabrīz in 1357. By this campaign and by his projected alliance with the Muẓaffarids (see above, p. 41), he hoped to open up another outlet to the south as an alternative to the Dardanelles. Notwithstanding the reluctance of the Muẓaffarid ruler, the conquest of Āẕarbāyjān gave the Tatar Khān an opportunity to establish direct communications with Syria and Mesopotamia. Jāni Beg, however, did not exploit his victory. He left Tabrīz almost immediately and entrusted the government of the area to his son. There is reason to suppose that he did so in order to escape from a new epidemic of the bubonic plague or "Black Death", which had already claimed large numbers of victims in the Crimea in 1348-9. Directly after his return to Sarai he died, having probably brought the fatal infection with him from Āẕarbāyjān. His son and successor *Berdi Beg*, fearing violent competition from his numerous brothers, sped forthwith to the north. The Persian conquests of the Golden Horde were thus abandoned, and the Caucasus was left to its appointed destiny.

These setbacks in the international position of the Golden Horde were soon followed by a complete internal disintegration. Berdi Beg only ruled two years before being ousted by one of his brothers, who shortly afterwards fell to an assassin's blow; and one revolt or murder then followed another. The structure of the state underwent a collapse from within like that seen shortly before in Persia. Numerous pretenders and army commanders feuded fiercely, but no single one could make himself master of the whole territory or keep power for long.

This collapse was all the more disastrous because it coincided not only with the rise of the Grand Princedom of Moscow but also with that of two new states, Moldavia (northern Rumania) and Lithuania. Moldavia occupied a highly strategic position, and its Hospodars succeeded in breaking the hold of the Tatars on the lower Danube, besides disputing their possession of what is now Bessarabia. A much more serious threat came from the growing power of the Grand Duchy of Lithuania. From its starting point in the Lithuanian homeland, this state had expanded further and further to the south-east, annexing the whole of the modern White Russia and large parts of the northern Ukraine. It now began to push relentlessly southwards, towards the Black Sea. At the battle of the Blue Waters (now the Sinyukha river) in 1362, the Lithuanians won an important victory over a league of the local Tatar magnates of Podolia. This led to the expulsion of the Tatar "Baskaks" and other local authorities from the area and to the appointment of a Lithuanian princely family, the so-called *Korydtovichi*, as protectors of Podolia, Volhynia and the Carpathians up to the Hungarian border. They kept guard on the frontier against the Tatars and harassed the Muslims of the coastal districts between the Dniestr and Dniepr mouths. Mainly as a result of their efforts, the Lithuanians succeeded about 1370 in capturing the city of Kíev and thereby acquiring a solid base for action against the powers of the steppe.

This event also presented a challenge to Moscow, which could not remain indifferent when an essentially alien power such as Lithuania conquered large parts of the old country of the "Rus" and might well deserve the title, to which the Lithuanian Grand Duke *Vitold* (1377-

1430)[1] began to lay claim, of "(Tribute) Gatherer of the Russian lands". A new source of tension which it was worth the while of the Tatars to exploit accordingly sprang up, though some time elapsed before the attitudes of the parties became clear. In 1380, however, the Tatar general *Mamai* was defeated by the Muscovites at the battle of Kulikovo Pólye (the "Snipe Field"), on the Don river; his forces were smashed and he himself was overthrown soon afterwards. As things turned out, this defeat did not fundamentally weaken the power of the Golden Horde, because it enabled *Tokhtamysh*, a claimant to the throne then favoured by the Central Asian ruler Tīmūr, to gain an eventual victory over his rivals and at last re-establish stable government in the Tatar realm. In 1382 he led a campaign against Moscow and after besieging the city compelled it to resume paying tribute.

The vitality of the Golden Horde state seemed fully restored when into its midst plunged the conqueror who was soon to dominate all Western Asia: *Tīmūr*.

EGYPT: THE BAḤRĪ MAMLŪKS

After this review of the Mongol states in the Muslim world and of the conflicts between the Īlkhānid state in Persia and its northern neighbours, the affairs of Egypt require scrutiny within the frame of the general picture. The Nile valley was the rallying ground of the forces which stemmed the Mongol torrent and most persistently opposed the Īlkhāns. It was also the land in which Muslim civilization continued to develop without any sharp break such as was experienced elsewhere; for the torch of Islāmic learning ceased for decades — in some cases for centuries — to burn in its old hearths in Central Asia, Persia and Mesopotamia and even to some extent in Syria, notwithstanding the Mongol failure to break the Egyptian hold on that country. During the later Middle Ages, Egypt became the centre of Near Eastern intellectual life. In particular, the related sciences of Islāmic law and theology found an asylum by the Nile where they could maintain a continued though somewhat fossilized existence.

Like other Near Eastern countries, Egypt underwent a great transformation in the middle years of the 13th century. After the downfall of the Ayyūbid dynasty, the imported *Mamlūk* slave-troops seized power and chose a commander, *Qotuz*, to whose ability was due the

[1] In modern Lithuanian, *Vytautas*.

decisive first victory over the Mongol invaders in 1260 (see above, p. 20). Though Qotuz was murdered for a personal grudge just after the battle, his murderer and successor, *Baybars*, proved to be one of the great figures of Muslim history; his heroic feats are still remembered in popular romances. During his reign, the finishing touches were put to the Mamlūk system of governing Egypt. At the top stood an aristocracy drawn from the military caste. The Sulṭān guarded the privileges of this caste and kept its numbers replenished by carefully planned imports of additional slaves. These came chiefly from southern Russia and Caucasia, and were shipped to Alexandria by Byzantine and Italian middlemen; but since the Caucasian element was quickly assimilated with the Turkish, the ruling class kept a definitely Turkish character, not only in its speech, which showed certain affinities with the language used on the Volga, but also in its general culture and social life. In short, the internal structure of the Mamlūk state broadly resembled that of the Mongol states being built up during the same period. This inherent similarity helps to explain how Egypt could be the birthplace of a powerful military organization, including a highly efficient intelligence service, especially designed for defence against the Mongols. To the success achieved by this organization, Egypt owed her continued territorial independence. Not only were the military systems, weapons, notions of valour and methods of fighting much alike on both sides, but in Egypt as in Persia a military caste with Turkish characteristics was grafted onto an alien population. The Mamlūk and the Mongol feudal systems were very largely identical, and both of them influenced the subsequent development of Ottoman-Turkish feudalism. The essential feature was the concentration of much of the soil as "military fiefs" in the hands of the dominant alien group. This feudal pattern of the state was typical of the period everywhere.

The legal and other learned professions were organized on somewhat analogous lines. Their economic basis lay in income from the *waqfs*, pious endowments founded by wealthy benefactors through bequests or donations of some part of their estates to the religious community — on the understanding that the founders' descendants would be provided therefrom with stewardships or other sinecures adequate for their livelihood and immune against the risk of confiscation by the ever impecunious Mamlūks. Large holdings of agricultural land and even more of urban real estate thus became available for religious and charitable purposes. Since learning and theology were the only professions in which native Egyptians could attain high office, abundant growth ensued in these fields. The main activity, however, was compiling and commenting;

hardly a single creative work appeared during the 13th and 14th centuries. History writing did not exhibit much originality either, though vast chronicles were composed, along with biographical dictionaries like that of *al-Ṣafadī* (c. 1296-1383) and manuals of administration like that of *al-Qalqashandī* (d. 1418). A movement for religious reform was initiated by *Ibn Taymīyah* of Damascus (1263-1328), but met with drastic repression; its call for a return to primitive Islām presented too much of a challenge to the generally accepted, and in Egypt officially established, schools of law. Ibn Taymīyah's opinions nevertheless lived on quietly and have greatly affected the modern Wahhābī movement.

The specifically administrative side of the government was also left alone by the Mamlūks, who preferred military pursuits; but it was only filled to a relatively small extent by Muslim Egyptians. This was the domain of the Christians (especially the Copts) and the Jews, who despite persecutions — for instance in 1301 and 1321 — continued as for centuries past to form the dominant element in the bureaucracy of the Nile valley, particularly in the record offices and tax-collecting departments. The traditional bureaucratic methods remained likewise in use; and the Egyptian state machine continued to turn through all the repeated upsets of its masters. The Mamlūk aristocracy did not ordinarily see fit to recognize the hereditary principle, but preferred to let control pass into the hands of the momentarily strongest general. The position, however, remained uncertain through the period (1259-1382) in which power was held by the *Baḥrī* Mamlūks — so named because their barracks were on the island of Rōḍah in the *River* Nile (*Baḥr* al-Nīl). The son of Baybars was ousted within two years of his father's death in 1277 on an expedition to Asia Minor against the Mongols. His successor *Qalā'ūn* (1279-1290), who won great renown as conqueror of the remaining Crusader footholds along the Syrian coast and as organizer of the Mamlūk army, was followed on the other hand by four generations of his own descendants. One of these, *al-Malik al-Nāṣir*, who came to the throne as a child in 1293 and reigned (with two early breaks) till 1341, gave the country a rather long spell of relatively stable government after repelling the Persian Mongols (see above, p. 38) and putting down a rebellion in Upper Egypt. Thereafter palace revolutions became the order of the day. During such upheavals, the so-called Caliph seemed a pillar of stability as titular sovereign of the realm. This extended, at the height of Mamlūk power, to Cyrenaica on the west and Maṣawwaʿ on the south, besides comprising the whole of Syria as far as the middle Euphrates. The last Crusader castles in Syria fell to the Mamlūks in 1289 and 1291. It has already been seen how after the fall of Baghdād Baybars had welcomed a fugitive ʿAbbāsid prince to Cairo and formally acknowledged him as sovereign. This step was intended to add weight to the Mamlūk government's stand against the initially pagan Mongols and assure it of special prestige among Muslims as protector of the Caliph; but the extent to which the desired effect ensued was very modest. The ʿAbbāsid Caliph at Cairo was only acknowledged in northern India and initially in the Golden Horde realm (see above, p. 24). His presence nevertheless conferred on the régime a semblance of legitimacy. In fact though not in constitutional theory, the ʿAbbāsids now were spiritual overlords, unarmed with temporal powers, which by established usage they were required to transfer to the Sulṭāns installed by the Mamlūks. The recognition of Egyptian suzerainty by the Sharīfs of Mecca and Madīnah (see Vol. I, p. 93) also helped to enhance the prestige of the Mamlūk Sulṭāns.

Besides building up a military strength sufficient to hold off the Mongols and giving shelter to the world of learning, the Egyptian state as thus constituted produced notable achievements in architecture — mosques, baths and royal tombs — and in the minor arts and crafts. It also began to resume a central position in the trade and related politics of the Mediterranean similar to that which Egypt had held in antiquity and until the coming of Islām (as discussed in the works of HENRI PIRENNE). The country kept up close commercial and political relations with Constantinople and also joined hands with her against the Persian Mongol menace. A firm front against the Mongols was maintained in Syria, whose northern frontiers had long since passed from the control of the Byzantines into that of the Saljūqs, the Little Armenians and now the Īlkhāns. (Little Armenia was finally conquered and annexed to the Mamlūk empire in 1375). The old rivalry with Byzantium had consequently abated. Venice and Genoa, however, were vigorously expanding their commercial activities in the Levant. The Crusades had greatly assisted their efforts. The success of the two Italian maritime republics proved that Christian Europe and the Muslim East could work together and profit from one another in spite of all their differences. The interdict which had kept the Christian and Muslim worlds with their many common religious and cultural legacies so far apart for centuries was now lifted. Instead there began a period of mutual association, such as had once been seen in Spain and notably in Sicily. It is impossible here to to go into details of the steadily growing Mediterranean trade; but special mention must be made of the political alliances which covered Egypt, Sicily, the Italian republics and Spain, and provoked the Persian Mongols in turn to seek contacts with Western and Central Europe. During this period the Near East, North Africa and Europe were drawn into a common diplomatic system, and East and West achieved an intimacy in their relations such as had not been known since ancient times. Herein lay the origins of the later oriental policies of the European powers, of the incipient "capitulation" system and of the much discussed "Eastern Question".

From Egypt it will be convenient to set sail for a land in the south east of the domain of Islām, whose Muslim inhabitants had at first lived remote from their coreligionists elsewhere and did not emerge from this isolation till the 11th and 13th centuries: that is, for India.

INDIA BEFORE TĪMŪR

It was during the second great wave of Muslim expansion — in the same year 711 in which Spain fell to the Arabs — that the Muslims first reached India. Only limited areas of the huge subcontinent — Sindh and the lower Panjāb — were penetrated by the victorious force commanded by *Muḥammad ibn Qāsim*, whose target was the city of Multān near the confluence of the five great tributaries of the Indus. For several centuries to come, this city remained the centre of Indian Islām. The question of the treatment to be accorded to the subject Hindu population was decided in accordance with the precedent set in Persia; just as the Zoroastrians of that country had been assured of religious freedom despite the literal meaning of the Qur'ānic text, few qualms were felt about leaving the Hindus to themselves, and no objections to this policy appear to have been raised by the tolerant Umayyads of Damascus. The Muslims showed wisdom in thus refraining from attempts to convert the Hindus by force; for otherwise they would certainly have brought about their own destruction in revolts by their subjects or invasions by neighbouring Indian princes. In fact, however, things settled down amicably, and the Muslims kept possession of the territory for several centuries. When the various provincial governors of Persia shook off all central control from Baghdād, the Indian territory likewise could no longer be governed as a province and was taken over by two independent principalities, which passed around 900 under Carmathian overlordship (see Vol. 1, p.p. 68). Internal conditions probably evolved on lines roughly parallel with those observed in Egypt and Mesopotamia; though the tax burden on the subject inhabitants was not insupportable, the prospect of joining the ruling class probably led to conversions among them on much the same scale as in those two countries.

The first great change in the situation came when the Turkish Ghaznavid dynasty of eastern Īrān intervened in India. The origin of the Ghaznavids and their place in Persian history have been discussed earlier, and it has already been emphasized that their policy (like that of other nations and tribes occupying eastern Īrān) had India as its main objective. The greatest figure of the dynasty, *Maḥmūd of Ghaznah* (997-1030), was eager to demonstrate his zeal for the Islāmic faith so recently adopted by his ancestors and compatriots; and as the Turks of that period were far behind the Arabs and Persians in all branches of intellectual and cultural activity, he set himself up as a patron of art and learning, Firdawsī and al-Bīrūnī, the explorer of India, being his most illustrious protégés. In the ensuing centuries, the Turkish attitude towards Islām was often characterized by the same two qualities; munificent patronage of art and learning, and a warlike eagerness to spread the Prophet's doctrine by conquering new territories and founding new states. The Indus valley, where there were Carmathian heretics as well as Hindu pagans to be dealt with, offered a tempting goal for Maḥmūd's ambition. In about two dozen campaigns in 1006 and subsequent years, he imposed or confirmed Muslim sovereignty with fire and the sword. He felt no compunction whatever about propagating Islām by force, which indeed was permitted according to the literal interpretation of the Qur'ān and seemed all the more justifiable because Muslims have always regarded the Hindu religion with its numerous and sometimes obscene idols as a particularly abominable form of paganism. The Hindus offered tenacious but ineffective resistance, and the entire Panjāb fell to the Muslims; but Gujarāt, further to the south, held out with sufficient success to be able to keep its independence, now and for the next two hundred years.

Events in Īrān after Maḥmūd's death obliged his son *Mas'ūd* to entrust the administration of the Indus provinces to governors, who acted ineptly and developed proclivities to independence from Ghaznah. Finally Mas'ūd had to commission an Indian in his service, *Tilak*, to organize and lead an expedition. This achieved complete success and left the Ghaznavids in secure possession of the Indus valley with its metropolis *Lahore (Lahāwur)*, though a second offensive begun in 1044 was halted by the stiffening resistance of the native Indian princes. It is at this point that the Panjāb and the Indus valley must be considered to have become definitely part of the Muslim world, as they still are today. The Ghaznavids maintained their authority over this region and over a diminishing area of eastern Īrān (corresponding to parts of the modern Afghānistān) for another century and a half. From 1117 onwards they acknowledged the suzerainty of the Saljūq Sulṭān Sanjar (see Vol. 1, p. 96) over their Īrānian territories, which they lost in 1151 to the Ghūrids. The Panjāb remained under Ghaznavid rule till 1186 and was then likewise conquered by the Ghūrids, whose brutal and destructive conduct has already been mentioned (see Vol. 1, p. 97).

The Ghūrid conquests did not merely lead to the establishment of a new régime within roughly the limits of the old Ghaznavid realm; they also galvanized the Muslims into new expansive action. No sooner had the Ghūrid ruler *Ghiyāth al-Din Muḥammad* made sure of his Indian foothold than he set out eastwards at the head of his seasoned troops to invade the middle Ganges valley. Since the Indians at that time (as in other ages) fell short of their north-western neighbours in military capacity, the ultimate issue could not be in doubt. First the Ghūrid *Muʿizz al-Dīn Muḥammad,* then his trusted "mamlūk" *Aybak* and finally a Turk of the Khalaj tribe, *Ikhtiyār al-Dīn Muḥammad,* pressed forward with only occasional setbacks past *Delhi (Dihlī),* which fell in 1190-91, to Bengal and the mouths of the Ganges (1202), destroying on their way the last Buddhist kingdoms of upper India. In this brief stretch of time, Muslim sovereignty was extended over the north of the subcontinent and the ground was prepared for the dissemination of Islām in large parts of north-western India and Bengal — including the areas which since August 15, 1947, have been grouped into the state of Pākistān with its racially and linguistically complex population of about 80,000,000 Muslims.

A long time was needed, however, before the foundations of the new empire in northern India became consolidated. Ghūrid power ceased to be formidable when its prime movers, the brothers Ghiyāth al-Dīn and Muʿizz al-Dīn, died in 1203 and 1206 respectively; and the dynasty was shortly afterwards extinguished. After the death of Aybak in 1210, the country was torn by civil wars, whose origin was to be found in its peculiar governmental structure. It was a distinctive feature of the Muslim world during the 13th century that the régimes which then emerged in many of its parts (in Spain somewhat earlier) were of a type which may be termed *"mamlūk"*. An intrusive military group, in the east generally of Turkish origin, made itself master of a country with an alien population, and power was seized by a clique of officers risen from the rank and file of the slave-soldiers or "mamlūks". These officers appropriated to their own use a great part of the financial resources and landed property of the country. From among them came the reigning sovereign, who might sometimes belong to a family in which hereditary right was recognized, but more often owed his position to some form of election or to his personal military prowess. In the Saljūq and Mongol states, it was only after several decades, when the heirs of Saljūq and Jingiz Khān turned out to be incapable or under age, that this type of régime appeared (though the legitimate rulers were generally kept on as puppets); but eventually some such system prevailed even there, as also in Egypt, Spain and parts of North Africa, and now in India. There could of course be no permanence in these régimes; but they left their mark on later medieval Islām and made it possible for a number of vigorous and talented military leaders to rise to the top and win power and prestige for their respective countries. One such leader was Aybak's son-in-law *Iltutmysh (Iletmish)*, the greatest of the *"Slave Kings"* of Delhi and the first Muslim ruler of India to receive the Caliph's brevet, who after long struggles got the better of the local mamlūk aristocracy called "The Forty" and ruled with energy for over 25 years till his death in 1236. Another was the grim tyrant *Balbān (Balabān)*, a Turk of a lordly family from Central Asia, who first held power for twenty years in the typical role of "guardian" *(atabeg)* of the puppet descendants of Iltutmysh, and then thrust them aside in 1266 to take possession of the throne himself. He died in 1287. Earlier India had experienced a phenomenon also seen during this century among the Ayyūbids of Egypt, the Mongols and a local dynasty in the Persian province of Fārs: for a few years a strong-willed woman ruled[1]. Such a state of affairs had never been tolerated by the Arabs and Persians, but was consistent with the different status of women among the early Turks; the 13th century Turks were by no means wholly subject to Near Eastern influences. The middle and lower administrative functions, as well as the practice of Islāmic theology and therewith law, were exercised in India, no less than in the Saljūq, Mongol and Egyptian Mamlūk realms, by natives of the country. To some extent, therefore, the old governmental apparatus and the old indigenous way of life continued as before, though the native population was liable to constant oppression and extortion. Administrative employments provided a livelihood for the former upper classes after the higher leadership, particularly of military and external affairs, had been wrested from them.

In external affairs, the "Slave Kingdom" played a rôle which was also analogous to that of the Egyptian Mamlūk state; for besides holding off attacks by immediate neighbours it was also largely engaged in resisting Mongols. The positions of the two states were, however, somewhat differently balanced. Although in direct proximity to Egypt itself

[1] *Raḍīyah Begum*, 1236-40 (see Dynastic Tables).

only the Nubians and a few Beduin tribes were of any importance as trouble-makers and even so were hardly serious adversaries, the whole weight of Īlkhānid Mongol might was brought to bear on the Syrian borderland, a country accessible to both contending parties. In India, on the other hand, the local enemies were considerably more formidable, whereas the Mongols came mainly in isolated marauding waves. They first appeared when Jingiz Khān ordered that the fugitive heir to the Khwārizmian throne be pursued across the Indus (see above, p. 10); but they never, it seems, received any definite support from the Īlkhāns — which probably explains why there is scarcely a mention of their activities in the Persian chronicles. Against full-scale Mongol invasion India enjoyed a certain immunity in her high and inaccessible mountain borderland, which formed a natural dividing line between the interests, military forces and civilizations on either side.

During the ensuing decades, India was the scene of further repeated Mongol incursions and frequent changes on the throne, while measures were decreed for the observance of Islāmic precepts and the strict enforcement of the Qur'ānic restraints on infidels, that is on Hindus. At the same time, new campaigns were launched into Central India and the Deccan (Dakhan) and into Gujarāt, which was now brought under Muslim rule. In these undertakings, the *Khal(a)jī* Sulṭān of Delhi *'Alā' al-Dīn* (1295-1316) and his generals displayed qualities of leadership far superior to those evinced by their adversaries; it was now clear that with sufficient effort the Muslims would have the military capacity to conquer the whole of India. Between 1305 and 1311 they penetrated the entire southern half of the peninsula and subjected all but a few areas to their suzerainty. 'Alā' al-Dīn also found time to patronize culture at his court and distributed lavish sums to scholars and men of letters. At Delhi during his reign, the greatest Persian poet of India, *Amīr Khusraw* (d. 1325), composed his numerous verses. Even in 'Alā' al-Dīn's lifetime, however, signs of decay began to appear; his death was followed by a series of palace revolutions in which power was seized by usurping slaves and favourites, while members of the ruling family were massacred down to the youngest child and enemies and rebels received equally barbarous treatment. In 1320, however, the Turkish general *Tughluq (Tughlak)*, who was a sincere Muslim, put a grim but salutary end to this state of affairs and was chosen to be Sulṭān. Under his capable guidance, some degree of order began to be restored; but he only reigned five years. In 1325 he was murdered by his son *Muḥammad II*, whose arbitrary tyranny provoked rebellions all over the country. Not even the ruthless methods used by this ruler availed to suppress them; and his schemes for reforming the taxation and currency systems and for transplanting whole populations led to famines and mass impoverishment. After leading a powerful army to complete destruction in an attempted invasion of China by way of Tibet (1337), he was in no position to prevent the definite secession of Bengal in 1339 and then of other provinces. The Deccan was taken over by an insurgent revenue collector who founded the *Bahmanid* dynasty of that country, and in other parts of south India the Hindus regained their independence. Muḥammad ibn Tughluq was succeeded by his cousin *Fērōz (Fīrūz)*, who in a reign lasting from 1351 to 1388 brought renewed prosperity to the area under his control through wise economic policies; he moderated the taxes, spent prudently, promoted agriculture and constructed roads and canals. He made no attempt to reconquer the Deccan and failed to subdue Bengal. In preference to military ventures, which were kept down to a minimum, he devoted his energy to architectural activity in the Indo-Islāmic style evolved over the foregoing centuries, and has left many fine buildings whose beauty compares well with that of the Mamlūk monuments. His way of governing, however, was too mild for those unruly times. The internal cohesion of the state was weakened by excessive grants of fiefs to influential Turkish officers and by further harsh treatment of the Hindus (though persecutions, together with financial inducements, won many a new convert to Islām). After the death of Fērōz came a period of general disintegration, soon to become utter ruin under the hammer-blow of the second great Mongol conqueror, Tīmūr, whose career now needs attention.

TĪMŪR

From the deluge of troubles which engulfed Transoxiana and Persia in the second half of the 14th century, a new military genius emerged in the person of a petty tribal princeling, *Tīmūr*. Born in 1336, he was the son of *Taragai*, head of the *Barlas* Turco-Mongol tribe. From an early age he associated with influential princes and generals, and in time he contrived to assemble a fair-sized force of his own. From about 1360 onwards, his star began to rise, though he was still to meet with many a sharp reverse in the incessant and historically quite unimportant warrings of contemporary Transoxiana. Accounts differ on the question whether it was in such a skirmish or when out sheep-stealing that he received the severe wound which crippled him for life and gave him the Persian surname *Lang ("the Lame")*, corrupted in the European languages into "Tamerlane". After years of fighting, much of it against his early friends, Tīmūr subdued the Kāshghar area and Khwārizm, and built up a powerful army consisting predominantly of Turks and Turkish-speaking remnants of the old Mongol tribes. Out of respect for the sentiments of his subjects, he arranged for one of Jingiz Khān's descendants to be elected as nominally supreme Khān and took for himself only the modest title of Beg (Amīr).

Even so, Tīmūr could not at once restore complete order in Transoxiana; for he now turned his thoughts to campaigns in other lands. In the Qypchaq country, he successfully installed his protégé *Tokhtamysh* (see above, p. 56); and with a view to the conquest of Persia, he crossed the Oxus in 1379. By means of barbarous cruelties such as building pyramids or towers from the skulls and corpses of his adversaries killed during or after battles, he sent a wave of horror throughout Western Asia and thereby broke down or greatly weakened all will to resist. When actually faced with resistance, he did not rely on his military skill alone; he would also attempt negotiations with possible traitors among the enemy, which more often than not led to the desired result, so that at the crucial moment great masses of the enemy would desert. The conquests of Tīmūr are not to be attributed solely to his qualities of generalship.

Tīmūr's career was an uninterrupted sequence of wars and predatory raids, which in frightfulness certainly equalled and probably outdid the campaigns of Jingiz Khān. This frightfulness is all the more shocking because it was devoid of any higher purpose. Jingiz Khān and his successors at least built up a well ordered empire and promoted economic and cultural growth by bringing together so many different regions of the globe. Moreover Jingiz Khān's successors soon developed a genuine taste for the finer sides of civilization. Tīmūr, on the other hand, though highly intelligent, was fundamentally uncultured. He judged human learning merely by its practical utility and never saw in it any intrinsic worth. Nothing that he did contributed to the subsequent development of civilization in Asia, and many of his campaigns were undertaken solely for plunder. Only his more important military feats need therefore be considered here (see map); the details, which are often repulsive, will be passed over. Between 1379 and 1385, Tīmūr subdued the whole of eastern Persia, defeated various local princes including the redoubtable Kurtids of Harāt (see above, p. 41) and suppressed rebellions which were constantly flaring up. He was then drawn westwards by the defiant attitude of Tokhtamysh, who had first attempted without success to organize the states of Western Asia into a system of alliances against his former patron and then, after the failure of these schemes, swooped down on Tabrīz. During 1385 and the next two years, Tīmūr's legions marched through Āzarbāyjān, Georgia, Armenia and northern Mesopotamia, expelling Tokhtamysh's garrisons, massacring tens of thousands of the inhabitants and laying waste untold numbers of towns and cities. He deemed it his special duty as a staunch Muslim to chastise the Christians, who suffered appalling torments at the hands of his troops. As an outcome of this campaign he turned aside to Iṣfahān and Shīrāz, overthrew the local princes and perpetrated unheard of atrocities, especially at the former city. An invasion by Tokhtamysh and a series of revolts in Transoxiana brought him hurriedly back to his homeland. After suppressing the revolts, he set out in pursuit of Tokhtamysh and marched diagonally accross the whole expanse of Central Asia to the Volga. The campaign continued until Tokhtamysh was put to flight at the battle of the Kandurcha river in 1391. Tīmūr then had his hands free.

He went back to Samarqand, which he had chosen as his summer capital and sumptuously embellished for the greater glory of his name. This by no means disinterested enthusiasm for rebuilding Samarqand was the one and only instance of concern on Tīmūr's part for things of the spirit. He caused a number of splendid buildings to be erected in the city; and sent artisans, artists and learned men from all the lands which he had conquered to live there and work for his purposes. The conqueror did not, however, stay long at his capital. In the following year he sallied forth anew. After marching through Persia into Mesopotamia and Syria and forcing the local potentates to flee or submit, he finally destroyed the power of Tokhtamysh in 1395 and thus made himself master of the entire area up to the Mediterranean coast and the frontiers of Asia Minor. Then, with an eye to yet richer spoils for his troops and with evident confidence that he had adequately secured his existing conquests, he decided to invade India, whose Muslim rulers he denounced as lukewarm champions of Islām. His passage over the Indus to Delhi brought sheer disaster to the area. Thousands of prisoners were butchered, and on December 18, 1398, after a trifling incident between his troops and some native soldiers, Delhi was given over to the sack — an ordeal from which it took many decades to recover. Having restored his finances with the booty acquired in India, Tīmūr resolved on war against the Ottoman Sulṭān *Bāyazīd I*, whose unsubmissive messages had long incensed him. Before opening the campaign, he took care to secure his left flank by subjugating Syria, as the Egyptian rulers of that country had adopted an equivocal attitude; and the citadels of Aleppo and Damascus fell before his onslaught. Egypt itself, however, was spared; an expedition to the Nile would have drawn the conqueror too far away from his goal, and he knew that the toughest fighting of his career lay ahead of him in Asia Minor. In fact the Sulṭān Bāyazīd had acted imprudently and neglected to make necessary preparations. Tīmūr was able to advance up to Ankara (Angora) before coming up against the Ottoman army, which shortly before had been besieging Constantinople; and as he once more contrived to suborn a fair number of the opposing troops, the battle ended in his favour (1402). The Sulṭān, who had refused all advice to flee, fell into his victor's hands and remained a prisoner till his death a year later; whether he was kept in an iron cage as the story runs, or carried round in a sedan chair with bars, cannot be clearly determined.

Tīmūr was now master of all Western Asia and could feel that his control of this vast empire, in extent hardly less than that of Jingiz Khān, was thoroughly secure. From beyond its frontiers, numerous rulers entered into diplomatic relations with him, one of them being the King of Castille, whose envoy, *Clavijo*, has left an interesting record. Yet his restless, warlike spirit was unsuited to tasks such as organizing an efficient administrative system or cementing together a hastily assembled aggregate of provinces.

Despite the exhaustion of his army and the growing reluctance of his senior officers, whose main ambition now was to secure and enjoy their hard-won riches, Tīmūr began planning a new war, this time with a view to the conquest of China. Scarcely had he set out, however, before he fell sick and died at Otrār on the Jaxartes river, on January 19, 1405.

The effects of Tīmūr's failure to integrate his conquests were felt immediately. The estate which he left had none of those qualities of permanence which had marked the empire of Jingiz Khān; and his enterprises, seen as a whole, were shown to have been not only hurtful in the extreme but also intrinsically futile. To Western Asia and the civilization of Islām, as also to Caucasia and oriental Christianity, they brought nothing but destruction and decay, with no such benefits as had accrued from the opening up of world-wide communications a century and a half earlier.

Unlike the sons of Jingiz Khān, who after their father's death agreed on a new Great Khān and lived in harmony for at least several decades, Tīmūr's descendants[1] plunged headlong into mutual strife. The decease

[1] See genealogical tree on p. 103.

of the sovereign was kept secret by the army commanders, who suspended the war against China and placed one of his grandsons in provisional charge of the government. This arrangement did not endure. Ferocious rivalries between the late conqueror's sons and grandsons led to several years of fighting, in which the advantage was eventually gained by *Shāhrukh*, a son of Tīmūr who was at first only viceroy of Khurāsān and had never been contemplated by his father for the succession. Though well endowed with military talents, he had a pacific temperament quite unlike that of his father and did his best to heal the wounds which the latter had inflicted on Western and Central Asia. Together with one of his sons, *Bāisunqur*, he gave great encouragement to the arts and founded an important library at Harāt. His authority, however, was not accepted without question. He had to deal with several insurrections by his own army commanders and sustain protracted hostilities with the "Black Sheep" (Qara Qoyunlu) Turcoman state (see below, p. 74). For all this, his reign gave the stricken population a respite for recovery and growth, and ushered in the last great productive period of Persian poetry and historiography. His son, *Ulugh Beg*, who succeeded him in 1447, was more conspicuous for learning (especially astronomy) than statecraft, and though moved by the best intentions, was unable to stand up against his turbulent relatives; before long he was dethroned and then blinded. The victor in the resultant family struggles was *Abū Sa'īd* (1452-1469), under whose energetic, moderate and shrewd leadership the eastern Īrānian lands (Khurāsān, Afghānistān and Transoxiana) were once more reunited. In the western regions of Īrān, his sovereignty was contested by the "White Sheep" (Aq Qoyunlu) Turcoman state of Uzun Ḥasan (see below, p. 75) with whom he warred unsuccessfully. Eventually he was captured by the latter and put to death.

Abū Sa'īd's death was followed by a new fragmentation of the Tīmūrid realm. The prince *Ḥusayn Bāiqara*, who resided at Harāt, had to fight for many years before he could reunite under his sceptre a part of the ancestral patrimony. He too was a friend of learning and of the arts, and during his long reign (1469-1506) the Īrānian genius found a refuge in Afghānistān[1]. As he grew older, however, Sulṭān Ḥusayn became afflicted with painful maladies and took to a dissolute life, with the result that his

[1] In Sulṭān Ḥusayn Bāiqara's reign Harāt was the home of *Jāmī* (1414-92), the poet and mystic, and numerous Persian historians and philosophers. His wazīr, *Mīr 'Alī Shīr Navā'ī* (d. 1501) has left works in Eastern (or *Jagatai*) Turkish as well as Persian. Under the Tīmūrids Persian art in the forms of architecture, carpet-weaving and miniature-painting reached its zenith — though unlike literature it continued to flourish under the Ṣafavids. Especially noteworthy are the XVth century shrines and mosques at Meshhed and the miniatures of *Behzād* (d. c. 1525).

realm suffered internal disruption and his sons began to rebel against him. He was unable to arrest the tendencies towards Īrānian unification which the rise of the Ṣafavid *Ismāʿīl* had set in motion in western Persia. Ismāʿīl trusted not only to military luck but to the power of the religious current which he headed — and which was to culminate in the triumphant surge of Twelver Shīʿism all over Persia. He gained control of most of Persia proper while Ḥusayn Bāiqara was still living. By the time of the latter's death, the position of the Tīmūrids at Harāt had become so weak that Ḥusayn's son had to acknowledge Ṣafavid suzerainty; and he eventually died at the court of the Ottoman Sulṭān.

All was thus over with the last representatives of Mongol statehood on Īrānian soil. The dynasty of Tīmūr cannot, of course, be categorically qualified as Mongol because, even if he did come of a Mongol family, his and still more his successor's régimes displayed essentially Turkish features. The triumph of the *Ṣafavids* in 1502 did not produce any fundamental change in this state of affairs; they too were of Turkish origin, and for a century to come the language of their court at Qazvīn and then at Iṣfahān, the new Persian capital, continued to be Turkish. They were accordingly not a national dynasty in the strict sense of the term. Geopolitical factors, however, obliged them, like the Īlkhāns, to attend to the national interests of Persia; and after so many decades of fragmentation and destructive civil war, the reunification of the Īrānian lands under a home-based government opened the way to a national rebirth.

The loss by Tīmūr's descendants of their Transoxianan sovereignty did not condemn them to banishment from the stage of history. One of the conqueror's great-grandsons, *Bābar (Bābur)*, was destined to be the founder of a mighty and durable new empire, not in Īrān but in India; and the fortunes of that country must now again be examined.

INDIA: FROM TĪMŪR TO BĀBAR

In Western and Central Asia, the shrinkage of Tīmūrid authority left room for the deployment of new forces. In India, Tīmūr's invasion so shattered the pre-existing order that the ground was likewise left clear for new developments. At Delhi after the death of Fērōz in 1388, one short-lived Sulṭān had followed another, disorders had broken out, Hindus had refused to pay the poll-tax and wazīrs had contended with one another for the real power. By 1393 the Sulṭān *Maḥmūd II*, a grandson of Fērōz, had managed to establish a fairly stable government; but conditions had continued to be such that he and his advisers could not throw any effective military force across Tīmūr's path after the latter's passage over the Indus in 1398. In the decisive battle near Delhi on December 17 of that year, the Indian troops were utterly routed, and the city and the entire surrounding area were mercilessly plundered. Tīmūr, who had accused the Indian princes of treating their Hindu subjects with undue leniency, chastised the country with his wonted brutality and departed leaving it a wilderness. Several years were needed before some sort of order could be restored. Eventually Maḥmūd, who had taken refuge in Gujarāt, succeeded in eliminating various rivals and once more got control of the government, though with his hands increasingly tied by the pretensions of his advisers, until his death in 1413. A year later, Delhi and the adjacent districts were seized by *Khiẓr Khān*, the viceroy placed by Tīmūr in charge of the Panjāb. He himself died in 1421, and his successors did not last long. Because of their purported descent from Prophet Muḥammad, they are known as the *"Sayyid"* dynasty. In 1451 the government was taken over by the *Lōdī* family, Turkish in origin but known as the Pathān — that is, Afghān — dynasty because their ancestors had been established in Afghānistān. The first of these rulers, *Bahlūl (Buhlūl)*, possessed considerable military ability and reasserted the ascendancy of Delhi over extensive territories where the central authority had almost ceased to be felt. The most important of these was Jawnpūr, which had made itself independent in 1394 and was reconquered by the Pathān Sulṭān in 1479, after protracted fighting[1]. Further expansion was achieved by Bahlūl's son *Sikandar* (i.e., *Alex-*

[1] The *"Sharqid"* rulers of this small state have left behind a number of fine mosques and other surviving architectural monuments.

ander), who reigned from 1489 to 1517. The realm came to stretch, at least nominally, from the Satlaj river in the Panjāb to the Bundelkhand district in the east, though the provincial governors and vassal princes within it enjoyed considerable freedom of action. Sikandar took particular care not to overstrain the economic resources of the country or provoke rebellion through excessive financial demands; and under his rule India enjoyed a period of comparatively peaceful development. The only difficulties which arose, and which recurred frequently, were attributable to his vigorous endeavours to promote Islām among the Hindus. After his death, his son *Ibrāhīm* overcame a number of rivals but remained weak on account of popular dissatisfaction with his rule and successive uprisings. Some of the malcontents sought help from abroad and addressed themselves to *Bābar*, the great-grandson of Tīmūr then reigning at Kābul. The latter's intervention in 1525-6 opened a new chapter in Indian history, that of the *Mughal* empire, which eventually incorporated the territories not only of the Delhi Sulṭānate but also of the other Muslim dynasties which had sprung up in India since the 14th century. The rôles of these latter must now be briefly considered.

The most important were in two areas which had cast off the domination of Muḥammad ibn Tughluq during the 14th century and continued thereafter to be subject to Muslim rulers. The greater part of South India had recovered its independence during the same period, but under the leadership of Hindu princes. Though Bengal broke loose comparatively early, in 1339, the fact was not admitted by Delhi until seventeen years later; and before another half century was out, the country fell into the power of a Hindu ruler, *Ganesh* (1404-1414), who instituted an anti-Muslim policy. By one of history's ironies, his son embraced Islām and under the name of *Jalāl al-Dīn Muḥammad* set to work in turn with all the zeal of a convert against the Hindus. The policies which he pursued during his reign of seventeen years were in all probability largely responsible for the adoption of Islām by a high proportion of the inhabitants of Bengal, where it is today the religion of the majority in many districts. Tīmūr's invasion did not affect Bengal, which indeed profited from the weakening of the north-west Indian empire; its position became more secure and it was able to preserve its independence till the latter part of the 16th century, notwithstanding violent upheavals of rulers and dynasties and repeated disorders caused by struggles for power among the local "mamlūks", who were imported from Africa.

The Muslim rulers of Bengal faced less acute difficulties than the *Bahmanid* dynasty in the *Deccan*, as the latter had to fight continual wars with the new Hindu states which had arisen on both the southern and the north-eastern frontiers of its domain and were continuously encroaching on it. The capital of the Muslim Deccan was at first Gulbarga (also called Aḥsanābād), then from about 1425 onwards Bīdar. Besides the founder of the dynasty, who died in 1358, several of the subsequent rulers were bloodthirsty tyrants, who often persecuted the Hindus and had in consequence to take the field against repeated uprisings, which in turn led not only to conflicts with the neighbouring Hindu states but also to secessions of various districts under their former Muslim governors (*"Ṭarafdārs"*). Palace revolutions, insurrections by the all-important mercenary garrison and clashes between Sunnites and Shīʿites also often occurred. These defects weakened the Bahmanid state internally and lowered its capacity to resist external enemies, with the result that the Hindu neighbours made frequent incursions; and during 1461 and the following years, it was only by dint of intense efforts that a nucleus of the state was kept in being. The moving spirit behind these exertions was an outstandingly able wazīr, *Maḥmūd Gāvān*, who was ultimately rewarded not with gratitude but, in 1481, with death. In 1490 the Bahmanid realm fell to pieces and in 1518 the dynasty disappeared. In its place five Muslim states arose: Bijāpūr, Aḥmadnagar, Berār (till 1574), Golconda (near the modern Hyderābād) and Bīdar. To the north lay another Muslim state, Malwa (1401-1531). The five Sulṭānates of the Deccan consumed most of their energies in continual fighting with one another, with the Hindus, with the newly arrived Portuguese and with domestic rebels; but at the battle of Talikota in 1565 they together destroyed the powerful southern Hindu kingdom of Vijayanagar and thus eliminated their most dangerous external enemy. After this great victory, they were able to continue their independent existences until at various dates during the 17th century they were incorporated into the Mughal empire.

It was in the Bahmanid and subsequent Muslim states of the Deccan that the *Urdū* language first came into literary use — as yet only for poetry. At Delhi, Persian held undisputed literary sway and Urdū only began to be written in the 18th century.

The west coast province of *Gujarāt*, which had been conquered by ʿAlāʾ al-Dīn (see above, p. 64), asserted its independence under a Muslim dynasty at the end of the 14th century. Its inland capital, Aḥmadābād, was founded by a capable early Sulṭān, *Aḥmad Shāh* (1410-1442). Its ports, especially Cambay, were now as earlier the scene of great activity by Muslim merchants and sea-farers, to whom must be ascribed the implantation of Islām in Malaya and Indonesia. During the 16th century,

Gujarāt struggled vigorously but on the whole unsuccessfully against the new maritime power of the Portuguese, and after suffering the usual internal breakdown was annexed to the Mughal empire in 1572.

The beautiful valley of *Kashmīr* in the Himalayas north of the Panjāb was also to become part of the Mughal empire, though it had never been subject to the Sulṭāns of Delhi. According to the Muslim chronicles, the country's first Muslim sovereign was an adventurer who had entered the service of its Hindu ruler and then seized power, in 1349. His grandson, *Iskandar* (1386-1410), stayed neutral during Tīmūr's invasion of India and treated his Hindu and Buddhist (Tibetan) subjects with much severity; it was probably during his reign that the great majority of the population became Muslim. On the other hand his grandson *Zayn al-ʿĀbidīn* pursued during a reign of fifty years (1420-1470) a policy of unqualified toleration, besides giving all possible encouragement to learning and the arts and to the economic welfare of his realm. His death was followed by a confused period of succession disputes, civil wars, invasions from Kāshghar and Lahore and dynastic changes, which only came to an end when Kashmīr was added to the domains of the Great Mughal in 1586.

The early fortunes of the Mughals were much influenced by the new situation which had arisen in Persia.

QARA QOYUNLU AND AQ QOYUNLU

After the death of Tīmūr, Mesopotamia and Āẕarbāyjān broke loose from the rule of his descendants. The Jalā'irid Aḥmad (see above, p. 42) at first made some headway, but could not muster enough strength to match the cohorts of the *Qara Qoyunlu ("Black Sheep")* Turcomans. Once the vassals of his ancestors, these Shīʿite tribesmen had since around 1375 been settled in the Mosul area of Northern Mesopotamia and adjacent parts of Armenia and Āẕarbāyjān and had since 1390 been led by an ambitious and warlike chieftain, *Qara Yūsuf*. The latter, who was on fairly good terms with the Mamlūks in Syria, first swept away Tīmūr's son *Mīrān-Shāh* and then, while the Tīmūrids were frittering away their strength in internecine struggles, defeated Aḥmad near Tabrīz in 1410 and put him and his sons to death. Aḥmad's capital, Baghdād, now fell into Qara Yūsuf's hands, and a branch of the Jalā'irid family still ruling in southern ʿIrāq and at Shūshtar was eliminated in 1421. The 300 year old dominion of the *Artuqid* family at Mārdīn and in parts of the Mosul area (see Vol. 1, p. 91) was also overthrown, in 1412, by Qara Yūsuf, who led minor expeditions in all directions and was preparing for a major collision with the powerful Tīmūrid Shāhrukh (see above, p. 69) when he died in 1420. Before the disputes attendant upon his succession had been resolved, Shāhrukh inflicted heavy losses on the Qara Qoyunlu but failed to gain effective control over their original territory of Āẕarbāyjān. Qara Yūsuf's eldest son *Iskandar* led a roving life full of adventures and battles, not unlike that of Jalāl al-Dīn Mangūbirdī (see above, p. 10), until one of his sons murdered him in 1437. Conditions then became more stable, as Iskandar's successor, who was his brother *Mīrzā Jahān-Shāh*, enjoyed the favour of Shāhrukh and had been invested by the Tīmūrid government with jurisdiction over Āẕarbāyjān; and he at first maintained cordial relations with his patron. After the latter's death, he was able step by step to occupy large parts of western and southern Persia, especially in the years 1452-1456; and though later forced back by the Tīmūrid Abū Saʿīd, he kept control of Āẕarbāyjān, Jibāl or Media, Mesopotamia (after ousting the local rulers, who came of his own clan), Kirmān and even the coasts of Oman (ʿUmān) in eastern Arabia. His authority was called in question by rebellions of his own sons, but remained intact until 1466 when he was defeated and killed by *Uzun Ḥasan*, whose career will shortly be discussed; and within two years of that event, all was over with the Qara Qoyunlu state.

Its heritage passed to the Turcomans of the *"White Sheep" (Aq Qoyun)* tribe, near kin of the "Black Sheep" but Sunnite in faith, who towards the end of Tīmūr's reign had established themselves in the country round Edessa (ʿUrfah), Āmid (Diyār Bakr) and Sivas under the leadership of *ʿUthmān Beg*, surnamed *Qara Ilük* (the "Black Leech"). After the founder's death, the realm was partitioned in 1435 among his numerous sons on the suggestion of the Qara Qoyunlu prince Iskandar and thus rendered provisionally harmless; but the "White Sheep" Turcomans soon resumed their turbulent career. At home and abroad, among themselves, and against the Qara Qoyunlu, the Turkish tribes of Asia Minor (especially the Dhū'l-Qadr and the Qaramānly) and the Mamlūks, they fought without intermission.

In the international scene, the Aq Qoyunlu only became important after 1449, when *Uzun ("Long") Ḥasan*, a grandson of the founder, prevailed over his relatives and began to expand at the expense of the Qara Qoyunlu, whom he finally vanquished in 1466-1468. His success in repelling a simultaneous attack by the Tīmūrid Abū Saʿīd, whom he captured and executed near Tabrīz in 1469, added Jibāl, Iṣfahān, Kirmān and Fārs to his domains, which now included the whole of western and southern Persia. With the Tīmūrid Ḥusayn Bāiqara (see above, p. 69), he prudently avoided hostilities in view of the growing threat with which his realm was confronted in the west. This came not from the Mamlūks — though he had frequent clashes with them — but from the Ottomans, lords of Constantinople since 1453, who in the teeth of his protests and of his attempt to intervene had taken possession in 1462 of the Greek state of Trebizond (where an uncle of his wife had been ruling), and had put an end in 1460 and 1466-68 respectively to the Turkish principalities of Kastamonu and Qaramān (Caramania) in Asia Minor. To offset this danger, Uzun Ḥasan followed the precedents set by the Mongols and the Mamlūks and sought alliances with Western Europe. As the Genoese had to keep on good terms with the Ottomans for the sake of their Crimean possessions (see above, p. 50 f.), he opened negotiations in 1463 with the Venetians, to whom the Ottoman power presented an equally serious menace; they had already been dislodged by the Ottomans from the Peloponnese and since 1462 had been carrying on open warfare with them in Albania. The alliance did not in fact lead to any concrete co-operation between the two parties, because the Aq Qoyunlu ruler was severely defeated by the Ottomans in 1472 and 1473 at the battles of Lake Kereli (Beyşehir Gölü) and Terjān (near the upper Euphrates between Erzinjān and Erzerum), while the Venetians were pinned down in Greece and Cyprus. Uzun Ḥasan was able to withdraw to the safety of Āzarbāyjān, but could not afford to attack the Ottomans again, as the Venetians repeatedly urged him to do; and before he had finished reorganizing his realm, he died on January 4/5, 1478. Internal disorders then beset the Aq Qoyunlu state, which would have fallen an easy prey to its neighbours had not the new Ottoman Sulṭān *Bāyazīd II* (1481-1512) been of a more pacific disposition than his father. Uzūn Ḥasan's successors thus kept their independence for a few decades, as did the Turcomans of Albistān (Abulustain) in the zone between the Aq Qoyunlu, Ottoman and Mamlūk empires; while Cyprus, whose Lusignan (Crusader) Kings had been saddled with an Egyptian garrison since 1426, was ceded in 1489 by its last queen, *Catharine Cornaro,* to her native country, Venice.

With the rise of the Ṣafavids in Īrān under Shāh *Ismāʿīl I* (1501-1524) and the accession to the Ottoman throne of *Selīm I* (1512-1520), there could be no independent future for the lands between them. During the years 1500-1514, the Ṣafavids occupied Āẕarbāyjān, Jībal and Baghdād, while in 1515 the Ottomans annexed Albistān and imposed their suzerainty upon Dhū'l-Qadr (where Selīm had his own grandfather executed) at the expense of the Mamlūks. The resultant conflict ended in the Ottoman conquest of all Syria and of Egypt (see below, p. 79).

Though many episodes and aspects of the "Black Sheep" and "White Sheep" domination remain obscure, it is clear that the two Turcoman dynasties left no significant imprint on the Muslim civilization of the Near East. Apart from a certain number of architectural monuments, notably at Tabrīz, they cannot be credited with any cultural achievements comparable with those of their Ṣafavid and Ottoman successors or their Tīmūrid and Mamlūk contemporaries.

The destinies of Egypt and Syria during this second period of Mamlūk rule have yet to be reviewed.

EGYPT: THE BURJĪ MAMLŪKS

The Nile valley was the only important Near Eastern country which remained untouched by the second, no less than the first, Mongol deluge. On the second occasion, however, it owed its immunity not to the military prowess of its Mamlūk masters but to their submission to the suzerainty of Tīmūr. The supremacy of the Baḥrī Mamlūks had first been assailed in 1382 and came to an end after a fairly long period of disorder in 1390. It was replaced by that of another series of Mamlūk rulers, called the *Burjī* or *Circassian* Sulṭāns because the regiments which supported them were quartered in barracks near a tower (*burj*) and had at first been recruited mainly from Caucasia, though they had long since become Turkish in speech and manners. The change accordingly made no fundamental difference to the position of the Egyptian people; but it had certain political effects. The rule of the Burjīs was much more rapacious and harsh than that of the Baḥrīs, and there was rarely any question of hereditary transmission of the Sulṭānate. The founder of the Burjī régime, *Barqūq* i.e., (the "plum", or "apricot"), was himself quite a forceful ruler; after winning a hard and at first hopeless-looking struggle against his rivals (1389-92), he made good his authority over Syria and boldly gave shelter at his court to a bitter enemy of Tīmūr. This was the fugitive Jalā'irid prince Aḥmad, formerly ruler of Baghdād as his ancestors had been since the "Big Ḥasān" of the closing years of the Īlkhāns had established himself in that city (see above, p. 42). Tīmūr could not, of course, overlook such a hostile gesture; but his quarrel with the Ottomans kept him busy till after the death of Barqūq in 1399 and he never declared war against Egypt, though he sacked Aleppo and Damascus as a preliminary to his victorious campaign against Bāyazīd I. Barqūq's son and successor *Faraj* (1399-1412) chose to submit to the great conqueror and until Tīmūr's death in 1405 remained nominally his vassal. Egypt then went through an unsettled period, in which the most noteworthy event was an attempt made in 1412 to install one of the puppet 'Abbāsid Caliphs as the real ruler of the country. Stability was not restored until the throne passed to *Barsbāi* (1422-1438), the ablest general among the Burjī Sulṭāns, one or two of whom before him had also displayed qualities of military leadership. His victories in Cyprus in 1426 and against the "White Sheep" Turcomans (see above, p. 75) and other princelings in Syria and Mesopotamia did much to restore the international prestige of Egypt. On the other hand, his financial and tariff policies, both at home and abroad at Jiddah in Arabia, proved quite disastrous. He squeezed the wretched Egyptian peasants even drier than the millennial custom of the country allowed. Among the Sulṭāns after him few possessed any of his military ability but nearly all followed his financial example; indeed they went further, for besides satisfying the appetites of the military aristocracy they spent large sums on building the sumptuous Tombs of the Mamlūks which still stand near Cairo. As worthy exceptions, mention must be made of the pious and frugal Sulṭān *Chaqmaq*, who only spent lavishly in support of learned men, and his successor *Īnāl (Yinal)*, who fought an indecisive war in Cyprus. Another of Barsbāi's ill-considered measures was to burden the European and Indian trades, from which Egypt derived such profit, with transit dues and currency restrictions of a severity which evoked protests from the Italian maritime republics. Though a few concessions were granted to appease them, the general effect was to interest the Italians, and still more the now very enterprising Portuguese and Spaniards, in possible alternatives to the use of the route through Egypt and dependence on Egyptian intermediaries. The possibility became a reality when Vasco da Gama doubled the Cape of Good Hope in 1498 and discovered the sea route to India.

Not many years passed before the Portuguese began to attack the Egyptians from the rear. They prosecuted their assault on Muslim shipping and coastal positions in the Indian Ocean and Red Sea with such vigour that Egypt's trade arteries to India and the Persian Gulf were virtually severed. They also established a foothold in Abyssinia, and even though this did not endure, the Egyptians were faced with the prospect of having a powerful enemy in the south. It was fortunate for Egypt that the inhabitants of Nubia, who had formerly been Coptic Christians, had finally gone over to Islām in the 13th and 14th centuries and that there were accordingly no openings in that country for Portuguese intervention. Moreover, the spread of Islām had resulted in the collapse of the two main Christian kingdoms of the old Nubia, and any political potentialities which the country might have possessed had been nipped in the bud by its fragmentation during the following centuries into a multitude of petty states.

While the Mamlūk rulers of Egypt were harassed at home by internal difficulties and disorders, abroad the Dhū'l-Qadr, the Qaramānlys, the "White Sheep" Turcomans (see above, p. 75 f.) and finally the ever more formidable Ottoman Turks encroached upon the Egyptian sphere of influence in the northern Syrian borderlands. The prudent and magnanimous, though cruel, *Qāitbāi* (1468-1496) and the Sulṭāns after him did not lack military abilities, but failed to plan any definite foreign policy or strategy; and the position of *Qānṣūḥ II al-Ghūrī* (1501-1516) was so impaired by financial troubles and unsuccessful naval warfare with the Portuguese that the Ottoman Sulṭān *Selīm I* did not have much difficulty in defeating the Mamlūk forces near Aleppo on August 24, 1516, or in putting an end to the Burjī dynasty with his capture of Cairo in January 1517 [1]. The Ottoman conquest of Egypt thus took place in the same year in which, some months later, the Protestant reformation in Europe was launched by Martin Luther.

The origins and rise of the Ottoman empire will not be considered in the present volume; and this neglect may perhaps have some justification, because until after the end of the 15th century that empire played only a peripheral part in the affairs of the Muslim world as a whole. With other Muslim states, aside from the petty Turkish principalities of Asia Minor, its contacts during the period were few. Its importance lay rather in the success with which it carried forward the banner of the Prophet into regions never before subject to Muslim rule. The domain of Islām was enlarged by the Ottoman Turks, as it had been earlier enlarged by the Mongols; but the Muslim Near East did not experience Ottoman political intervention before the time when Selīm I began a struggle against the new Turkish, but Shī'ite, dynasty which had reunited Persia, and then drove out the last Turcoman rulers from the intervening territories and conquered Syria and Egypt.

The rest of this volume will be concerned with the destinies of the Muslims in East Europe.

---

[1] See Herbert Jansky, *Die Chronik des Ibn Tūlūn als Geschichtsquelle über den Feldzug Sultan Selīm's I. gegen die Mamluken*, in *Islam* XVIII (1929), p. 24-33; Ibn Iyâs, *Journal d'un bourgeois du Caire*, tr. and annotated by Gaston Wiet, Paris 1955; George W. F. Stripling, *The Ottoman Turks and the Arabs*, Urbana 1942 (see Bibliography); David Ayalon, *Gunpowder and firearms in the Mamluk kingdom*, London 1956.

THE MUSLIMS IN EAST EUROPE

One of the lands smitten by the sword of Tīmūr was the East European empire which had been added to the domain of Islām by the Golden Horde. The ruling Khān of that empire, *Tokhtamysh*, had only been able to win his throne by reason of the help which had been given to him by Tīmūr (see above, p. 56); but not long afterwards he rashly intruded into Tīmūr's sphere of influence by leading an expedition to Caucasia and Tabrīz (the last ever undertaken by a Golden Horde ruler), and thus incurred the great conqueror's displeasure. In 1391, the latter went to war with his former protégé, and after the initial fighting in Transoxiana had ended disastrously for Tokhtamysh, the road lay open before Tīmūr, who advanced to the Volga but soon withdrew. Tokhtamysh then fought hard to regain his throne, but in 1395 a second campaign by Tīmūr ruined his fortunes for good. He eventually had to flee the country, and in view of his old enmity with Moscow sought refuge at the court of the Lithuanian Grand Duke *Vitold* (see above, p. 55-56), who had concluded a defensive and offensive alliance with him in 1392 and now undertook to restore him to the Golden Horde throne. In return for Vitold's help, it was understood that Tokhtamysh would recognize him as the future lord of all Russia and invest him with the immediate possession of a great many districts, most of which belonged to the Grand Prince of Moscow but some directly to the Horde. Vitold thus acquired an excellent pretext to intervene in Golden Horde territory with the object of extending his authority to the Black Sea. His calculations, however, proved false. After a number of exploratory raids had further convinced him that the Horde could be overthrown without much difficulty, he began to advance southwards down the Dniepr in 1399; but on August 12 of that year he met with a decisive defeat on the Vorskla river, near the modern town of Poltava. The Horde had in fact recovered rapidly after the fall of Tokhtamysh, as effective power had passed from the hands of the transient Khāns then reigning into those of a mayor of the palace, *Edigü* (Russian: *Yedigéi*), who was a competent general.

This recovery went so far that at times the Tatars could again extract tribute payments for Podolia. Vitold's ambitions suffered a severe setback, and the Lithuanian menace to the Golden Horde was eliminated for many years to come. The authority of the Koryátovichi also came to an end during this period. Edigü next turned against Russia, where Tokhtamysh had found his last refuge; in the winter of 1406-7 he finally destroyed the pretender, and in 1408 he subjected Moscow to another siege and put a stop to its insubordination. These wars nevertheless caused such a drain on the resources of the Horde that Edigü could not prevent a partial recrudescence of the Lithuanian influence on the Volga; and Vitold was able on occasions to procure the accession of Khāns, including sons of Tokhtamysh, who were acceptable to himself, and to counteract Edigü's authority in this way to an extent which made it difficult for the latter to maintain his position. After Edigü's death in 1419, the Lithuanians kept the Golden Horde in leading strings for a decade, and Vitold very largely achieved his goal of an outlet on the Black Sea. The area between the Dniepr and Dniestr rivers became virtually a Lithuanian sphere of influence, and Vitold was able to build a castle near the site of the modern Odessa.

The ascendancy of the Lithuanians in these parts only lasted till the death of their great ruler in 1430. His constant interventions, however, left such confusion in the ranks of the Golden Horde that before many years passed it was to break up from within. His policy had had the effect of making it customary in the Horde for the rival parties to seek supremacy by elevating Khāns of their own choice; and it was only because one party had hitherto always been strong enough to overcome its rivals and restore the unity of the monarchy that the empire had continued to be a single whole. In 1438, however, a lasting disruption occurred when one of two contending aspirants to the throne, *Ulugh Meḥmed* by name, was beaten but not eliminated. He established himself at the city of Kazán, near the great bend of the Volga, and made it the headquarters of a state of his own which maintained an independent existence alongside the realm of *Küchük Meḥmed* to the south. The Golden Horde empire thus came to be divided between two states generally known as the "*Great Horde*" and the "*Khānate of Kazán*" respectively. Soon afterwards (1441) another secession occurred in the south west, when a member of the ruling house set up an independent *Khānate of the Crimea*, which presently achieved great prosperity under the leadership of its energetic Khān *Ḥajjī Girai*. At the mouth of the Volga yet another Khānate came almost simultaneously into being, that of *Ástrakhan*.

Vitold's plan to disorganize Tatar strength by playing off one pretender against another thus bore ample fruit, though only after his death. There was never a lack of princes who could be won by promises to a particular party and then be planted on the throne. The once so powerful Golden Horde became a football in the game of the East European powers. The danger to Tatar statehood was checked, however, by the fact that

Christian East Europe was also divided and that its three principal component states were nearly always at loggerheads, largely because of their religious and cultural differences. On the one hand stood Lithuania and Poland, closely associated after 1386 in that members of the Lithuanian Jagellonian dynasty reigned in both countries; on the other stood the Grand Prince of Moscow and the lesser Russian states, whose number was continually being reduced by the successful tactics of the Muscovites, though reciprocal jealousies gave rise to many a tense situation.

The Tatars of the Great Horde were long dependent on Moscow, after the Muscovite Grand Prince *Basil (Vasílií) II, the Blind,* had been released from the custody of their Khān on quite favourable terms in 1446. Ḥajjī Girai, on the other hand, having spent part of his youth at the Lithuanian capital Vilna, worked closely with the Lithuanian Grand Duke *Casimir,* who in 1447 became King Casimir IV of Poland, and in this dual capacity disposed of no mean strength. The copious available source material makes it possible to follow the political permutations and combinations of these states in detail. The Crimean Horde did its best to undermine Moscow's influence at Kazán, where the Muscovites installed their own candidates as Khāns while treating the country as a sort of protectorate. The Muscovite Grand Princes, on the other hand, were endeavouring to advance south-eastwards, in the hope that they might somewhere establish direct commercial contact with the states bordering on the Black Sea; and to facilitate these endeavours, they sought the Great Horde's backing. The resultant disputes were long, complicated and bitter, and did not much affect the general diplomatic pattern as long as Ḥajjī Girai, who clung faithfully to his alliance with Lithuania, remained living; but his death in 1466 led to a complete reversal of the positions. After an interval of confusion, the Crimean throne was won by his son *Mengli Girai I,* the greatest prince in the the history of the Crimea. Mengli quarrelled with Casimir and approached the Grand Prince *Iván III, the "Great",* of Moscow (1462-1505) with proposals for an alliance, which the latter after some hesitation accepted. The two rulers, however, were pursuing different objectives. Mengli's main concern was to get the better of his Great Horde rivals; Iván's was to expand south-westwards towards Chernígov and Severia. This naturally moved the new Khān of the Great Horde, *Aḥmed,* who had succeeded around 1465, to make common cause with Casimir IV of Poland-Lithuania.

As things turned out, however, the alliance between Mengli Girai and Iván III remained in abeyance so long as each was busy with separate policies which did not call for practical co-operation between them. While the Muscovite ruler cast his eyes on the ancient mercantile city-republic of (Great) Nóvgorod and finally captured it in 1478, the Crimean Khān sought a reckoning with the Genoese in the Crimea. Their settlements, after surviving several ordeals in the period before the outbreak of the Tatar civil wars of the second half of the 14th century, had then grown and flourished exceedingly, while the Venetian settlements had faded away; from 1365 onwards practically the whole south coast of the Crimea was in the hands of the Genoese. Their interests, however, were mortally damaged by the expansion of Lithuania towards the Black Sea, as the trade was now largely diverted to the land route through Moldavia, Podolia and Galicia in consequence of the facilities and preferences granted by the Lithuanian Grand Dukes, Moldavian Hospodars and Polish Kings. Compared with this erosion of the economic basis of the settlements, the difficulties caused by the rise of the Ottoman empire, culminating in the capture of Constantinople in 1453, were not of great importance, as the Genoese and the Ottoman Turks reached a compromise which was embodied in commercial treaties. So unsatisfactory did conditions become for the Genoese in the Crimea that from 1449 onwards they took the side of the Polish kings, who were really their enemies in the commercial field, and accepted a form of Lithuanian protection [1]; and this prompted Mengli to deal them a finishing stroke.

In 1475 the last Italian stronghold in the Black Sea ports, Kaffa, fell after a stubborn defence; and with it came to an end the Latin hierarchy in the Crimea, whose century and a half of missionary effort had borne no fruit.

The destruction of the Genoese settlements coincided with another important development, the origins and circumstances of which are by no means clear. At the siege of Kaffa, Ottoman as well as Tatar troops took part; and while Mengli eliminated the last remnant of foreign influence in the Crimea, he himself had to submit to domination from outside by acknowledging the suzerainty of the Ottoman Sulṭān. This may well have been hard for the proud Crimean ruler to bear, but tended in the then existing state of affairs to reinforce rather than diminish his real power, even when a son of the Sulṭān Meḥmed II, the Conqueror, was posted to Kaffa as Ottoman resident.

With Kaffa and Nóvgorod respectively in their hands, the two rulers

---

[1] Marian Malowist, *Kaffa - Kolonia genueńska na Krymie i problem wschodni w latach 1453-1475* (Caffa, colonie génoise en Crimée et la question d'Orient dans les années 1453-1475), Warsaw 1947.

had achieved their separate goals and could thereafter deal in concert with affairs in South Russia (the Ukraine). To this situation King Casimir IV of Poland responded by entering into an alliance with Khān Aḥmed of the Great Horde; but he failed to give active support to his ally when the latter advanced against Moscow in the summer of 1480, with the result that Aḥmed, after spending several months encamped opposite Iván III along the Oka river, was obliged to retreat when winter set in. The Grand Prince, who had not displayed much fortitude during the critical hours, was able to return to Moscow as a "victor", while Aḥmed died during the Great Horde's retreat. His sons divided his heritage among themselves, but one of them, *Sayyid Aḥmed,* succeeded in gaining the upper hand.

Iván III took full advantage of his success of 1480 to consolidate his position in Russia. During the last several decades, the Muscovite Grand Princes had made treaties with the other Russian princes obliging them to deliver the Tatar tribute to Moscow and not to deal direct with the Khān. This obligation was now peremptorily imposed on all the still reigning Russian princes and extended to cover relations with "the Hordes". The break-up of the Golden Horde empire into separate states thus received formal acknowledgement. To all intents and purposes the Russian people were now free of the Tatar shackles which had hitherto held them in check. The Great Horde, however, was not done for yet; and Mengli Girai, who after a brief exile had reestablished his authority in the Crimea, accordingly made a new compact with Ivan III to crush the rising power of Sayyid Aḥmed for good and all. The plan hung fire because the other interests of the parties were divergent. The Muscovite ruler was at first more intent upon war with Lithuania, and only promised help to the Crimean Khān on the understanding that he would make attacks on the southern parts of Lithuania and Poland in addition to preparing for action against the Great Horde. Meanwhile, Moscow was in a position to strengthen its influence at Kazán, where recurrent strife was constantly inviting intervention. Suddenly, however, Iván III made peace with the Lithuanian Grand Duke *Alexander,* who was his son-in-law and had come to the throne in 1492. This almost led to a breach between Moscow and the Crimea, as the latter had become deeply involved in warfare with Lithuania and would have been faced with disaster if left in the lurch; but a new accord was reached, thanks to the skilful diplomacy of Iván III and to the threat to Mengli's rule posed by Sayyid Aḥmed. As a result of this accord, the Grand Duke of Moscow was enabled to enter into diplomatic relations with the Sulṭān at

Constantinople for the first time in 1495-6; their dealings, which were for the present mainly of a commercial nature, were conducted through the Crimean Tatars as intermediaries. Sayyid Aḥmed, on the other hand, was obliged by the geographically unfavourable position of his realm to overlook his father's unhappy experiences in 1480 and resume a close association with Lithuania and Poland. This brought down on him the displeasure of the Ottoman Sulṭān, because in 1497 the combined Polish and Lithuanian forces entered Moldavia in a determined effort to gain direct access to the Black Sea; their aim was to reconquer the areas which they had lost to the Ottoman Turks in 1484 round Kilia (Chilia) and Aq Kerman (Cetatea Albă, now Byélgorod). The Sulṭān bade the Great Horde ruler to desist from his warlike designs against the Crimea; and in consequence many of Sayyid Aḥmed's best regiments, under the leadership of his principal general and wazīr, deserted to Mengli's side before the struggle was over. The final battle between Sayyid Aḥmed and Mengli was fought in June 1502. No detailed information about it has come down, but the upshot of the struggle was, as could be expected, that the remnant of Sayyid Aḥmed's army ceased to exist as an organized force. The survivors were absorbed into the Crimean army; Sayyid Aḥmed himself was taken prisoner and, in 1505, for some political reason, done to death. The state which was the direct successor of the Golden Horde, though in its later years it had lain at the mercy of neighbouring powers, thus came to an end. In the complex arena of East Europe, one uncertain player was now eliminated.

The Tatar states of Kazán, Astrakhan and the Crimea were nevertheless still in existence, and a new Tatar realm had recently been constituted in western Siberia. The political tokens of the Mongol conquest of 1240 had thus by no means yet been effaced. The geographical link between the Volga Khānates and the Crimea had, however, been broken down, and a wide stretch of country was left without protection against the southward thrust of Moscow. The Russians did not neglect their opportunity, especially as Iván III had by 1503 achieved his objectives against Lithuania. Kazán passed more than ever under Muscovite domination, as attempts by the Crimean Tatars to intervene were thwarted and the perennial internal dissensions made it possible for the Khānate to be treated much like one of the lesser Russian states [1]. Various princes of the ruling house joined the Russian service, and some embraced Christianity. In 1552, however, *Iván IV, "the Terrible"*, not many years

[1] See IGOR SMOLITISCH, *Zur Geschichte der russischen Ostpolitik des* 15. *und* 16. *Jahrhunderts*, in the *Jahrbücher für Geschichte Osteuropas*, VI (1941), pp. 55-84.

after he had come of age, led a carefully prepared expedition against Kazán; it met with no effective resistance, and on October 15th the city and with it the Khānate fell. In 1554 Ástrakhan also was conquered. It was these two events that marked the end of the Asian sway in East Europe which had endured since the invasion of 1240. The West Siberian Khānate ceased to exist in 1584. Only the Crimea survived, under the rule of the Girai dynasty and the suzerainty of the Ottoman Sulṭāns; it did not lie across the tracks of the Muscovites, whose Tsars regarded its existence as a problem of foreign rather than domestic policy. Its subsequent evolution will be traced in a separate chapter.

Down to the time of the fall of the Volga Khānates, independent statehood had secured the Tatar people in the possession of their distinctive religion and culture and in that of the lands which they had occupied during the 13th century. This security had facilitated the fusion of the Turks and Mongols of the Volga into the new entity of the *Tatars*, Muslim in faith and Turkish in speech, who in spite of much dialectical diversity regarded themselves as belonging to a single nation and differed markedly from the surrounding Russians and East Finns [1]. Religious toleration had left intact the Orthodox Christian heritage of the former; and the latter, on account of the remoteness of the areas which they occupied, had scarcely been touched by the preaching of Islām. All these peoples were of course affected by their centuries of living side by side. A fair measure of Finnish blood was absorbed into the veins of the Tatar nation, and Russian and Polish captives of both sexes added a certain Slavic element, though the Russian contribution was in all probability still very small in the mid 15th century. Not less important than the upbuilding of the Tatar nation was the fact that it had become sedentary; from the 14th century onwards, nomadism had shown a growing decline, and when the Khānates fell the population had become largely agricultural with trading interests.

At the same time, the Islāmic civilization on the Volga had thus far maintained a fairly pure consistency. No evidence exists to suggest that Russian civilization had as yet exercised any influence on the Tatars. On the contrary, Tatar ideas were undoubtedly reflected in the ceremonial of the Russian court, not indeed directly but in an amalgam with the strong Byzantine influences and numerous old Russian features which were also present; the subject has not yet, however, been fully investigated and remains somewhat obscure. The Russian vocabulary was

---

[1] See BERTOLD SPULER, *Die Mordwinen. Vom Lebenslauf eines wolga-finnischen Volkes*, in the *Zeitschrift der Deutschen Morgenlandsgesellschaft*, C (1950), pp. 90-111.

enriched with a number of Tatar words, indicating that the Russians took over certain cultural and technical accomplishments of the Tatars; on this ground it can be inferred that foreign influences were at work in the Russian postal and financial systems, and in many of the handicrafts, such as metal work. The strongest and most lasting Tatar influence was on Russian military methods; the organization of the army on the decade system was clearly borrowed from the Tatars, and the weapons and battle techniques, especially the cavalry tactics, in use in late medieval Russia were mainly developed from Tatar models.

The battle of Kulikovo in 1380. (illustration dating from the fifteenth century)

RUSSIAN RULE ON THE VOLGA

With the downfall of the Khānates other than the Crimea, the position of the the Tatars inevitably underwent a radical change. They no longer had rulers of their own to protect them, and the Volga region, having passed under Russian rule, ceased to play any political part in the life of the Muslim world. A forward look at its subsequent destinies may perhaps not be out of place here. The Tsar Iván IV followed up his victories by grouping the former Tatar dominions into a territory, still called the Khānate of Kazán but administered on Russian lines, which stretched from the Cheremiss country in the north to the Caspian Sea and included Ástrakhan and the North Caucasian steppe. The Russians showed little concern for the survival of Tatar nationhood. From the outset they engaged in proselytizing activity, which to a medieval Christian state seemed an obvious religious duty and in the Volga territory also served the purpose of russification. An Orthodox Archbishopric was created at Kazán, numerous monasteries were built and the message of the Gospels was spread throughout the land. In view of the rather large number of conversions of Tatar noble families during the preceding centuries, it was believed in Moscow that the prospects of success in the Tatar country were sure beyond question. In fact, however, these conversions had largely been determined by social considerations of much the same nature (allowance being made for the circumstances of time and place) as those which had brought about the rapid victory of Islām among the Persian nobility in the 7th and 8th centuries (see Vol. 1, p. 29) and among the Bosnian nobility in the 15th century. The broad mass of the Tatar population, on the other hand, soon began to offer that tenacious resistance which Christian missionary efforts have always encountered among Muslims. Violent uprisings also occurred, not long after the conquest; and one result of the measures taken to suppress them was that the *Bashkirs*, a Turkish or turkicized people living south east of the Kazán Tatars, submitted voluntarily to Muscovite rule in 1554.

Proselytizing activity was not the only irritant which provoked increased resistance by the Tatar population. An oppressive financial system aggravated the burden of the taxes, and more important still, the country was inundated by a largely uncontrolled influx of Russian immigrants. The newcomers not only effected a peaceful settlement of the fertile and commercially well placed lands along the Volga and Káma rivers, but also on occasions proceeded, with help from the government's forces, to evict and dispossess the inhabitants of Muslim towns and villages. During this period, Kazán was almost entirely cleared of Muslim inhabitants. Tatars were forbidden to dwell in the city, and a wide area surrounding it was planted exclusively with Russians. The flood of immigrants moved forward with elemental force, spreading Russian populations and Russian culture over immense new areas. The trend of the migration movement, which since the Tatar invasion of the 13th century had been to the north and north east, was now deflected to the south. As has been said, the only comparable phenomenon was the eastward emigration of the Germans; in continuity and volume, no other movement of peoples in the Middle Ages was commensurate with these two great migratory waves.[1]

Further revolts broke out towards the end of Iván IV's reign and were not put down till after his death in 1584. In these the Tatars were joined by the Volga Finnish peoples, who had also been affected by the Russian immigration movement. As a result of these revolts, the administrative system was reorganized in 1586, and a decree was issued in 1593 enjoining the destruction of existing mosques and prohibiting the construction of new ones. In actual practice, however, these and similar drastic ordinances were attenuated by the consideration that the Russians were in no small measure dependent on the Tatars. The long established trading relations of these latter with Central Asia were an irreplaceable asset. It was solely through the enterprise of Muslim merchants that Kazán developed into an important commercial centre, as Bulgār had been in an earlier age. The widespread respect among Russians for such practical considerations helped the Tatars to survive the sternest periods of official repression. There was at first no question of Russia's reciprocating the tolerance shown to the Balkan peoples by the Ottoman Sulṭāns, who were obliged by the Qur'ānic precepts to allow a certain legal status to their Christian subjects. It was not until 1665 that the Sublime Porte first threatened reprisals against the Balkan Christians if the Tsars would not place their Muslim subjects on a more nearly equivalent footing.

Another result of Moscow's encouragement of the activities of the rich Tatar merchants was that the interests of these latter, unlike those of the common people, came to be bound up with the policies of the Russian state. The Tsars thus began to have supporters among the Tatars. During the "Time of Troubles" (1606-1609), the mass of the Volga Tatars took

[1] Russian pioneers founded Okhotsk on the Pacific coast in 1647.

the side of the second "False Demetrius" and joined in the plundering of monasteries and noblemen's mansions, while the upper class stood for law and order and joined in the movement which led to the expulsion of the Poles and the election of a new Tsar, *Michael Románov*, in 1613. The diploma of his election bears seven Tatar signatures.

In the early years of the period which followed, milder laws were enacted and above all the deliberate promotion of Russian eastward emigration was abandoned. Before long, however, efforts to win the Tatars to Christianity were resumed, and economic measures to add weight to the missionary appeal were adopted. In 1628 it was decreed that no Muslim landowner might have Christian serfs, and at times during the 17th century attempts were made to put converted Christian Tatars in possession of lands owned by their Muslim relatives. Some of the Tatars who were deprived of their lands by such measures took to trade, as the Russian government stood in need of the Muslim merchant class and therefore left its members more or less undisturbed. But not all those affected were so steadfast in their faith as to renounce their worldly possessions, and once again a proportion of the Tatar nobility went over to the Christian religion. Less highly placed converts were rewarded with exemption from taxes and personal services such as compulsory labour, military duties, etc., and a fair number of members of the lower classes were thus also induced to make the change. Some whole villages and tribal groups adopted Christianity, with the result that in the course of the century a distinct community of Tatar Christians came into existence, numbering several tens of thousands and known by the name of *"Kresh" ("the Baptized")*. This group was rendered additionally compact by transplantations of neighbouring Muslim elements to other areas.

Notwithstanding these missionary successes, the Tatars continued to be overwhelmingly Muslim and were consequently subjected by the Russian government to a number of disabilities. All these restrictions on their liberty, and especially the liability to perform compulsory services (such as tree-felling for the shipyards, cultivating state lands, etc.), which was enforced mainly in the 18th century and was much resented, caused Tatars to be among the first to join in anti-governmental movements. There were Muslims in the company of *Sténka Rásin* (1667-1671), *Kondratiĭ Bulávin* (1708) and *Emelyán Pugachév* (1773-1774). Interspersed between these great revolutionary outbreaks in the Volga basin were various isolated uprisings which, like them, were all eventually put down. In reply to the rebel challenge, the existing laws were made more severe, the "Khānate of Kazán" was transformed in 1709 into a Russian "Government" (i.e. province), and further emphasis was given to the missionary policy and financial measures. During all these upheavals, however, it was evident that an important section of the Tatar upper class desired to co-operate with the Russians. The government was also able to play off the different national groups — Tatars, Bashkirs, Volga Finns — one against the other. Even the Islāmic religious leaders, who hoped for Ottoman aid and around 1608 had counted on an intervention by the Shī'ite Shāh *'Abbās the Great* of Persia, kept fairly quiet. They could not in the circumstances follow up the first modest efforts which had been made to propagate Islām among the Volga Finns; and in the course of the 18th century the Orthodox Church contrived to win almost the entirety of these hitherto pagan tribes. To avoid the Russian pressure, however, some of these Finns migrated to the land of the Bashkirs, where they at first lived according to their own customs but later gradually adopted the Muslim faith and for the most part also the Bashkir language. They thus eventually became very largely assimilated with the Bashkirs, though they have kept a certain identity down to the present under the names "*Mishér*" and "*Teptér*".

The migration movements and mass conversions of the 17th and 18th centuries had a far-reaching effect on the geopolitical position of the Tatars. The region in which they dwelt was now interlaced with zones of Russian settlement, so that their own areas came increasingly to consist of isolated fragments. The conversion of some of the Tatars and Volga Finns to Christianity facilitated the intermixture of these peoples with the Russians and with each other, while the emigration of some of the Finns to Tatar areas reinforced the Finnish strain in the blood of the Tatars. It thus came about that the Russians of the south-east have ever since shown signs of a Tatar admixture, while among the Tatars and Bashkirs two physical types are apparent: a Turanian type among those living further east, and an East European type among those with a Finnish or Russian strain.

The Russian policy of discriminating between the different classes of Tatars was carried to an extreme during the reign of *Catharine the Great* (1762-1796), after the rebellion of Pugachév had been suppressed. In 1784 Tatar nobles were placed on an equal footing with Russian nobles and granted a modicum of self-government. They might now judge minor civil cases themselves, elect a religious head of their own, the *Muftī of Orenburg*, and hold the rank of officer in a newly constituted Bashkir corps. Their prospects of social advancement depended, of course, on their readiness to collaborate with the Russian government; but on this basis the Tatar nation came to enjoy a fair degree of prosperity during the early part of the 19th century. In addition to their purely trading activites, they were able to start manufacturing enterprises such as tanneries, woollen-mills and paper-mills. They also set up a printing and publishing house, which busily turned out not only religious works but also medical treatises and studies of Tatar life. The Tatar peasants of the Volga, hardly any of whom had the status of serfs, could now breathe more freely and develop cottage industries as well as farming with some success. The peasant emancipation decree of 1861 nevertheless gave rise to certain social tensions, which found expression in a few local disorders, notably in 1881.

Meanwhile a new movement of ideas had begun to stir the Volga Tatars. In the early part of the century, orthodox Sunnite Islām still determined the whole rhythm of their intellectual life; but from about 1850 onwards a new note was struck by a handful of patriots, who gradually succeeded in swaying the general opinion. The most important [1] were *Shihāb al-Dīn Merjāni* (1818-1898) and the Crimean Tatar *Ismā'īl Bey Gaspyraly* or *Gasprinskiĭ* (1815-1914), both of whom were partly influenced by Ottoman-Turkish and Western European thought. They strove for a radical reform of the entire intellectual groundwork of Tatar life and were by no means foes of Islām, though on account of the innovations which they urged they naturally met with strong opposition from the Muslim religious leaders and at first made little headway. Eventually, however, they succeeded in persuading even the *mullās* of the importance of their cause. Their efforts led to the establishment of large numbers of new schools, which gave the children a sound knowledge of their native language by modern methods and prepared the ground for advances in all the professional fields. At the same time, Gaspyraly worked for the creation of a common language, intelligible to all the Tatar peoples, which was to be intermediate between the dialects and as near as possible to Ottoman Turkish [2]. Such a language would also serve to link the Volga Tatars with his own people of the Crimea, who since the annexation of 1783 and great emigration of 1856 (see below, p. 100) had suffered a particularly hard fate under Russian rule. Most of the reformers were also in favour of spreading a knowledge of Russian among their fellow-Tatars, as they saw in it a means of acquainting them

[1] The work of another reformer has recently been investigated by SAADET ÇAGATAY, *Abdül-Kayyum Nasirî*, in the *Ankara Üniversitesi Dil ve Tarih-Coğrafya Fak. Dergisi*, X 3/4 (1952), pp. 147-160.

[2] GUSTAV BURBIEL, *Die Sprache Ismā'īl Bey Gaspyralys*, typewritten thesis, Hamburg 1950; CAFER SEYDAMET, *Gaspirali Ismail Bey*, Istanbul 1934.

with Western culture, which had by that time become strongly rooted in the empire of the Tsars.

The awakening in these years of a national consciousness among all the Turkish peoples of Russia, the similarity of their cultural life as it had developed in modern times and the attempt to harmonize and transcend their dialects, all tended to intensify their sense of solidarity as Muslims and for a time made them responsive to the Pan-Islāmic teachings then coming from Constantinople. The Russian revolution of 1905 did not catch the Tatars off their guard. Immediately after its outbreak, the Russian Muslims called for a conference to consider and watch over their interests, and in the Duma they were represented by a fair number of deputies, associated for the most part with the "Cadet" and Socialist parties, which were expected to show most sympathy for Muslim aspirations.

An entirely new phase was introduced by the Russian revolution of 1917. To this the Tatars reacted in different ways. One group, while insisting on cultural autonomy, held mainly for economic reasons that the association with Russia should be preserved. Others advocated complete independence for the "*Idel-Uralian people*", as they called the Tatars dwelling between the Volga (in Turkish *Idel,* earlier *Etil*) and the Urals. Nothing of any significance, however, was actually achieved in that region, whereas the Crimea enjoyed independence for some months and northern Āẕarbāyjān for two years (1918-1920). In the last-named country, where Russian rule was only a century old and the Muslim population had remained relatively compact, the national movement was particularly strong and received support from nearby Turkey. Ultimately, however, the Bolshevik government overcame all the separatist forces. The new régime accommodated the various Turkish peoples with privileges of cultural autonomy, which were gradually elaborated and put into effect; but at the same time it put a stop to the articulation of these peoples by splitting them into separate autonomous regions or republics and elevating their dialects into literary languages. The Tatar and Bashkir regions were among those affected, as well as the Crimea and Āẕarbāyjān.

Under the Bolshevik plan, this autonomy had reference mainly to the use of language. The content of the national culture was required to be Marxist, and such it increasingly became. Original movements aiming at any sort of self-development were suppressed. The office of the *Muftī,* who had his seat at *Ufá* and was now elected by the believers, acquired particular importance after 1917 as the one and only common institution of the Turks of Russia. The anti-religious struggle was extended to Islām, and the scope of the Muftī's functions was kept as narrow as possible.

In the everyday life of the Turks of Russia, fundamental changes set in under the Bolshevik régime. The anti-religious attitude, which the Bolsheviks strongly emphasized in the early years, led many of the younger generation to grow up without religion, especially as attendance at mosques generally ceased to be feasible; and in this way one of their distinctive non-Russian characteristics has been effaced. Moreover, knowledge of the Russian language has made rapid strides, its advance being promoted by the state notwithstanding the grant of language-autonomy. Where Russian was previously understood only by individuals, it has now spread among the masses, and though its intelligibility to the great majority may still be somewhat limited, an increasing number have chosen for the sake of practical advantage to attend Russian rather than Tatar schools and have come to know Russian better than their mother tongue. The collectivization of agriculture in the Volga region and the Crimea between 1928 and 1930 impelled numerous peasants to migrate, partly to other areas of Russia and also on quite a considerable scale to Central Asia; and their place has mostly been filled with Russians. Tatar nationhood is thus menaced by far greater dangers than it was a generation ago. Even if the proportion of younger men who have become more or less strangers to their native language and culture is in fact still comparatively low, the increasing frequency of mixed marriages when both the parties are atheists shows the direction in which the tide is running. Whether the concessions to religion made in 1942 and the support now given by the Kremlin to politically reliable spiritual leaders [1] are checking the rise of religious indifference is a question which cannot be verified from outside. The Kresh (baptized) Tatars, who have traditionally kept apart from the Muslims right down to the most recent times, are also more than ever exposed to Russian influence. The Āẕarbāyjānīs alone still stand as a distinct national block, thanks to their peripheral location and compact area of settlement; but even they face a threat to their national individuality in the growth of the Russian industrial proletariat at Bākū. The descendants of the Turks and Mongols who once ruled in East Europe are thus approaching a crisis of their national existence, the outcome of which cannot be foreseen.

---

[1] For details see BERTOLD SPULER, *Die Lage der Muslime in Russland seit 1942*, in "*Islam*" XXIX (1950), pp. 296-300.

THE CRIMEA

The independent Khānate of the Crimea was, as has been seen, founded by Ḥajjī Girai, who seized control of the peninsula and adjacent areas to the north and east around the year 1441; and the first decades of its existence were mainly occupied with wars against the Great Horde, which naturally sought to re-establish its authority over the lost territory. The destinies of the Crimea were therefore closely bound up with those of its northern rival until the destruction of the latter by *Mengli Girai I* in 1502 made it possible for the Crimean Horde to embark on new, self-chosen policies. In spite of his vassalage to the Ottoman Sulṭān, this capable ruler carried the Crimean state to its highest point of external power and prestige. He failed, however, to keep up his alliance with Moscow, as after the downfall of the Great Horde *Basil (Vasiliĭ) III* 1505-1533) no longer had any motive for cooperating with him and indeed had reason for anxiety lest the Girai dynasty might acquire a position like that of the bygone Khāns at Sarai. In the last years of his long life, which ended in 1515, Mengli accordingly reverted to the policy of his father and sought the friendship of Poland-Lithuania.

In internal prosperity, the Crimea also reached its highest point during Mengli's reign. The close links with the Ottoman Sulṭānate laid the Crimea wide open to Anatolian influences, which now became more and more conspicuous in all fields of activity. Splendid buildings arose, including the palace of the Khāns at Bāghcheh Sarai, to which Mengli moved his residence from Old Krim (Qyrym), and the famous Zenjirly Medreseh (a theological college), which is still preserved. Among the architects of the period were a few Genoese who had remained in the Khān's service after the fall of Kaffa.

At the same time, the state administration was conducted on well planned lines. Surviving documents show that taxes were levied and justice dispensed in accordance with strict regulations. The country was divided into 28 judicial districts under a *dīvān* or high court. The women of the Crimea enjoyed a status of much greater freedom than their sisters in other Muslim countries, and there were some who took part in public life or devoted themselves to the poetic art. One custom to be gradually abandoned was that of sending young princes, and particularly heirs to the throne (who always held the title "*Qalga*") to spend part of their youth undergoing military training with the Circassians; the reputation of these latter as instructors endured, however, till the 19th century. The trend away from the old simplicity was parallelled by a growing demoralization in political life, which during the 17th century prompted the Ottoman Sulṭāns to depose Crimean Khāns on more and more frequent occasions. In these circumstances the stability of the government was seriously weakened.

During the 16th century, however, the Khāns of the Crimea were strong enough to make numerous interventions in the affairs of East Europe. In 1520 the Khān *Meḥmed Girai* led a campaign against Kazán and Ástrakhan, with the object of counteracting the growing Russian influence in these two Khānates, and his capture of Ástrakhan was an outstanding triumph; but as a result of internal intrigues he was murdered in 1521, and his death had serious consequences. The power of the Crimean Tatars now began to decline; and though still capable of an offensive against Moscow in 1541, they could not prevent the downfall of Kazán and Ástrakhan respectively. Henceforward they stood alone before the rising power of the Tsars. It was only because Iván IV's forces were now pinned down by Poland and Sweden that the Crimea had a respite for internal rehabilitation. The Ottoman Sulṭān and his wazīr were however of the opinion that the time had come to strike a decisive blow against Russia with a view to restoring the overthrown Volga Khānates; and in conjunction with the Crimeans an ambitious plan was drawn up in 1569. This was to join the Volga and the Don by a canal at the point where the two rivers come closest to each other (near the modern Stalingrád) in order that the Ottoman fleet might have access to the Caspian Sea, which would have been useful in the war against Persia. The severities of the climate, and the apathy of the Crimean Khān *Devlet Girai I* who had no desire to see Ottoman forces based permanently in his territory, prevented any realization of these schemes [1], which lost their point when the Ottoman fleet was destroyed at the battle of Lepanto on October 7, 1571. As soon as his fears of Ottoman interference were allayed, Devlet went to war against Moscow. For the last time in its history, the Tatars entered the city in 1571, and Iván IV was forced to assent to the reimposition of a Tatar tribute *(tysh)*.

Meḥmed Girai II, who came to the throne in 1577, was above all eager to reconquer Kazán and Ástrakhan. He accordingly entered into negoti-

---

[1] See Halil İnalcik, *Osmanlı-rus rekabetinin menşei ve Don-Volga Kanalı teşebbüsü* (*The beginnings of Ottoman-Russian rivalry and the scheme for a Don-Volga Canal*) in the *Belleten*, Ankara, XII (1948) pp. 349-402.

ations with *Stephen Báthory*, Prince of Transylvania and King of Poland, who was the bitter enemy of Iván IV, and went so far as to dangle false hopes of his impending conversion to Catholicism before the eyes of Jesuit missionaries who appeared at his court. Troop requisitions by the Sulṭān for the war against Persia, and internal disorders during which the Khān was murdered in 1584, prevented the conclusion of an alliance, while frequent raids by Tatar freebooters into the Ukraine and Poland placed a strain on the relations between the two states. Economic shortages, a recurrent phenomenon in Crimean life, probably lay at the root of these raids, which in general lacked any political motive; but the Polish king could not view with indifference the damage which they caused to his subjects, and he therefore refrained from an alliance with the Crimean Tatars.

The Khāns of the Crimea and the Kings of Poland were nevertheless again drawn together when the Cossacks, led by their Hetman *Bogdán Khmielnitskiĭ*, transferred their allegiance from Poland to Russia in 1654. The extension of the Russian sphere of influence to the lower Dniepr threatened both states alike. In 1655 the allied Tatars and Poles won the victory of Okhmátov over the Russians and the Cossacks, and at the battle of Warsaw in 1656 Tatars fought with the Poles against the Swedes and Brandenburgers. *Meḥmed Girai IV*, during his second reign (1654-1666), made a treaty with *John II Casimir* of Poland ap-apportioning between them the lands which they planned to conquer; those which Meḥmed had in view were the former Khānates of Kazán and Ástrakhan. Under this treaty the Crimean Tatars invaded Transylvania in 1657 in support of Poland, and together with the Poles won the victory of Tsudnov in 1660. The figures for their army strength given by contemporary writers are as exaggerated as those in similar reports from earlier periods; investigations into the matter have shown that the total fighting force of the Crimean Tatars must at the very most have amounted to only 30,000-40,000 men [1]. They could not, however, have put a force of this size into the field unless they had been capable of a high degree of organization, notwithstanding their reputation as undisciplined marauders.

The conclusion of a truce between Poland and Russia at Andrúsovo in 1667 transformed the general picture and particularly affected the relations between the Poles and the Crimean Tatars. The Cossack Hetman

[1] Olgierd Górka, *Liczebność Tatarów Krymskich i ich wojsk (The numerical strength of the Crimean Tatars and their armies)*, Warsaw 1936 (Special Supplement to the *Przegląd Historyczno-wojskowy*, VIII).

Peter Doroshénko, who complained of having been tricked by the Muscovites and felt the same resentment against them as his predecessor had felt against the Poles, placed himself under the suzerainty of the Ottoman Sulṭān and accordingly received political backing from the Crimean Khān *'Ādil Girai* (1666-1671). This of necessity put an end to King John Casimir's friendship with the Khān; and the subsequent war between the Ottoman empire on the one hand and Poland and Russia on the other, which lasted from 1682 to 1699, prevented any resumption of the Polish-Tatar partnership. Meanwhile the power of the Crimean state was weakened by disturbances at home and by the enforced participation of Tatar contingents in the unsuccessful campaign of 1683 against Vienna. When the Russians took the offensive in 1686 and 1687, the Crimeans were no longer strong enough to put up an effective defence, and in 1699 they had to acquiesce in the cession to *Peter the Great* of the fortress of Azóv on the Don estuary. Peter's rash proceedings in Moldavia in 1711 and the resultant peace treaty of the Pruth restored Azóv to the Crimean domains [1]; but Russia reannexed Azóv in 1739 after a war which had lasted three years. The power of the Tatars was now broken, and they were never again to play an active part in international affairs. Their cultural life, however, was to be marked by a last creative upsurge, the highest achievements of which were seen in the new palace of the Khāns at Bāghcheh Sarai, built in the years 1740-1743 to replace the old palace which the Russians had destroyed, and in the superb carpets then produced. Crimean carpet-weaving had a considerable influence on the development of the arts in Polish Galicia [2].

In 1761, King *Frederick II the Great* of Prussia, who was then in the most critical phase of his war with Russia, entered into relations with the Khān of the Crimea. He must have been prompted by counsels of despair, as he could have had no serious grounds for believing that the Tatars would attack Russia or that such an attack would significantly weaken Russian strength. Their relations, however, gave a pretext to Tsarina *Catharine II the Great* for a more active policy towards the Tatars. Through her publicists she spread abroad the opinion that their destruction would be in the interests of European civilization. The defeat of Turkey in the Russo-Turkish war of 1768-1774 and the ensuing peace treaty of Küçük Kaynarcı (1774) sealed the fate of the Crimea. It was

---

[1] Benedict Humphrey Sumner, *Peter the Great and the Ottoman Empire*, Oxford 1949.

[2] Tadeusz Mankowski, *Sztuka Islamu w Polsce w XVII i XVIII wieku* (Islamic art in Poland in the 17th and 18th centuries), Krakow 1935. (*P.A.U. Rozprawy wydziatu filologicznego LXXIV/3*).

left nominally independent but actually at the mercy of Russia. The Ottoman Sulṭān was nevertheless able to obtain Russian recognition, through the treaty of Aynalı Kavak (1779), of his continued suzerainty over the Muslims of the Crimea "in his capacity as Caliph" [1]. In carrying this point, the Ottomans took advantage of an illusion which had taken root in European minds. The mention of the Sulṭān's name before the Friday sermon was really not a religious but a political act, which served to keep alive the Sulṭān's dormant claim to the Crimea. The idea of a supreme religious authority, as in the Roman Catholic Church, is entirely foreign to Islām. In spite of this agreement, the Russians soon carried their policy to its logical conclusion. In the Khān *Shāhīn Girai*, who succeeded in 1777 and was familiar and sympathetic with European ideas, Russia had a good friend; but the governor and organizer of the Russian Black Sea province of Taurida, *Gregor Yefimovich Potyómkin (Potemkin)*, stirred up dissension in the Crimea and instigated the Beg of the Nogai tribe to intervene. Shāhīn let himself be persuaded to abdicate in 1783. The Crimea with its dependencies in the Nogai steppe and in the basin of the Kuban river became a Russian province.

The political consequences of the Mongol invasion of 1240 were thus finally effaced, and the Tatars of the Crimea were reduced to the same status as that in which their brothers on the Volga had subsisted for nearly 250 years. They did not, indeed, have to suffer from the empirical and consequently erratic policies which had characterized the Russian government's treatment of its Muslim subjects up to the reign of Catharine the Great; on the contrary, religious toleration was immediately proclaimed and the administrative system was improved by well conceived reforms. Far-reaching changes, however, were brought about in the population picture. Not only Russians and Ukrainians, but also Germans and Greeks, were invited to settle in the Crimea, and their presence so reduced the space available to the Tatars that many of them decided to quit their country.

Social changes also took place in the years after 1783, in consequence of land redistribution measures enacted by the Russian government; and in the 19th century the rise of Pan-Slavism tended to intensify the missionary zeal of the Tsars, who besides being actuated by religious motives felt that the winning of their subjects to Christianity would give greater homogeneity to the empire. Mosques and prayer leaders *(imāms)*

---

[1] Wilhelm Barthold, *Sultan i Chalif*, in *Mir Islama* (1912), pp. 203-226, 345-400; Carl Heinrich Becker, *Bartholds Studien über Chalif und Sultan*, in "*Islam*", VI (1916), pp. 350-412; Sir Thomas Walker Arnold, *The Caliphate*, Oxford 1924.

accordingly became fewer; a great many mosques were converted despite Muslim indignation into Christian churches. Then came the Crimean War (1853-1856), in which Russia and Turkey were enemies and much of the Crimea was laid waste. It is not surprising that a new movement of emigration set in, and that it was on a large scale. Within a few years over 200,000 persons, constituting more than half of the then Tatar population of the Crimea, moved to Ottoman territory. They and their dependents at first eked out an existence in the Dobruja and Bulgaria, but since the first world war have for the most part found shelter in Asiatic Turkey under the Republican government's land-settlement policy. The Russian authorities began by encouraging the emigration, but after a few years felt obliged by financial and economic considerations to take action against it; the measures adopted, however, did not suffice the hold back the movement to any great extent.

The spiritual, moral and economic life of the Tatars in the Crimea was thus at a low ebb when they found a leader in *Ismā'īl Bey Gaspyraly* (see above, p. 92) who, by revitalizing their schools and culture, guided them out of their dark valley and enabled them to make contact with the other Turkish populations of the empire of the Tsars. Through Gaspyraly and his periodical "*Tercümān*", the Crimean Tatar people made an all-important contribution to the growth of national consciousness among the Turks of Russia.

When the Russian revolution first broke out, it seemed likely that conditions would undergo a complete transformation; for the month of May 1917 saw the establishment of a Democratic Tatar Republic of the Crimea, which was recognized by the contemporary Russian and Ukrainian governments and later also by the occupying German military authorities. It was tolerated by the White Russian movement and survived until overthrown by the Bolsheviks in 1921. After the conquest and pacification of the peninsula had been carried through with great severity under the direction of the Hungarian communist leader Béla Kun, the Bolsheviks decided to allow the Crimean Tatars a degree of autonomy corresponding with that granted to the other national minorities in the Soviet Union; and for a few years this gave some impetus to Tatar culture. A sudden setback, however, came in 1927 when the Tatars resisted a plan to settle Jews in the country; the measures adopted by the Bolsheviks sufficed to overcome their resistance. In the Crimea, as on the Volga, the younger generation was exposed to intense Bolshevik influences, with much the same results. At the same time, the introduction of the Jewish settlers, the dissolution of the German settlements and a voluminous immigration of Russians and Ukrainians into the cities greatly changed the population picture and proportionately weakened the Tatar element. During the second world war, the German troops then occupying the Crimea gave permission early in August 1942 for fifty mosques to be reopened, thereby paving the way for a national revival. The Soviet government, after its reconquest of the peninsula in the spring of 1944, made this the pretext for a massive transplantation of the Crimean Tatars, which is said to have deprived the Crimea of the entire Muslim element in its population. Some of them are reported to have been sent to live near Grodno; others appear to have been removed to Siberia, and many to have perished. Whatever their individual fates may have been, it is probable that the history of the Crimean Tatars as a nation has come to an end.

THE POSTERITY OF JINGIZ KHĀN

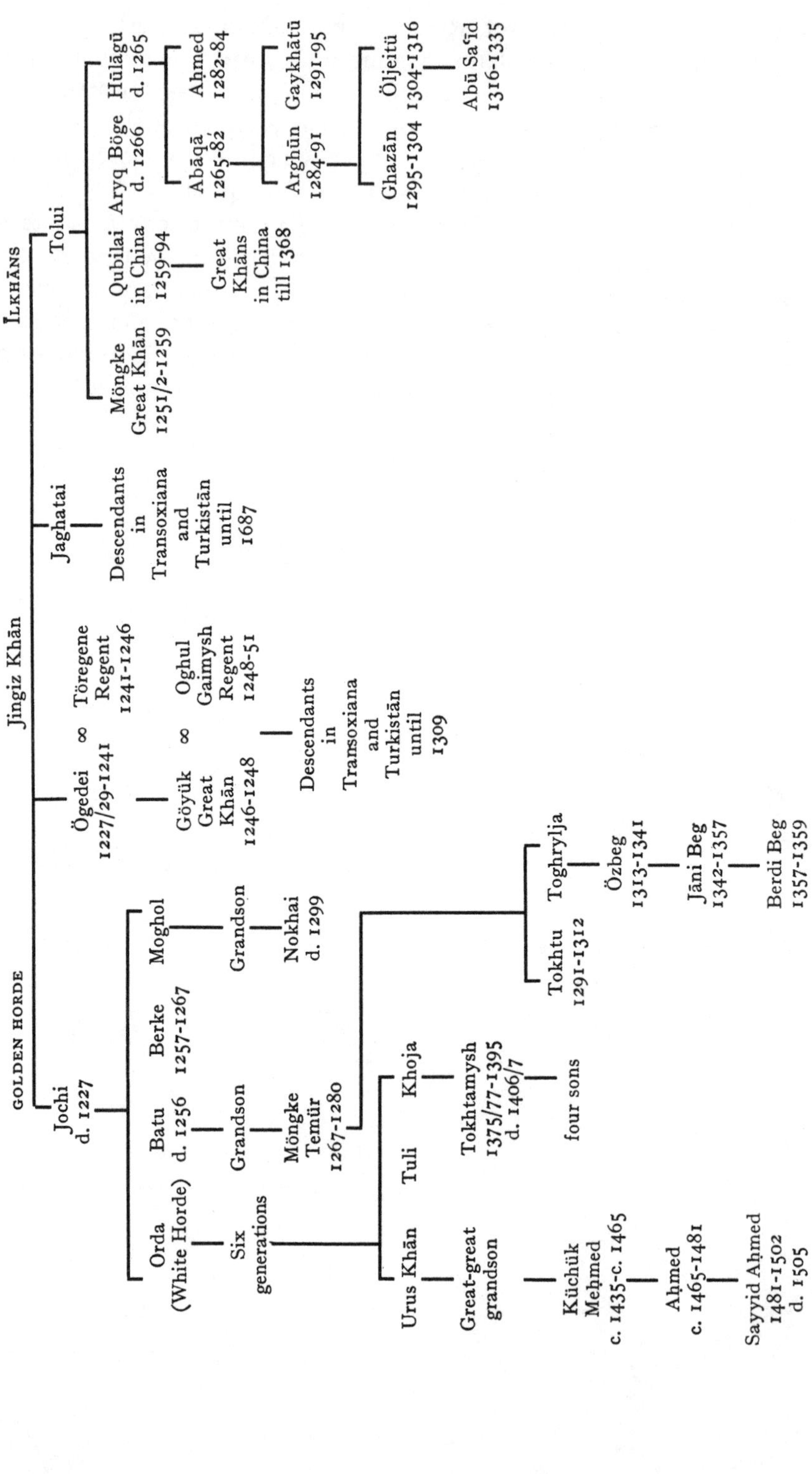

THE POSTERITY OP TĪMŪR

- Turaghai
  - Tīmūr Lang, b. 8. IV. 1336, d. 19. I. 1405
    - Jahāngīr, d. Samarqand 1375/6
      - Pīr Muḥammad (in India; from 1405 at Balkh) d. 1406/7
        - Qaidu (at Balkh, 1406/7-1409/10; at Qandahār, Kābul and Ghaznah, 1409/10)
      - Muhammad Sulṭān d. 1421
        - Sa'd al-Waqqāṣ (at Qumm 1414-1425) b. 1398/9; d. 1421
    - 'Umar Shaykh (in Turkistān, then in Fārs) d. 1394
      - Pīr Muḥammad (in Fārs from 1407/8) d. 1409/10
      - Rustam (in Iṣfahān 1405-1407/8) d. 1436/7
      - Iskandar (in Fārs and Iṣfahān 1409/10-1414) d. 1415
      - Bāiqara (at Hamadān, 1414-1415) b. 1393; d. 1423
        - Ghiyāth al-Dīn Manṣūr, d. 1445/6
          - Abū'l-Ghāzī Ḥusayn Bāiqara (in Harāt and Khurāsān from 1469); b. VI. 1438; d. V. 1506
    - Mīrān-Shāh (in Āzarbāyjān and 'Irāq, 1405-07) b. 1366/7, d. 20. IV. 1408
      - Khalīl (in Transoxiana 1405-1409/10, then at Rayy) b 1384; d 1409/10
      - Muḥammad
        - Abū Sa'īd (in Transoxiana from 1452; in Harāt, Balkh and Khurāsān from 1459) b. 1427, d. 4. 11. 1469
          - Aḥmad (in Transoxiana from 1468/9) d. 1493/4
          - Maḥmūd (in Māzandarān from 1460; in Transoxiana from 1494) d. 1499/5
          - Ulugh Beg (in Kābul and Ghaznah from 1460/61) d. 1501/2
          - 'Umar Shaykh (in Ferghānah from c. 1465/6) d. 1493/4
            - Bābur (conquered India, 1524-26) b. 1482, d. 26. XII. 1530
              - Mughal emperors in India till 1857
    - Shāhrukh (in Khurāsān and Māzandarān from 1405; in Iṣfahān and Shīrāz from 1414) b. 20. VIII. 1377, d. 12. III 1447
      - Ulugh Beg (in Transoxiana from 1409/10; in Khurāsān from 1446) b. 1393; d. 27. X. 1449
        - Rukn al-Dīn 'Abd al-Laṭīf (in Transoxiana) d. 6. X. 1450

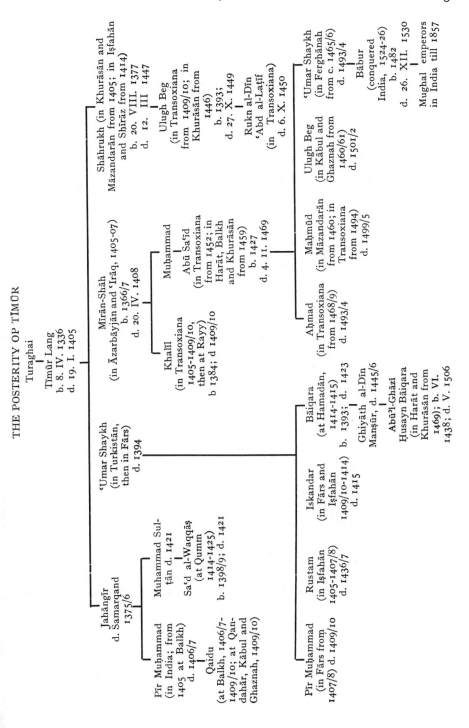

DYNASTIC TABLES

When the end of one reign coincided with the beginning of another reign, only the date of the first ruler's accession is given.

THE MAMLŪKS IN EGYPT

1. Baḥrī Mamlūks

... XI. 1259	al-Muẓaffar Sayf al-Dīn Qotuz.
24. X. 1260	al-Ẓāhir Rukn al-Dīn Baybars I. al-Bunduqdārī.
1. VII. 1277	al-Malik al-Saʿīd Nāṣir al-Dīn Berke Khān, son of the above (d. March 1280).
... VIII. 1279	al-Malik al-Manṣūr Sayf al-Dīn Qalā'ūn (Qilāwūn).
10. XI. 1290	al-Malik al-Ashraf I., Ṣalāḥ al-Dīn Muḥammad, son of the above.
12. XII. 1293	al-Malik al-Nāṣir Nāṣir al-Dīn Muḥammad, brother of the above.
... XII. 1294	al-Malik al-ʿĀdil Zayn al-Dīn Ketbogha.
7. XII. 1296	al-Malik al-Manṣūr I., Ḥusām al-Dīn Lāchīn.
16. I. 1299	al-Malik al-Nāṣir (second time).
5. IV. 1309	al-Malik al-Muẓaffar Rukn al-Dīn Baybars II. (Burjī).
5. III. 1310	al-Malik al-Nāṣir (third time).
6. VI. 1341	al-Malik al-Manṣūr II. Sayf al-Dīn Abū Bakr, son of the above.
1341	al-Malik al-Ashraf II. ʿAlā' al-Dīn Küchük, brother of the above.
1342	al-Malik al-Nāṣir II. Shihāb al-Dīn Aḥmad, brother of the above.
1342/3	al-Malik al-Ṣāliḥ I. ʿImād al-Dīn Ismāʿīl, brother of the above.
1345/6	al-Malik al-Kāmil Sayf al-Dīn Shaʿbān I., brother of the above.
1346/7	al-Malik al-Muẓaffar Sayf al-Dīn Ḥājjī I., brother of the above.
... XII. 1347	al-Malik al-Nāṣir III., Nāṣir al-Dīn al-Ḥasan, brother of the above.
1351	al-Malik al-Ṣāliḥ II., Ṣalāḥ al-Dīn Ṣāliḥ, brother of the above.
1354	al-Ḥasan (second time).
1361	al-Malik al-Manṣūr III., Ṣalāḥ al-Dīn Muḥammad, son of Ḥājjī I.

1362/3 al-Malik al-Ashraf III., Nāṣir al-Dīn Sha'bān II, cousin of the above.
1376/7 al-Malik al-Manṣūr IV. 'Alā' al-Dīn 'Alī, son of the above.
1381/2 al-Malik al-Ṣāliḥ III., Ṣalāḥ al-Dīn Ḥājjī II., brother of the above.

2. Burjī Mamlūks

26. XI. 1382 al-Malik al-Ẓāhir Sayf al-Dīn Barqūq ibn Anas.
1. VI. 1389 al-Malik al-Ṣāliḥ III. Ḥājjī II. (second time, d. 1411/2).
1. II. 1390 Barqūq (second time).
20. VI. 1399 al-Malik al-Nāṣir Nāṣir al-Dīn Faraj, son of the above.
20. IX. 1405 al-Malik al-Manṣūr 'Izz al-Dīn 'Abd al-'Azīz, brother of the above, (d. 20. IX. 1406).
20. XI. 1405 Faraj (second time).
28. V. 1412 The 'Abbāsid Caliph al-Musta'īn.
6. XI. 1412 al-Malik al-Mu'ayyad Sayf al-Dīn Shaykh al-Maḥmūdī.
13. I. 1421 al-Malik al-Muẓaffar Aḥmad I., son of the above.
29. VII. 1421 al-Malik al-Ẓāhir Sayf al-Dīn Ṭaṭar.
30. XI. 1421 al-Malik al-Ṣāliḥ Nāṣir al-Dīn Muḥammad, son of the above.
1. IV. 1422 al-Malik al-Ashraf Sayf al-Dīn Yūsuf, Bars Bāi, son of the above.
7. VI. 1438 al-Malik al-'Azīz Jamāl al-Dīn Chaqmaq.
13. II. 1453 al-Malik al-Manṣūr Fakhr al-Dīn 'Uthmān, son of the above.
19. III. 1453 al-Malik al-Ashraf Sayf al-Dīn Īnāl al-'Alā'ī al-Ẓāhirī al-Ajrūd.
26. II. 1461 al-Malik al-Mu'ayyad Shihāb al-Dīn Aḥmad II, son of the above.
28. VI. 1461 al-Malik al-Ẓāhir Sayf al-Dīn Khoshqadam.
9. X. 1467 al-Malik al-Ẓāhir Sayf al-Dīn Bilbay.
3. XII. 1467 al-Malik al-Ẓāhir Tīmūr Bogha.
31. I. 1468 al-Malik al-Ashraf Sayf al-Dīn Qāitbāi (d. 7. VIII. 1496).
6. VIII. 1496 al-Malik al-Nāṣir Muḥammad, son of the above.
31. X. 1498 al-Malik al-Ẓāhir Qānṣūḥ I.
28. VI. 1500 al-Malik al-Ashraf Jānbulāṭ
25. I. 1501 al-Malik al-'Ādil Sayf al-Dīn Ṭūmān Bāi I.
20. IV. 1501 - 24. VIII. 1516 al-Malik al-Ashraf Qānṣūḥ II. al-Ghūrī.
17. X. 1516 - 23. I. 1517 al-Malik al-Ashraf Ṭūmān Bāi II. (d. 14. IV. 1517).

THE MUSLIM RULERS OF INDIA

Ghaznavids

997 Maḥmūd (b. 971).
30. VI. 1030 Muḥammad, son of the above (b. 998).
... X. 1030 Mas'ūd I., brother of the above (b. 998, d. 6. I. 1042).
1041 Muḥammad (second time).
... IV. 1042 Mawdūd, son of Mas'ūd I. (b. 1010/1).
... XII. 1048 Mas'ūd II., son of the above (d. 1048).
... XII. 1048 - ... I. 1049 'Ālī, uncle of the above.
1049/50 'Abd al-Rashīd, brother of the above.
1052/3 Farrukhzād, son of Mas'ūd I. (b. 1036).
1059 Ibrāhīm, brother of the above (b. 1033).
1099 (?) Mas'ūd III. (b. 1061).
1114/5 Shīrzād, son of the above.
1115/6 Arslān, brother of the above (b. 1084/5).
... VIII./IX. 1118 Bahrām Shāh, brother of the above.
1152/3 Khusraw Shāh, son of the above.
1160–1186 Khusraw Malik, son of the above (d. 1191).

Ghūrids

1186 Ghiyāth al-Dīn Muḥammad, son of Sām.
11. II. 1203 Mu'izz al-Dīn Muḥammad Ghūrī, brother of the above.

Turkish, called "Pathān" (i.e. Afghān), Dynasty

24. VI. 1206 Aybak Quṭb al-Dīn.
... X/XI. 1210 Arām Shāh.
1211 Iltutmysh (Iletmish) Shams al-Dīn al-Quṭbī.
... IV/V. 1236 Fērōz Shāh I, Rukn al-Dīn.
... XI. 1236 Raḍīyah Begum Jalālat al-Dīn.
22. IV. 1240 Bahrām Shāh Mu'izz al-Dīn.
... IV. 1242 Mas'ūd Shāh 'Alā' al-Dīn.
9. VI. 1246 Maḥmūd Shāh I. Nāṣir al-Dīn.
17. II. 1266 Bal(a)bān Ghiyāth al-Dīn Ulugh Khān.
1287 Kai Qubād Mu'izz al-Dīn.
... V/VI. 1290 Kayūmarth Shams al-Din.

Khaljī or Khalajī (Afghān) Dynasty

13. VI. 1290 Fīrūz (Fērōz) Shāh II. Jalāl al-Dīn.
24. XI. 1294 Ibrāhīm Shāh I. Rukn al-Dīn (d. 26. XI. 1295).
... X. 1295 - 3. I. 1316 Muḥammad Shāh I. 'Alā' al-Dīn.
... III. 1316 'Umar Shāh Shihāb al-Dīn.
1. IV. 1316 Mubārak Shāh I. Quṭb al-Din.
15. IV. 1320 Khusraw Shāh Nāṣir al-Dīn

Tughluqids

... IX/X. 1320 Tughluq Shāh I., Ghiyāth al-Dīn, Ghāzī Malik.
... II/III. 1325 Muḥammad II. Jūnā, son of the above (d. 20. III. 1351).
mid III. 1351 Maḥmūd, son of the above.
20. III. 1351 Fērōz (Fīrūz) Shāh III.
21. IX. 1388 Tughluq Shāh II. Ghiyāth al-Din Sālārshāh.
15. II. 1389 Abū Bakr Shāh.
25. XII. 1389 (?) Muḥammad Shāh III.
1. III. 1393 Sikandar Shāh I. Humāyūn.
12. IV. 1393 Maḥmūd Shāh II. Nāṣir al-Dīn.
1394/5 Naṣrat Shāh.
1398/9 Maḥmūd II. (second time).
(1399/1400-1405/6 Iqbāl Khān ibn Ẓafar, pretender).
(1411/2 or 1413/4)-1414/5 Dawlat Khān Lōdī (interregnum).

Sayyids

19. VII. 1414 Khiẓr Khān.
19. V. 1421 Mubārak Shāh II. Mu'izz al-Dīn.
27. I. 1435 Muḥammad Shāh IV.
... I. 1446-1451 'Ālam Shāh 'Alā' al-Dīn, (d. 1478/9)

Lōdī Dynasty

17. I. 1452 Bahlūl Lōdī.
1. VII. 1489 Sikandar II. ibn Bahlūl.
15. II. 1517 (?) - 19. IV. 1526 Ibrāhīm II.

RULERS OF THE AQ QOYUNLU

1378/9 Bahā' al-Din Qara Ilük 'Uthmān ibn Fakhr al-Dīn.
1434/5 Nūr al-Dīn Ḥamzah, son of the above.
1444/5 Mu'izz al-Dīn Jahāngīr ibn 'Alī ibn Qara Ilük.
1453 Uzun Ḥasan ibn 'Alī.
5./6. I. 1478 Khalīl, son of the above.
1479/80 Ya'qūb, brother of the above.
1491 Bāysonqor, son of the above.
(1491 Masīḥ, son of Uzun Ḥasan).
(1491 'Alī, son of Khalīl).
1492 Rüstem ibn Maqṣūd.
1496/7 Aḥmed Gevde ibn Meḥmed.
1497/8 Murād ibn Ya'qūb.
1499-1500 Elvend (Alwand) ibn Yūsuf.
1500/1 Meḥmed ibn Yūsuf (at Iṣfahān, Alwand and Kirmān).
1501/2-1502/3 Murād (second time).

BIBLIOGRAPHY

Reference works, general studies of Islām and of Muslim civilization, history etc., are listed in the bibliography at the end of *"The Age of the Caliphs"* and are not repeated here. The list below is a selection of the more valuable modern studies, with a few mentions of important sources. Particulars of the available source material can be found in many of the works which are listed and in the *Encyclopaedia of Islam* and *İslâm Ansiklopedisi*.

GENERAL

OHSSON, ABRAHAM CONSTANTIN MOURADGEA D', *Histoire des Mongols depuis Tchinguiz-Khan jusqu'à Timour Bey ou Tamerlan*, 2nd ed., 4 vols., Amsterdam 1852.

HOWORTH, Sir HENRY HOYLE, *History of the Mongols, from the 9th to the 19th century*, 4 vols., London 1876-88, supplement and indices, London 1927.

DEGUIGNES, JOSEPH, *Histoire générale des Huns, des Turcs, des Mongols et des autres Tartares occidentaux, ouvrage tiré des livres chinois*, 4 vols., Paris 1756-58.

GROUSSET, RENÉ, *Histoire de l'Asie*; vol. III, *Le monde mongol*, Paris 1921-22.

——, *L'empire des steppes. Attila, Gengis-Khan, Tamerlan*, Paris 1939.

——, *L'empire mongol (1ère. phase)*, Paris 1941.

BLOCHET, EDGAR, *Introduction à l'histoire des Mongols de Fadl Allah Rashid ed-Din*, Leiden and London 1910. (Gibb Memorial Series, XII).

PAWLIKOWSKI-CHOLEWA, ALFRED VON, *Die Heere des Morgenlandes. Militärische Beiträge zur Geschichte des Nahen und Fernen Ostens*, Berlin 1940.

——, *Militärische Organisation und Taktik der innerasiatischen Reiter-Völker von den Parthern über Mao-tun, Attila und Tschinggiz-Chan bis Timur*, Leipzig 1937 *(Deutsche Kavallerie-Zeitung, Beiheft I)*.

JUVAINI, 'ALĀ' AL-DIN 'ATĀ' MALIK. *The history of the world conqueror*, tr. by JOHN ANDREW BOYLE, 2 vols., Manchester 1958.

EARLY PERIOD

HAENISCH, ERICH, *Die Geheime Geschichte der Mongolen aus einer mongolischen Niederschrift des Jahres 1240 von der Insel Kode'e im Keluren-Fluss, erstmalig übersetzt und erläutert*, 2nd ed., Leipzig 1948. (Das Mongolische Weltreich I).

PELLIOT, PAUL, *Yüan-ch'ao pi-shih — Histoire secrète des Mongols. Restitution du texte mongol et traduction française des chapitres I à VI*, Paris 1949.

VLADIMIRTSOV, BORIS YAKOVLEVICH, *Obshchestvennyi stroy Mongolov. Mongol'skiĭ kochevoy feodalizm* (The social structure of the Mongols. The Mongol nomad feudal system), Leningrad 1934. Tr. by MICHEL CARSOW, *Le régime social des Mongols: le féodalisme nomade*, Paris 1948.

BARTHOLD, WILHELM (VASILIĬ VLADIMIROVICH), *Turkestan down to the Mongol invasion.* 2nd ed. Tr. from the original Russian and revised by the author with the assistance of H. A. R. GIBB. London 1928. (Gibb Memorial Series, N.S., V).

——, *Zwölf Vorlesungen über die Geschichte der Türken Mittelasiens.* Deutsche Bearbeitung von THEODOR MENZEL. Berlin 1935. Tr. by Mme. M. DONSKIS, *Histoire des Turcs d'Asie Centrale*, Paris 1945.

ALINGE, KURT, *Mongolische Gesetze*, Leipzig 1934. (*Leipziger Rechtswissenschaftliche Studien*, 87).

RECORDS, COINS ETC.

WADDING, LUCAS, *Annales Ordinis Minorum*, vols. V-VII, Rome 1731.

RAYNALDUS, ODORICUS, *Annales Ecclesiastici ab Anno MCXCVIII*, 21 vols., Lucca 1747.

GOLUBOVICH, GEROLAMO, *Biblioteca Bio-Bibliografica della Terra Santa e dell' Oriente Francescano*, 5 vols., Quaracchi near Florence 1906-27.

LANE-POOLE, STANLEY, *The coins of the Mongols in the British Museum* ... ed. by REGINALD LANE-POOLE, vols. VI, VII and X, London 1881, 1890.

FRÄHN, CHRISTIAN MARTIN, *De Il-Chanorum seu Chulaguidarum numis commentationes duae*, in *Mém. de l'Ac. Imp. des Sciences de St.-Pétersbourg*, Series 6, vol. 2, St. Petersburg 1833, pp. 479-562.

TRAVELS

WYNGAERT, ANASTASIUS VAN DEN, *Itinera et relationes fratrum minorum saeculi XIII et XIV*, Quaracchi near Florence 1929 *(Sinica Franciscana, I)*.

YULE, Sir HENRY, *Cathay and the way thither, a collection of medieval notices of China, revised by* HENRI CORDIER, 4 vols., 1913-1916. (Published for the Hakluyt Society).

SYKES, Sir PERCY MOLESWORTH, *The quest for Cathay*, London 1936.

BEAZLEY, Sir CHARLES RAYMOND, ed., *The texts and versions of* JOHN DE PLANO CARPINI *and* WILLIAM DE RUBRUQUIS, *as printed for the first time by* HAKLUYT *in* 1598, *together with some shorter pieces*, Cambridge 1903. (Pub. for the Hakluyt Soc.).

JOHANN VON PLANO CARPINI, *Geschichte der Mongolen und Reisebericht* 1245-1247, tr. and explained by FRIEDRICH RISCH, Leipzig 1930.

WILHELM VON RUBRUCK, *Reise zu den Mongolen*, tr. by FRIEDRICH RISCH, Leipzig 1934.

MARCO POLO, *The description of the world*, ed. and tr. by ARTHUR CHRISTOPHER MOULE and PAUL PELLIOT. 4 vols. planned. Vols. 1-2, London 1938.

——, *The book of Ser Marco Polo, the Venetian, concerning the kingdoms and marvels of the East.* 3rd ed., *revised in the light of recent discoveries by* HENRI CORDIER. London 1903, reprinted 1929.

BRETSCHNEIDER, EMIL VASILIEVIČH, *Medieval researches from eastern Asiatic sources*, 2 vols., London 1910.

IBN BAṬṬŪṬA(H), ABŪ 'ABD ALLĀH MUḤAMMAD, *Voyages*; *texte arabe accompagné d'une traduction* par CHARLES DEFRÉMERY and BENJAMIN RAPHAEL SANGUINETTI, 4 vols., Paris 1854-74.

——, *The Travels of I. B.*, tr. and annot. by Sir HAMILTON GIBB, vol. I, Cambridge 1958.

JINGIZ KHĀN

VLADIMIRTSOV, BORIS YAKOVLEVICH, *The life of Chingis Khan*, tr. by Prince DMITRI SVYATOPOLK-MIRSKY, London 1930; *Gengis Khan*, tr. by MICHEL CARSOW, Paris 1948.

FOX, RALPH, *Genghiz Khan*, London 1936.

LAMB, HAROLD, *Jinghiz Khan, the emperor of all men*, New York 1930.

PÉTIS DE LA CROIX FRANÇOIS, *Histoire du grand Genghiscan* . . ., Paris 1710.

CHARA-DAVAN, ÉRENŽEN, *Chingiz-Chan kak polkovodec i ego nasledie* (Jingiz Khān as a military leader and his successors), Belgrade 1929.

IVANIN, MIKHAIL IVANOVICH, *O voennom iskusstvě i zavoevaniyakh Mongolo-Tatar i sredneaziatskikh narodov pri Chingiz-Khaně i Tamerlaně* (The military methods and conquests of the Mongols, Tatars and Central Asian peoples in the age of Jingiz Khān and Tīmūr), St. Petersburg 1875.

VERNADSKIĬ, GEORGIĬ VLADIMIROVICH, *O sostave Velikoy Yasy Chingiz Khana* (The content of the Great Yasa of Jingiz Khān), Brussels 1939. (Issledovaniya i materialy po istorii Rossii i Vostoka, Vyp. I).

——, *The scope and contents of Chingis Khan's Yasa*, in *Harvard Journal of Asiatic Studies*, III (Dec. 1938), 3 and 4, pp. 337-360.

THE ĪLKHĀNS

a. Politics

SPULER, BERTOLD, *Die Mongolen in Iran. Politik, Verwaltung und Kultur der Ilchanzeit* 1220-1350, Leipzig 1939, 2d ed. Berlin 1955.

JAHN, KARL, *Das iranische Papiergeld*, in *Archiv Orientální*, X (1935), pp. 308-40.

'AZZĀWI, 'ABBĀS AL-, *Ta'rīkh al-'Irāq bayn Iḥtilālayn: I, Ḥukūmat al-Mughul* ('Irāq under Ilkhānid rule), Baghdād 1353/1934/5.

b. Religion

PELLIOT, PAUL, *Les Mongols et la papauté*, in *Revue de l'Orient Chrétien*, Series 3, Vol. XXIII (1922-23), pp. 1-30, and vol. XXVIII (1931-32), pp. 3-84.

SORANZO, GIOVANNI, *Il papato, L'Europa cristiana e i Tartari*, Milan 1930. *(Pubblicazioni dell'università cattolica del Sacro Cuore*, Series 5, Vol. XII).

OPPERT, GUSTAV SALOMON, *Der Priester Johannes in Sage und Geschichte*, 2nd ed., Berlin 1870.
ZARNCKE, FRIEDRICH, *Der Priester Johannes*, in *Abhandlungen der kgl. sächsischen Gesellschaft der Wissenschaften*, Vol. VII (Leipzig 1879), pp. 827-1039; Vol. VIII (1883), pp. 1-186.
RICHARD, JEAN, *L'extrême Orient...:... Prêtre Jean*, in "*Annales d'Éthiopie*" II (Paris 1957), p. 225-42.

c. Economics

HEYD, WILHELM, *Histoire du commerce dans le Levant au moyen âge*, 2nd enlarged ed., Leipzig 1923.
PETRUSHEVSKIĬ, I. P., *Gorodskaya znat' v gosudarstve Khulaguidov* (The urban intelligentsia in the Īlkhānid state), in *Sovetskoe Vostokovedenie*, V (1948), pp. 85-110.
BELENITSKIĬ, A. M., *K voprosu o social'nykh otnosheniyakh Irana v Khulaguidskuyu épokhu*, (On the question of social relationships in Persia dwing the Īlkhānid period), ibid. pp. 111-128.

PERSIA AND 'IRĀQ IN THE 14TH CENTURY

DEFRÉMERY, CHARLES, *Mémoire historique sur la destruction de la dynastie dès Mozaffériens* Paris 1854. (Offprint from the *Journal Asiatique*).
'AZZĀWĪ, 'ABBĀS AL-, *Ta'rīkh al-'Irāq bayn Iḥtilālayn: II, Ḥukūmat al-Jalāyirīyah*, Baghdād 1304/1936. (Jalā'irids).

FRASER TYTLER, Sir WILLIAM KERR, *Afghanistan: a study of political developments in Central Asia*, London 1953.
SYKES, SIR PERCY MOLESWORTH, *A history of Afghanistan*, London 1940.

TĪMŪR AND THE TĪMURĪDS

BOUVAT, LUCIEN, *L'empire mongol (2e. phase)*, Paris 1927.
IQBĀL, 'ABBĀS, *Tārīkh-i mufaṣṣal-i Īrān az istīlā-yi Mughul tā inqirāẓ-i Qājārīyeh* (Detailed history of Persia from the Mongol conquest to the fall of the Qājārs), Tehrān 1941.
SKRINE, FRANCIS HENRY BENNETT, and ROSS, Sir EDWARD DENISON, *The heart of Asia; a history of Russian Turkestan and the Central Asian Khanates from the earliest times*, London 1899.
SANDERS, J. H., *Tamerlane, or Timur, the Great Amir*, tr. from IBN 'ARABSHĀH London 1936.
TAUER, FELIX, *Histoire des conquêtes de Tamerlan de Niẓām ed-Dīn Šāmī*, vol. I, Prague 1937 (*Monogr. Archivu Orientálního, V*).
ALEXANDRESCU-DERSCA, MARIA MATILDA, *La campagne de Timur en Anatolie* 1402, Bucarest 1942.
CLAVIJO, RUY GONZÁLEZ DE, *Narrative of the embassy to the court of Tamerlane at Samarcand*, A.D. 1403-1406, tr. from the Spanish with introd., by GUY LE STRANGE, London 1928.
SCHILTBERGER, JOHANNES, *The bondage and travels of Johann Schiltberger ... 1396-1427*, tr. by BUCHAN TELFER with notes by P. BRUUN, London 1879. (Pub. for the Hakluyt Society).

HINZ, WALTHER, *Quellenstudien zur Geschichte der Timuriden*, in the *Zeitschrift der Deutschen Morgenländischen Gesellschaft*, 90 (1936), pp. 357-398.
BOUVAT, LUCIEN, *Essai sur la civilisation timouride*, in the *Journal Asiatique*, CCVIII (1926), pp. 193-299.
BARTHOLD, WILHELM (VASILIĬ) VLADIMIROVICH, *Ulug Beg und seine Zeit*, Deutsche Bearbeitung von WALTHER HINZ, Leipzig 1935.
——, *Herat unter Ḥusein Baiqara*, Deutsche Bearbeitung von WALTHER HINZ, Leipzig 1937.
BOLDYREV, A. N., *Ocherki iz geratskogo obshchestva na rubezhe XV-XVI vekov* (Sketches of Herat society at the turn of the 15th and 16th centuries), in the *Trudy otd. Vostoka, Leningrad. Gos. Ėrmitazh, otd. its. kul't. i isk. Vostoka*, IV (1947), pp. 313-422.
ALISHER NAVOI (Commemoration volume for the jubilee of 'Alī Shīr Navā'ī), Moscow and Leningrad 1948.
BERTHELS, EVGENIĬ ĖDUARDOVICH, *Navoi*, Moscow and Leningrad 1948.

TARLAN, A. N., *Ali Şir Nevâyi*, Istanbul 1942.

QUATREMÈRE, MARC ÉTIENNE, *Mémoire sur le règne du Sultan Schah-Rokh*, in the *Journal Asiatique*, 1836.

TOGAN, ZEKI VELIDI, *Büyük Türk hükümdari, Şahruh* (The great Turkish ruler Shāhrukh), in the *Türk Dili ve Edebiyatı Dergisi*, III, 3-4 (1949), pp. 520-538.

THE GOLDEN HORDE

a. General Histories

SPULER, BERTOLD, *Die Goldene Horde. Die Mongolen in Russland* 1223-1502, Leipzig 1943.

HAMMER-PURGSTALL, JOSEF, Freiherr VON, *Geschichte der Goldenen Horde in Kiptschak*, Pest 1840.

GREKOV, BORIS DMITRIEVICH and YAKUBOVSKIĬ, ALEKSANDR YUR'EVICH, *Zolotaya Orda i eë padenie* (The Golden Horde and its fall), Moscow and Leningrad 1950; tr. (of a first, abridged ed.) by FRANÇOIS THURET, *La Horde d'Or*, Paris 1939.

PELLIOT, PAUL, *Notes sur l'histoire de la Horde d'Or*, Paris 1950. (Essays on about 20 local and personal names).

b. External relations

ŻDAN, MICHAL, *Stosunki litewsko-tatarskie za czasów Witolda, w. ks. Litwy* (Lithuanian-Tatar relations at the time of the Lithuanian Grand Prince Witold) in the *Ateneum Wileńskie VII* (1930), pp. 529-601.

KUCZYŃSKI, STEFAN MARJA, *Ziemie czernihowsko-siewierskie pod rządami Litwy* (The Chernígov-Severian region under Lithuanian rule), Warsaw 1936. (*Praci ukraïnškoho naukovoho instytutu* XXXIII).

BÄCHTOLD, RUDOLF, *Südwestrussland im Spätmittelalter (Territoriale, wirtschaftliche und soziale Verhältnisse)*, Basle 1951. (Basler Beiträge zur Gesch.wiss. 38).

NASONOV, A. N., *Mongoly i Rus. Istoriya tatarskoy politiki na Rusi* (The Tatars and (Old) Russia. History of Tatar policy in Russia), Moscow and Leningrad 1940.

RHODE, GOTTHOLD, *Die Ostgrenze Polens* I (bis 1401), Köln/Graz 1955.

JAHN, KARL, *Turken en Oostslaven. Enkele beschouwingen over hun onderlinge betrekkingen*, Leiden 1953.

---

b. Internal affairs

BEREZIN, IL'YA NIKOLAEVICH, *Ocherk vnutrennago ustroystva ulusa Dzhuchieva* (Sketch of the internal structure of the Ulus Jochi), in *Trudy vost. otd. Imp. archeol. ob-va*, VIII (St.Petersburg 1864), pp. 385-480.

SABLUKOV, GORDIĬ SEMËNOVICH, *Ocherk vnutrennago sostoyaniya Kipchakskago Tsarstva* (Sketch of internal conditions in the Qypchaq Khānate), 2nd ed., Kazan 1895 (Izvestiya Kazanskago Universitèta VII).

c. Coins

FRÄHN, CHRISTIAN MARTIN (CHRISTIAN DANILOVICH), *Über die Münzen der Chane vom Ulus Dschutschi's oder der Goldenen Horde* ..., St. Petersburg and Leipzig 1832.

SAVEL'EV, PAVEL STEPANOVICH, *Monety Dzhuchidov, Dzhagataidov, Dzhelairidov i drugie, obrashchavshiesya v Zolotoy Ordě v épochu Tokhtamysha* (Coins of the Jochids, Jagataiids, Jalā'irids and others which circulated in the Golden Horde at the time of Tokhtamysh), St. Petersburg 1857-58.

d. Excavations

BALODIS, FRANZ, *Alt- und Neu-Sarai, die Hauptstädte der Goldenen Horde*, in *Latvijas universitātes raksti*, XIII (Riga 1926), pp. 3-82.

BALLOD, FRANTS V., *Privolzhskie Pompei* (Pompeii on the Volga), Moscow and Petrograd 1923.

e. Trade

BRĂTIANU, GEORGES I., *Recherches sur le commerce génois dans la Mer Noire au XIIIe siècle*, Paris 1929.

KUTRZEBA, STANISLAW, *Handel Polski ze wschodem w wiekach średnich* (Poland's eastern trade in the Middle Ages), Krakow 1903.

NISTOR, JOHANN, *Handel und Wandel in der Moldau bis zum Ende des 16. Jahrhunderts*, Tschernowitz (Çernăuţi) 1912.

——, *Die auswärtigen Handelsbeziehungen der Moldau im 14., 15. und 16. Jahrhundert*, Gotha 1911.

RUSSIAN RULE ON THE VOLGA

a. Records

ISTORIYA TATARII *v materialakh i dokumentakh* (History of Tatary in records and documents), ed. by N. L. RUBINSTEIN, Moscow 1937.

Tatarskaya ASSR. Materialy po istorii Tatarii vtoroy polovine XIX veka; Part I, *Agrarnyi vopros i krest'yanskoe dvizhenie* 50 *do* 70-*kh godov XIX v.* (The agrarian question and the peasant movement of the 50s to 70 s of the 19th century), ed. by VYACHESLAV PETROVICH VOLGIN, Moscow and Leningrad 1936 *(Akademiya Nauk SSSR. Trudy istoriko-archeograficheskogo instituta XVI - Materialy po istorii narodov SSSR VI).*

KLIMOVICH, LYUCIAN IPPOLITOVICH, *Islam v tsarskoy Rossii. Ocherki* (Islām in the Russia of the Tsars. Sketches), Moscow 1936.

Materialy po istorii Bashkirskoy ASSR. Bashirskie vosstaniya v 17 *i pervoy polovine* 18 *vv.* (Materials for the history of the Bashkir Republic. Bashkir revolts in the 17th and first half of the 18th centuries), Part I, Moscow and Leningrad 1936 *(Akademiya Nauk SSSR. Trudy ist.-archeogr. Inst. Akad. Nauk SSSR XVIII).*

TUKHVATULLIN, FATIKH, *Materialy k istorii Bashkir* (Materials for the history of the Bashkirs), Ufa 1928.

Polnoe Sobranie Zakonov Rossiĭskoy Imperii (Complete collection of the laws of the Russian Empire), St. Petersburg 1830 ff.

b. Travels

BRONIOVIUS DE BIEZDZFEDEA, MARTIN, *Tartariae descriptio*, Cologne 1595.

PALLAS, PETER SIMON, *Reise durch verschiedene Provinzen des Russischen Reiches in den Jahren* 1768 bis 1774, 3 vols., St. Petersburg 1771-76.

GMELIN, SAMUEL GOTTLIEB, *Reise durch Russland*, Part 2, St. Petersburg 1774.

GEORGI, JOHANN GOTTLIEB, *Beobachtungen während einer Reise im Russischen Reiche*, St. Petersburg 1775.

HAXTHAUSEN-ABBENBURG, AUGUST, Freiherr VON, *Studien über die inneren Zustände, das Leben und insbesondere die ländliche Einrichtungen Russlands*, 2 vols., Hanover 1847.

c. General

SPULER, BERTOLD, *Idel-Ural. Völker und Staaten zwischen Volga und Ural*, Berlin 1942.

——, *Die Wolga-Tataren und Baschkiren unter russischer Herrschaft*, in *Islam XXIX* (1949), pp 142-216.

MENDE, GERHARD VON, *Der nationale Kampf der Russlandtürken. Ein Beitrag zur nationalen Frage in der Sovetunion*, Berlin 1936 (*Mitteilungen des Seminars für Orientalische Sprachen*, supp. to year XXXIX).

GUBAYDULLIN, GAZIZ S., *Iz proshlogo tatar* (From the past of the Tatars), in *Materialy po izuchéniyu Tataristana II* (Kazan 1925), pp. 71-111.

VOROB'ËV, NIKOLAĬ YOSIFOVICH, *Material'naya kul'tura Kazanskikh Tatar* (The material culture of the Kazan Tatars), Kazan 1930, *(Trudy doma tat. Kul't. II).*

TIPEEV, SAMSON, *Ocherki po istorii Bashkirii* (Sketches for the history of Bashkiria), Ufa 1930.

KUFTIN, BORIS ALEKSEYEVICH, *Material'naya kul'tura russkoy meshchery* (The material culture of the Russian Mishérs), Part I, Moscow 1926 *(Trudy Ges. Muzeya Central'no-promyshlenoy oblasti III).*

PERETYATKOVICH, GEORGIĬ IVANOVICH, *Povolzh'e v XV i XVI věkakh. Ocherki iz istorii kolonizatsii kraya* (The Volga region in the 15th and 16th centuries; sketches from the history of the colonization of the region), 1877.
——, *Povolzh'e v XVII i nachalě XVIII věka* (The Volga region in the 17th and early 18th centuries), Odessa 1882.
WASTL, JOSEPH, *Baschkiren. Ein Beitrag zur Klärung der Rassenprobleme Osteuropas*, Vienna 1938 (*Rudolf Pöchs Nachlass, Serie A. Physische Anthropologie*, vol. V).
TUPPA, KARL, *Mischeren und Tipteren. Beiträge zur Anthropologie der Türkvolker Russlands*, Vienna 1941.

THE CRIMEA

SMIRNOV, VASILIĬ DMITRIEVICH, *Krymskoe khanstvo pod verkhovenstvom Ottomanskoy Porty do nachala XVIII věka* (The Khānate of the Crimea under the suzerainty of the Ottoman Porte until the beginning of the 18th century), St. Petersburg 1887.
SMIRNOV, VASILIĬ DMITRIEVICH, *Krymskoe khanstvo pod verkhovenstvom Ottomanskoy Porty v XVIII stol.* (The Khānate of the Crimea under the suzerainty of the Ottoman Porte in the 18th century), Odessa 1889.
SOYSAL, ABDULLAH ZIHNI, *Z dziejów Krymu* (From the history of the Crimea), Warsaw 1938 (*Prace Młodzieży Krymskiei na emigracii I*).
HAMMER-PURGSTALL, JOSEF, Freiherr VON, *Geschichte der Chane der Krim unter Osmanischer Herrschaft*, Vienna 1856. (Of little value).
BARTOSZEWICZ, JULJAN, *Poglqd na stosunki Polski z Turcjq i Tatarami* (Survey of Poland's relations with the Turks and Tatars), Warsaw 1860. (Uninformative).
ZAVADOVSKIĬ, A., *Sto lět zhizni Tavridy* 1783-1883 (A hundred years of the life of Taurida), Simferopol 1885.
SPULER, BERTOLD, *Die Krim unter russıscher Herrschaft*, in "*Blick in die Wissenschaft*" (Berlin), August 1948, pp. 356-363.
KIRIMAL, EDIGE, *Der nationale Kampf der Krimtürken*, Emsdetten (Westphalia) 1952. (Covers period 1917-1945) — (Highly informative work).

ARTUQIDS

FERDI, KATIP, *Mardin Artukları tarihi* (History of the Artuqids of Mardin), İstanbul 1939.
ARTUK, İBRAHIM. *Mardin Artuk oğullarl tarihi*, İstanbul 1941.

QARA QOYUNLU AND AQ QOYUNLU

HINZ, WALTHER, *Irans Aufstieg zum Nationalstaat im 15. Jahrhundert*, Berlin and Leipzig 1936.
MINORSKY, VLADIMIR FEODOROVICH, *La Perse au XVe. siècle entre la Turquie et Venise*, Paris 1933. (Pub. de la Soc. des Etudes Iraniennes 7).
'AZZĀWI, 'ABBĀS AL-, *Ta'rīkh al-'Irāq bayn Iḥtilālayn: III, Al-ḥukūmah al-Turkumānīyah*, Baghdād 1357-1938/9.
UZUNÇARŞILI, İSMAIL HAKKI, *Anadolu Beylikleri, Karakoyunlu ve Akkoyunlu devletleri* (The Anatolian principalities and the Qara Qoyunlu and Aq Qoyunlu empires), İstanbul 1937.
BERCHET, GUGLIELMO, *La repubblica di Venezia e la Persia*, Turin 1859.
SASSOON, DAVID SOLOMON, ed. *A history of the Jews in Baghdad*, Letchworth 1949.

INDIA

BĪRŪNĪ, ABŪ RAYḤĀN MUḤAMMAD AL-, *Alberuni's India*, tr. by EDUARD SACHAU, 2 vols., London 1888, reprinted 1910.
ELLIOTT, Sir HENRY MIERS, and DOWSON, JOHN, ed., *The history of India as told by its own historians; the posthumous papers of the late Sir H. M. Elliott ed. by Prof. John Dowson*, 8 vols., London 1867-77. Partially reprinted, Calcutta 1952-.
FIRISHTAH, MUḤAMMAD QĀSIM, *The history of Hindostan*; tr. from the Persian by ALEXANDER DOW, 2nd ed., 3 vols., London 1770-1772.

The Cambridge History of India; vol. III, *Turks and Afghans*, by Sir WOLSELEY HAIG, Cambridge 1928.

SMITH, VINCENT ARTHUR, *The Oxford history of India*, 2nd ed., Oxford 1923. (Vol. II).
POWELL-PRICE, JOHN CADWGAN, *A history of India*, London 1955.
DUNBAR, SIR GEORGE, *A history of India from the earliest times to the present day*, London 1933; tr. *Geschichte Indiens von den ältesten Zeiten bis zur Gegenwart*, Munich and Berlin 1937.
MORELAND, WILLIAM HARRISON, and CHATTERJEE, Sir ATUL CHANDRA, *A short history of India*, London 1935, 2nd ed. 1945.
LANE-POOLE, STANLEY, *Medieval India under Mohammedan rule*, London 1906.
PRASAD, ISHWARI, *A short history of Muslim rule in India, from the conquest of Islam to the death of Aurangzeb*, Allahabad 1939. Tr. by H. DE SAUGY, *L'Inde du VIIe. au XVIe. siècle*, Paris 1930.
SHARMA, SRI RAM, *The Crescent in India, a study in medieval history*, revised ed., Bombay 1954.
HASSAN, ABID, *Der Islam in Indien. Indien im Weltislam*, Berlin and Magdeburg 1942.

JAFFAR, S. M., *Mediaeval India under Muslim kings*; II, *The rise and fall of the Ghaznavids*, Peshawar 1940.
——, *Some aspects of Muslim rule in India*, Peshawar 1956.
HASHMI, YUSUF ABBAS: *The latter Ghaznavids* 1030-1187, (Thesis), Hamburg 1957.
MOINUL HAQ, SYED, *A short history of the Delhi Sultanate*, Aligarh 1945.
AHMAD, MUHAMMAD AZIZ, *Political history and institutions of the early Turkish empire of Delhi* (1206-1290 *A.D.*), Lahore 1949.
QURESHI, ISHTIAQ HUSAIN, *The administration of the Sultanate of Delhi*, 2nd revised ed., Lahore 1944.
LAL, KISHORI SARAN, *History of the Khaljīs* (1290-1320), Allahabad 1950.
ḤUSAIN, AGHA MAHDI, *The rise and fall of Muḥammad bin Tughluq*, London 1938.
BIYIKTAY, HALIS, *Timuriler zamanında Hindustan Türk İmparatorluğu* (The Turkish empire in India at the time of the Tīmūrids).
SHERWANI, HAROON KHAN, *The Bahmanis of the Deccan*, London 1953.
ṢŪFĪ, GHULĀM MUḤYI'D-DĪN, *Kashmīr, being a history of Kashmīr from the earliest times to our own*, Lahore 1948.

TITUS, MURRAY T., *Indian Islam*, London 1930.
HOLLISTER, JOHN NORMAN, *The Shī'a of India*, London 1953.

MORELAND, WILLIAM HARRISON, *The agrarian system of Moslem India, an historical essay*, Cambridge 1929.
YUSUF ALI, *Medieval India; social and economic conditions*, London 1932.
ASHRAF, KUNWAR MUHAMMAD, *Life and conditions of the people of Hindūstān* (1200-1550 *A.D.*), Calcutta 1935.

RAWLINSON, HUGH GEORGE, *India, a short cultural history*, London 1952.
SARKAR, Sir JADUNATH, *India through the ages; a survey of the growth of Indian life and thought*, Calcutta 1928.
GARRETT, GEOFFREY THEODORE, ed., *The legacy of India*, Oxford 1937.

EGYPT

MUIR, Sir WILLIAM, *The Mameluke or slave dynasty of Egypt*, London 1896; Arabic tr., Cairo 1342-1924.
WEIL, GUSTAV, *Geschichte der Chalifen*, vols. IV and V, Heidelberg 1862.
QUATREMÈRE, MARC ÉTIENNE, *Histoire des sultans mamelouks*, 2 vols., Paris 1837-45.
LANE, EDWARD WILLIAM, *Arabian society in the Middle Ages*, London 1883.
ZETTERSTÉEN, KARL VILHELM, *Beiträge zur Geschichte der Mamlukensultane in den Jahren 690-741 der Hiğra, nach arabischen Handschriften*, Leiden 1919.
IBN IYÂS, *Journal d'un bourgeois du Caise*, tr. by GASTON WIET, Paris 1955.
NIEMEYER, WOLFGANG, *Ägypten zur Zeit der Mamluken, eine kultur- und landeskundliche Skizze*, Berlin 1936. (Later Mamlūk period).

Wüstenfeld, Ferdinand, *Die Geographie und Verwaltung von Egypten*, Göttingen 1879. (Based on Qalqashandī).
Björkman, Walther, *Beiträge zur Geschichte der Staatskanzlei im islamischen Egypten*, Hamburg 1928. (Based on Qalqashandī).
Reitemeyer, Else, *Beschreibung Ägyptens im Mittelalter*, Leipzig 1903.
Poliak, Abraham N., *Feudalism in Egypt, Syria, Palestine and the Lebanon* 1200-1900, London 1939.

Grousset, René, *L'empire du Levant; histoire de la Question d'Orient*, revised ed., Paris 1949.
Atiya, Aziz Suryal, *Egypt and Aragon. Embassies and diplomatic correspondence between* 1300 *and* 1330, Leipzig 1938. (*Abhandlungen für die Kunde des Morgenlandes*, XXIII/7).
——, *The crusade in the later Middle Ages*, London 1938.
Stripling, George William Frederick, *The Ottoman Turks and the Arabs* 1511-1574, Urbana 1942. (*Illinois studies in the social sciences*, XXVI, 4).
Ayalon, David, *Gunpowder and firearms in the Mamluk kingdom*, London 1956.

SYRIA-PALESTINE

Gaudefroy-Demombynes, Maurice, *La Syrie à l'époque des Mamelouks d'après les auteurs arabes*, Paris 1923.
Z!adeh, Niöola A., *Urban life in Syria under the early Mamlūks*, Beirut 1953.

INDICES

Some of the names and terms which appear are subjects of articles in the Encyclopaedia of Islam. (N.B. Č = Ch, Dj = J and Ḳ = Q in E.I.).

INDEX A

Names of persons, families, tribes, religious communities, political parties

Abāqā *(Īlkhān)* 26-33, 34
'Abbās I the Great (Ṣafavid *Shāh*) 91
'Abbāsids (Caliphal dynasty) 19, 20, 24, 45, 59, 78
Abdül-Kayyum Nasirî (Tatar reformer) 92 note
Abū Sa'īd (Īlkhānid ruler) 39-40, 42
Abū Sa'īd (Tīmūrid ruler) 69, 75
'Ādil Girai (Crimean *Khān*) 98
Aḥmad ibn Uways (Jalā'irid ruler) 42, 74, 77
Aḥmad Nakūdār *(Īlkhān)* 33 f.
Aḥmad Shāh (ruler of Gujarāt) 73
Aḥmed (*Khān* of the Great Horde) 82, 84
'Alā al-Dīn Khaljī (*Sulṭān* of Delhi) 64, 73
Alexander (Lithuanian ruler) 84
Algu (Jagataid *Khān*) 43 f.
'Alī Shāh *(wazīr)* 37, 39
Amīr Khusraw (poet) 64
Aq Qoyunlu ("White Sheep") (dynasty) 69, 75-77, 78, 79
Arghūn *(Īlkhān)* 34, 35, 37
Artuqids (Turkish dynasty) 74
Aryq Böge (Mongol prince) 21 f., 24, 43 f.
Assassins (Nizārī Ismā'īlites) 18 f.
Aybak ("Slave" *Sulṭān* of Delhi) 62, 63
Ayyūbids (dynasty) 56, 63

Bābar (or Bābur) (Mughal emperor) 10, 12
Bahlūl Lōdī (*Sulṭān* of Delhi) 71
Bahmanids (dynasty) 65, 72 f.
Bahrī Mamlūks (rulers of Egypt) 58 f., 77
Bāidū *(Īlkhān)* 35
Bāisunqur (Tīmūrid prince) 69
Bal(a)bān (*Sulṭān* of Delhi) 63
Bar Hebraeus *see* Gregory Bar Hebracus
Barlas (Turco-Mongol tribe) 65
Barqūq (Mamlūk *Sulṭān*) 77
Barsbāi (Mamlūk *Sulṭān*) 78
Basil II, the Blind (Muscovite ruler) 82
Basil III (Muscovite ruler) 95
Batu (founder of the Golden Horde) 11-16, 22, 48
Bāyazīd I (Ottoman *Sulṭān*) 67 f., 77
Bāyazīd II (Ottoman *Sulṭān*) 76
Baybars I (Mamlūk *Sulṭān*) 20, 23, 27, 57, 58, 59
Behzād (miniaturist) 69 note
Béla IV (Hungarian king) 13
Berdi Beg (Golden Horde prince) 41, 55
Berke (Golden Horde *Khān*) 22-24, 26, 29, 44, 47, 49, 50
"Big" Ḥasan *(Ḥasan-i Buzurg)* (Mongol *amīr*) 39 f., 42, 77
al-Bīrūnī (author) 61
"Black Sheep" *see* Qara Qoyunlu
"Black Tatars" 2
Bolsheviks (Russian party) 93 f., 100
Borte (wife of Jingiz Khān) 3
Buddhists 16, 26, 30 f., 34-36, 39, 50, 62, 74
Buhlūl *see* Bahlūl
Bulāvin, Kondratiĭ (Russian rebel) 90
Burāq Ḥājib *(wazīr)* 32
Burjī Mamlūks (rulers of Egypt) 77-79

"Cadets" (Constitutional Democrats) (Russian party) 93
Carmathians *(Qarāmiṭah)* (Ismā'īlite sect) 60 f.
Carpini, Giovanni di Plano (Papal enissary) 14 f.
Casimir IV (King of Poland) 82, 84
Catharine II the Great (Tsarina of Russia) 91, 98 f.
Catharine Cornaro (Queen of Cyprus) 76
Catholic Christians 28, 30, 37, 53, 83, 97, 99
Chaqmaq (Mamlūk *Sulṭān*) 78
Christians 2, 4 f., 15-20, 25-31, 34, 36-37, 39, 47 f., 50, 53 f., 58, 59, 67 f., 78 f., 82, 83, 86, 88-91, 99, 100
Chūbān (Mongol *amīr*) 39 f.
Clavijo, Ruy Gonzālez de (Castilian envoy) 68
Çoban *see* Chūbān
Crusaders 28, 29, 58, 59, 76

Devlet Girai I (Crimean *Khān*) 96
Dhū'l-Qadr (Turkish principality) 75, 76, 79
Doquz Khātūn (wife of Hūlāgū) 19, 25, 30
Doroshénko, Peter (Cossack *hetman*) 98

Edigü (Crimean general) 80 f.
Ergene Khātūn (Mongol princess) 44

"False Demetrius" (Russian pretender) 90
Faraj (Mamlūk *Sulṭān*) 78
Fērōz (*Sulṭān* of Delhi) 65, 71
Firdawsī (poet) 61
Fīrūz *see* Fērōz
"The Forty" (oligarchy at Delhi) 63
Frederick II the Great (Prussian king) 98

Ganesh (ruler of Bengal) 72
Gaspyraly (Gasprinskiĭ) *see* Ismā'īl Bey Gaspyraly
Gaykhātū *(Īlkhān)* 34 f., 37
Ghazān Maḥmūd (Īlkhānid ruler) 35-38, 51
Ghaznavids (dynasty) 61 f.
Ghiyāth al-Dīn Muḥammad (Ghūrid ruler) 62
Ghūrids (dynasty) 62
Girai (dynasty) 81-86, 95-99
Golden Horde 14, 20, 21-25, 26, 28, 29, 34, 38 39, 40 f., 42, 44, 47-56, 59, 80 f., 84
Göyük *(Great Khān)* 14-16
Great Horde (dynasty) 81, 82, 84 f., 95
Gregory IX (Pope) 29
Gregory Bar Hebraeus (author) 31

Ḥāfiẓ (poet) 41
Ḥajjī Girai (Crimean *Khān*) 81, 82, 95
Ḥasan *see* "Big Ḥasan" and "Little Ḥasan"
Haytonus (author) 29, 37
Henry II (Duke of Silesia) 13
Hethum *see* Haytonus
Hindus 60-65, 71-74
Hohenstaufen (dynasty) 28
Hūlāgū (Hülegü) *(Īlkhān)* 18-23, 25 f., 27, 30
Ḥusayn Bāiqara (Tīmūrid ruler) 69 f., 76
Ḥusayn ibn Uways (Jalā'irid ruler) 42

Ibn Taymiyah (theologian) 58
Ibrāhīm Lōdī (*Sulṭān* of Delhi) 72
Ikhtiyār al-Dīn Muḥammad Khaljī (general) 62
Iletmish *see* Iltutmysh
Īlkhānids (dynasty) 25-41, 42, 44, 48 f., 50, 53, 59, 64, 70, 77
Iltutmysh (*Sulṭān* of Delhi) 106
Īnāl (Mamlūk *Sulṭān*) 78
Innocent IV (Pope) 29
Iskandar (ruler of Kashmīr) 74
Iskandar (Qara Qoyunlu ruler) 75
Islām 5, 6, 8, 9, 21, 26, 31, 38 f., 56, 58, 60, 61, 64, 92 f. *See also* Muslims
Ismā'īl (Ṣafavid *Shāh*) 70, 76
Ismā'īl Bey Gaspyraly (Tatar reformer) 92 f., 100
Iván I, Kalitá (Muscovite ruler) 53
Iván III, the Great (Muscovite ruler) 82, 85
Iván IV, "the Terrible" (Tsar of Russia) 85 f., 88 f., 96, 97

Jacobite (Syrian Monophysite) Christians 19, 26, 30, 31
Jagatai (Mongol prince) 10, 43
Jagataids (dynasty) 43-46
Jagellonians (dynasty) 82
Jahān-Shāh *see* Mīrzā Jahān-Shāh
Jalā'irids (dynasty) 41, 42, 74, 77
Jalāl al-Dīn Mangūbirdī (Mengüberdi) *(Khwārizm-Shāh)* 10, 64, 75
Jalāl al-Dīn Muḥammad (ruler of Kashmīr) 72
Jāmī (poet) 69 note
Jamukha (Mongol chieftain) 3, 4
Jāni Beg (Golden Horde *Khān*) 40, 54 f.
Jebe (Mongol general) 10
Jesuits (Catholic order) 97
Jews 31, 34, 37, 58, 100
Jingiz Khān (Temujin) 3-11, 13, 14, 16, 17, 18, 31, 43, 63, 64, 66, 68
Jochi (Mongol prince) 10 f., 16
John XXII (Pope) 53
John II Casimir (King of Poland) 97

Kartids *see* Kurtids
Keräit (Mongol tribe) 2, 3, 4
Khalaj (Turkish tribe) 62
Khal(a)jī (dynasty) 64
Khiẕr Khān Sayyid (*Sulṭān* of Delhi) 71
Khwārizm-Shāhs (dynasty) 8-10, 64
Khmielnitskiĭ, Bogdán (Cossack *hetman*) 97
Kin (dynasty) 3, 7
Kök Turk (Turkish tribe) 1
Koryátovichi (Lithuanian princes) 55, 80
"Kresh" ("Baptized" Tatars) 91, 94
Küchlüg (Mongol chieftain) 4
Küchük Meḥmed (Great Horde *Khān*) 81
Kun, Béla (communist leader) 100
Kurtids (dynasty) 33, 41, 66

"Latin" Christians 23, 53, 83
Liao (dynasty) 2
Little Ḥasan *(Ḥasan-i Kūchik)* (Mongol *amīr*) 40, 42
Lōdī (dynasty) 71 f.
Louis IX (King of France) 15, 29
Lur (Īrānian tribe) 19
Lusignan (dynasty) 76

Maḥmūd of Ghaznah *(Sulṭān)* 61
Maḥmūd II (*Sulṭān* of Delhi) 71
Maḥmūd Gāvān *(wazīr)* 73
Maḥmūd Yalavach (governor) 43
al-Malik al-Nāṣir (Mamlūk *Sulṭān*) 58
Mamai (Tatar general) 56
Mamlūks (rulers of Egypt) 20, 23, 27-29, 33 f., 41, 42, 49, 56-60, 63, 65, 74, 75, 76, 77-79
Mangkhol (tribe) 2, 3, 4
Mangū *see* Möngke
Marco Polo (voyager) 32 note
Marxism 93
Mas'ūd (Ghaznavid *Sulṭān*) 61
Mas'ūd Beg (governor) 43, 44
Meḥmed II, the Conqueror (Ottoman *Sulṭān*) 83
Meḥmed Girai I (Ç̧rimean *Khān*) 96
Meḥmed Girai II (Crimean *Khān*) 96 f.
Meḥmed Girai IV (Crimean *Khān*) 97
Mengli Girai I (Crimean *Khān*) 82-85, 95
Merkit (Mongol tribe) 2, 3, 4
Michael of Chernígov (Grand Prince of Russia) 12

Michael VIII Palaeologus (Byzantine emperor) 23, 29, 48
Michael Románov (Tsar of Russia) 90
Mir 'Alī Shīr Navā'ī (*wazīr* and author) 69 note
Mīrān-Shāh (Tīmūrid ruler) 74
Mīrzā Jahān-Shāh (Qara Qoyunlu ruler) 75
Mishér (tribe) 91
Möngke (*Great Khān*) 16-18, 21, 24, 43
Möngke Tīmūr (Golden Horde *Khān*) 49
Monophysite Christians 26. *See also* Jacobites, Armenians, Copts
Mubāriz al-Dīn Muḥammad (Muẓaffarid ruler) 41
Mughal empire 70, 72, 73, 74
Muḥammad II, 'Alā' al-Dīn (*Khwārizm-Shāh*) 8-10
Muḥammad ibn Qāsim (Arab general) 60
Muḥammad II ibn Tughuq (*Sulṭān* of Delhi) 64 f., 72
Mu'izz al-Dīn Muḥammad (Ghūrid ruler) 62
Muslims 16, 19-20, 22 f., 27, 28-31, 33-37, 38 f., 45, 49 f., 52, 56, 58, 59, 60-65, 67, 68, 72-74, 78-79, 86, 88-91, 92 f., 94, 99, 100, 101
Muẓaffarids (dynasty) 41, 42, 54

Naiman (Mongol tribe) 2, 4
al-Nāṣir ('Abbāsid *Caliph*) 8
Naṣīr al-Dīn Ṭūsī (philosopher) 18, 19
Navā'ī *see* Mīr 'Alī Shīr Navā'ī
Nogai (Tatar tribe) 51, 99
Nokhai (Tatar prince) 29, 47, 51, 51

Ögedei (*Great Khān*) 10, 11, 13, 14, 16, 18, 43, 44, 45
Oghul Gaimysh (widow of Göyük) 16
Oirat (Mongol tribe) 2
Öljeitü see Uljaytū
Öngüt (Turkish tribe) 31
Orda (Mongol prince) 16
Orgyna see Ergene
Orthodox Christians 26, 27, 30, 47 f., 53, 86, 88-91
Ottomans (dynasty) 54, 67 f., 70, 76 f., 79, 83, 85, 86, 89, 92 f., 95, 96, 98, 99, 100
Özbeg (Golden Horde *Khān*) 52-54

Palaeologi (dynasty) 29
Pan-Islāmism 93
Pan-Slavism 99
Peter the Great (Tsar of Russia) 98
Potyómkin (Potemkin), G. Y. (Russian governor) 99
Pugachév, Emelyán (Russian rebel) 90

Qalā'ūn (Mamlūk *Sulṭān*) 58
Qaidu (Mongol prince) 44
Qāitbāi (Mamlūk *Sulṭān*) 79
al-Qalqashandī (author) 58
Qara Khiṭai (dynasty) 2, 4, 32
Qara Qoyunlu ("Black Sheep") (dynasty) 42, 69, 74-75, 77
Qara Yūsuf (Qara Qoyunlu ruler) 74 f.
Qaramān(ly) (Turkish principality) 75, 76, 79
Qotuz (Mamlūk *Sulṭān*) 20, 56 f.
Qubilai (*Great Khān*) 18, 21, 22, 24, 32, 36

Raḍīyah Begum (Queen of Delhi) 63
Rashīd al-Dīn Faẓl Allāh (*wazīr* and historian) 37, 38, 39
Rasin, Sténka (Russian rebel) 90
von Rubruck (de Rubruqis), Wilhelm (Papal Legate) 16 f.
Rurik (founder of the "Rus") 52
"Rus" (Viking dynasty) 12, 55

Sa'd al-Dawlah (*wazīr*) 34
Sa'dī (poet) 32
al-Ṣafadī (author) 58
Ṣafavids (dynasty) 70, 76, 77
Saljūqs (Selcük) (dynasty) 62, 63
Saljūqs of Rūm (dynasty) 27, 29, 40, 48 f., 59
Sanjar (Saljūq *Sulṭān*) 62
Sarbadārs (dynasty) 41 f.
Sartaq (Golden Horde *Khān*) 22 note
"Savage Tatars" 2
Sayyids (dynasty in India) 71
Sayyid Aḥmed (Great Horde *Khān*) 84 f.
Selīm (Ottoman *Sulṭān*) 76, 79
Shāh Shujā' (Muẓaffarid ruler) 44
Shāhrukh (Tīmūrid ruler) 69, 75
Shāhīn Girai (Crimean *Khān*) 99
Shamanists (animists) 2, 15, 30, 50
Sharqids (dynasty) 71 note
Shihāb al-Dīn Merjāni (Tatar reformer) 92
Shī'ite Muslims 19 f., 30, 35, 39, 42, 70, 73, 74, 79, 91
Sikandar Lōdī (*Sulṭān* of Delhi) 71 f.
"Slave Kings" (*Sulṭāns* of Delhi) 63
Socialists (Russian party) 93
Soviet government 101
Stephen Báthory (King of Poland) 97
Sübödei (Mongol general) 10
Suldūz (Turco-Mongol tribe) 39
Sunnite Muslims 19, 30, 35, 38, 39, 73, 75, 92

Tamerlane *see* Tīmūr
Taragai (father of Tīmūr) 65
Tarmashīrīn (Jagataid *Khān*) 45
Tatar (tribe) 1, 3
Temujin *see* Jingiz Khān
Teptér (tribe) 91
Tilak (Hindu general) 61
Tīmūr 41, 42, 56, 65-69, 71, 72, 74, 77, 78, 80
Tīmurids (dynasty) 69 f., 74, 75, 77
Tīni Beg (Golden Horde *Khān*) 53, 54
Tokhtamysh (Golden Horde *Khān*) 56, 66 f., 80, 81
Tokhtu (Golden Horde *Khān*) 51 f., 53
Toghril (To'oril) (Mongol chieftain) 3

Tolui (Mongol prince) 1;, 16
Töregene (widow of Ögedei) 14
Tughluq (Tughlak), Ghiyāth al-Dīn (*Sulṭān* of Delhi) 64
Tuqta'a *see* Tokhtu
Twelver Shī'ites 19, 70. *See also* Shī'ite Muslims

'Ubayd-i Zakānī (satirist) 42 note
Uljaytū Khudābandeh (Īlkhānid ruler) 38 f.
Ulugh Beg (Tīmūrid ruler) 69
Ulugh Meḥmed (*Khān* of Kazán) 81
Uniat churches 28, 30
Umayyads (Caliphal dynasty) 21, 60
'Uthmān Beg Qara Ilük (Aq Qoyunlu ruler) 75
Uways (Jalā'irid ruler) 42
Uzun Ḥasan (Aq Qoyunlu ruler) 69, 75 f.

Vasco da Gama (explorer) 78
Vasílii *see* Basil
Vitold (Vytautas) (Lithuanian ruler) 55 f., 80 f.

Wahhabīs (Sunnite sect) 58
Wajīh al-Dīn Mas'ūd (Sarbadār ruler) 42
Wang Khān (title of Toghril) 4
White Russians (party) 100
White Sheep *see* Aq Qoyunlu
"White Tatars" 2

Yabhalāhā III (Nestorian Patriarch) 31, 36
Yedigéi see Edigü
Ye-lü-chu-ts'ai (minister) 8
Yesughai (father of Jingiz Khān) 2 f.
Yinal see Īnāl
Yüan (dynasty) 21

Zayn al-'Ābidīn (ruler of Kashmīr) 74
Zoroastrians 60

INDEX B

Names of places, nations, languages

Abulustain *see* Albistān
Abyssinia *(Ḥabashah)* 78
Acre *('Akkā)* (port in Palestine)
Afghānistān 61, 69, 71
Africa 72
Aḥmadābād (city in Gujarāt) 73
Aḥmadnagar (city in the Deccan) 73
Aḥsanābād *see* Gulbarga
Alamūt (fortress in N. Persia) 18 f.
Albania *(Arnawutluq)* 76
Albistan *(Elbistan)* (town in E. Asia Minor) 76
Aleppo *(Ḥalab)* (city in N. Syria) 20, 27, 68, 77 79
Alexandria *(al-Iskandarīyah)* 57
Almalygh (former city in N. E. Turkistān) 46
Altai mountains 1, 2
Āmid *(Diyār Bakr)* (city in Upper Mesopotamia) 75
Anatolia *(Anadolu)* (western Asia Minor) 49, 95
Andrúsovo (treaty of) 97
Ankara (Angora) 68
Aq Kermān (Cetatea Albă, now Byélgorod) port in Bessarabia) 85
Arabs 25, 41, 61, 63
Arabia 21, 75, 78
Arabic language 31, 58
Aral Sea 11
Armenians *(Arman)*, Armenia 23, 26, 27, 29 31, 32, 40, 59, 67, 74
Asia Minor 20, 27, 29, 34, 40, 42, 48, 54, 58, 67, 68, 75, 76, 79
Ástarābād (city in Gurgān) 42
Ástrakhan (port near Volga mouth) 81, 85, 86, 96, 97
'Ayn Jālūt (Goliath's Well) (in Palestine) 20, 23, 27
Aynalı Kavak (treaty of) 99
Āẕarbāyjān (N. W. Īrānian region) 10, 25, 36, 41, 42, 54, 55, 67, 74-76, 93, 94
Azov *(Azaq)* (town at Don mouth)

Bāghceh Sarai (town in the Crimea) 95, 98
Baghdād 8, 19, 20, 22, 25, 30, 41, 42, 59, 74, 76, 77
Baikal (Lake) 1
Bākū (city in N. Āẕarbāyjān) 94
Balkan (peninsula) 89
Baltic (Sea) 12
Bashkir *(Bashkurt)* (Turkish people in the Urals) 88, 91, 93
Battle near Aleppo (Marj Dābiq) 79
" " Ankara (Chibūqābād) 68
Battle of 'Ayn Jālūt 20, 23, 27
" " the Blue Waters 55
" " Chmielnik 12
" " the Kalka river 10
" " " Kandurcha river 67
" " Kulikovo Pólye 56
" " Lake Kereli 76
" " Lepanto 96
" " the Plain of Mohi 13
" " Talikota 73
" " Terjān 76
" " the Walstatt plain 13
Bengal (region in N. E. India) 62, 65, 72
Berār (district in the Deccan) 73
Besh Balygh (former city in N. E. Turkistān) 43
Bessarabia (province N. of Danube delta) 55
Bīdar (town in the Deccan) 73
Bijāpūr (town in the Deccan) 73
Black Sea 13, 14, 23, 49, 51, 55, 80 f., 82, 83, 85
Blue Waters (Sinyukha river) (battle of)

Bolgáry *see* Bulgār
Bosnia (Balkan territory) 88
Brandenburg (territory in N. Germany) 97
Breslau (city in Silesia) 13
Bukhārā (city in Transoxiana) 9, 43, 44, 49
Bulgār (former city on the Volga) 11
Bulgars *see* Volga Bulgars, Danubian Bulgaria
Bundelkhand (district in C. India) 72
Byzantines 23, 24, 29, 30, 48, 51, 54, 57, 59

Cairo *(al-Qāhirah)* 20, 22, 24, 28, 29, 42, 45, 53, 54, 59, 78, 79
Cambay (port in Gujarāt) 73
Cape of Good Hope 78
Carpathian mountains 55
Caspian Sea 11, 18, 33, 88, 96
Castille (territory in C. Spain) 68
Catalonia (territory in N. E. Spain) 28
Caucasus mountains, Caucasia 10, 14, 18, 22, 23, 26, 27, 28, 33, 35, 38, 40, 44, 47, 48, 51, 54, 55, 57, 68, 77, 80, 88
Central Europe 12, 51, 60
Central Asia 1, 9, 11, 14, 16, 17, 24, 25, 32, 43-46, 49, 53, 56, 63, 67, 69, 89, 94
Cheremiss (Finnish people, N. of Kazán) 88
Chernígov (town in N. Ukraine) 12, 82
China, Chinese 1, 2, 3, 5, 6, 7 f., 9, 11, 17, 18, 21, 22, 24, 25, 26, 32, 35, 36 f., 65, 68, 69
Chinese language 35
Chmielnik (battle of) 12
Cilicia (territory in S. Asia Minor) 27
Circassians *(Cherkess)* (Caucasian people) 77, 96
Constantinople *(İstanbul)* 23, 29, 48, 51, 53, 59, 68, 76, 83, 85, 93
Copt(s) *(Qibṭ)* 58, 78 f.
Cossacks 97
Crimea *(Qyrym, Qirim)* 10, 28, 49, 50 f., 53, 54, 55, 76, 81-86, 92, 93, 94, 95-101
Croatia (territory in C. Europe) 13
Cyprus *(Qubrus)* 76, 78
Cyrenaica *(Barqah)* (territory in N. Africa) 58

Damascus *(Dimashq)* 20, 27, 58, 60, 68, 77
Damghān (town in N. Persia) 42
Danube (river) 13, 55
Danubian Bulgaria 13 f., 48, 53
Dardanelles (Straits) 28, 54
Deccan *(Dakhan)* (region in the Indian peninsula) 64, 65, 72 f.
Delhi *(Dihlī)* 62-65, 71 f., 72
Diyār Bakr *(Āmid)* (city in Upper Mesopotamia) 75
Dniepr (river) 55, 80, 81, 97
Dniestr (river) 55, 81
Dobruja (province S. of Danube delta) 100
Don (river) 56, 96, 98

East Europe 10, 12, 24, 47-56, 80-101
Eastern Turkish languages 50, 69 note

Edessa *('Urfah)* (city in Upper Mesopotamia) 75
Egypt *(Miṣr)* 20, 22, 23 f., 27 f., 34, 37, 40, 41, 42, 49, 51, 53, 54, 56-60, 63, 68, 76, 77-79
England 39
Erzerum (city in E. Asia Minor) 76
Erzinjān (town in E. Asia Minor) 76
Euphrates *(al-Furāt)* (river) 27, 58, 76

Farghānā (province in C. Asia) 2
Fārs (province in S. Persia) 32, 33, 41, 63, 75
Finns 50, 86, 89, 91
France, French 15, 17, 28, 29
Franks 49

Galicia (Polish province) 12, 47, 51, 83, 98
Ganges (river) 62
Genoa, Genoese 28, 50 f., 53, 59, 76, 83, 95
Germans, Germany 13, 16, 17, 48, 89, 98, 99, 100, 101
Georgians *(Gurj)*, Georgia 10, 14, 23, 26, 32, 33, 34, 38, 40, 51, 67
Ghaznah (E. Īrānian city) 61 f.
Gīlān (province in N. Persia) 33
Golconda (former city in the Deccan) 73
Great Nóvgorod see Nóvgorod
Greece 76
Greeks 76, 99. *See also* Byzantines
Grodno (city now in White Russia) 101
Gujarāt (province in W. India) 61, 64, 73 f.
Gulbarga (town in the Deccan) 73
Gurgān (province in N. Persia) 42

Halycz (town in Galicia) 12
Harāt (city in Khurāsān) 33, 38, 40, 41, 66, 69 f.
Himalaya (mountains) 74
Hindū Kush (mountains) 26
Huns 1
Hungary, Hungarians 13, 14, 17, 55, 100
Hurmuz (island and port in the Persian Gulf) 32 note
Hyderabad *(Ḥaydarābād)* (city in the Deccan) 73

"Idel-Uralian people" 93
Ilmen (lake in N. W. Russia) 12
India 10, 11, 20, 32, 59, 60-65, 67, 70, 71-77, 78
Indian Ocean 78
Indo-European peoples 1
Indonesia 73
Indus (river) 10, 60, 61, 64, 67, 71
Īrān see Persia
al-'Irāq see Mesopotamia
Irtysh (river) 2
Iṣfahān (city in C. Persia) 67, 70, 75
Italians, Italy 28, 50 f., 57, 59, 78, 83

Jagatai (people) 43. See also Eastern Turkish
Japan 17

Jaxartes *(Sayḥūn* or *Syr Daryā)* 26, 44, 68
Jerusalem *(al-Quds)* 37
Jawnpūr (town in N. India) 71
Jibāl (province in C. Persia) 75, 76
Jiddah (Red Sea port) 78

Kābul (city in Afghānistān) 72
Kaffa (now Feodosia) (Crimean port) 28, 50 f., 83, 95
Kalka (river) 10
Káma (Volga tritutary) 89
Kandurcha (river in Russia) 67
Karbalā' (town in Lower Mesopotamia) 35
Kāshghar (city in E. Turkistān) 66, 74
Kashmīr 74
Kastamonu (town in N. Asia Minor) 76
Kazán (city on the Volga) 11, 81, 82, 85 f., 88, 89, 90, 96, 97
Kereli (now Beyşehir Gölü) (lake in S. W. Asia Minor) 76
Khitai (Turco-Mongol people) 2, 8
Khoqand (or Khojent) (city in Farghānah) 43
Khurāsān (N. E. Īrānian region) 9, 10, 18, 25, 26, 35, 40, 44, 69 f.
Khwārizm (territory on the lower Oxus) 8 f., 43, 44, 66
Kilia (Chilia) (port near Danube mouth) 85
Kíev 12, 47, 48, 55
Kirghiz (Turkish people) 2
Kirmān (city and territory in S.E. Īrān) 32, 41, 75
Konya (city in C. Asia Minor) 49
Kozélsk (town in Russia) 12
Krakow (city in Galicia) 12
Kuban (river in N. Caucasia) 99
Küçük Kaynarcı (treaty of) 98
Kulikovo Pólye (battle of) 56
Kūr (river in Georgia and Āẕarbāyjān) 26
Kurds 10

Lahore (Lahāwur) (city in the Panjāb) 61, 74
Lepanto (Navpaktos) (port in W. Greece) 96
Levant (E. Mediterranean) 59
Liegnitz (town in Silesia) 13
Lithuania 55 f, 80-85, 95
Little Armenia (kingdom in Cilicia) 27

al-Madīnah 59
Malatya (city in E. Asia Minor) 27
Malaya 73
Malwa (territory in C. India) 73
Marāghah (town in Āẕarbāyjān) 19, 25
Mārdīn (city in Upper Mesopotamia) 74
Marv (city in Khurāsān) 9
Maṣawwa' (Red Sea port)
Mayyāfāriqīn (fortress in Upper Mesopotamia) 20
Māzandarān (province in N. Persia) 32, 38
Mecca (Makkah) 59
Mediterranean Sea 17, 20, 27, 29, 49, 54, 59, 67
Meshhed *(Mashhad)* (city in Khurāsān) 69 note
Mesopotamia (Lower, *al-'Irāq al-'Arabī*; Upper, *al-Jazīrah*) 1, 10, 19, 20, 25, 27, 28, 30, 31, 34, 40, 42, 54, 56, 60, 67, 74, 75, 78
Moldavia (Rumanian territory) 51, 55, 83, 85
Mohi (plain in Hungary) 13
Mongolia 1-7, 10, 11, 16 f., 21, 43 f.
Mongols 1-25, 25-36, 38, 41, 42, 43-46, 47-52, 56, 57, 58, 59, 63 f., 65 f., 70, 76, 77, 85, 86, 94, 99
Mongol language 21, 35, 36, 44, 50
Moravia (territory in C. Europe) 13
Moscow, Muscovites 12, 48, 52, 53, 55 f., 80, 82-86
Mosul *(al-Mawṣil)* (city in Upper Mesopotamia) 42, 74
Mtsketh (former city in Georgia) 26
Mughān (steppe in Āẕarbāyjān) 25
Mulṭān (city in S. Panjāb) 60
Múrom (city in Russia) 12

Near East 17, 27, 39, 45, 60. *See also* Western Asia
Nile *(al-Nīl)* (river) 58. *See also* Egypt
Nīshāpūr (city in Khurāsān) 42
North Africa 60, 63
Nóvgorod (city in N. W. Russia) 12, 83
Nubians *(al-Nūbah)* 64, 78 f.

Oder (river) 12
Odessa (Black Sea port) 81
Oirats (Mongol people) 2
Oka (Volga tributary) 84
Okhmatov (battle of) 97
Okhotsk (town) 92 note.
Old Krim *(Qyrym, Qirim)* 95
Olmütz (city in Moravia) 13
Oman see 'Umān
Onon (river in Mongolia) 3
Orenburg (now Chkalov) (city in the S. Urals) 91
Orkhon (river in Mongolia) 2, 8
Otrār (former city in Turkistān) 44, 68
Oxus *(Jayḥūn* or *Amu Daryā)* (river) 10, 26, 27, 43, 66
Özbegs (Turkish people) 53
Pacific Ocean 89 note.
Pākistān 62
Palestine *(Filasṭīn)* 20
Pamīr (plateau) 26
Panjāb "(Five Rivers") (province in N. W. India) 60-62, 71, 72, 74
Pathān (Afghān) 71
Peking 21, 22, 24
Peloponnese *(Morea)* 76
Persia *(Īrān)*, Persians 1, 9, 10, 17, 18 f., 22-24, 25-42, 45, 49, 50, 51 f., 53, 54 f., 56, 57, 59, 60-62, 63, 65-70, 74-77, 79, 88, 91, 96, 97

Persian language 32, 35, 41, 50, 60, 64, 69, 73
Podolia (province in W. Ukraine) 12, 55, 80, 83
Poland, Poles 12 f., 82-85, 86, 90, 95, 96-98
Poltava (town in the Ukraine) 80
Portugese 73, 74, 78
Prussia (German kingdom) 98
Pruth (river) (treaty of the) 98

Qara Qorum (former city) 8, 11, 13, 14, 16 f., 21, 30
Qaramān (Caramania) (principality in Asia Minor) 76
Qazvīn (city in N. Persia) 38, 70
Qypchaq *(Qipçāq)* (plain N. of Black and Caspian Seas) 50, 52, 66

Red Sea 78
Rōḍah *(al-Rawḍah)* (island) 58
Rome 28, 30, 37
Rumania 51
Russia, Russians 3, 10, 12, 14, 16, 17, 22, 23, 29, 47-56, 57, 80-101
Russian language 86 f., 92 f., 94

Sabzāvar (town in Khurāsān) 42
Samarqand (city in Transoxiana) 9, 43, 49, 67
Sarai (Old and New; former cities on the lower Volga) 14, 16, 18, 23, 28, 29, 41, 47, 49-55, 95
Sarts (Īrāniān people) 45
Satlaj (river in the Panjāb) 72
Selenga (river in Mongolia) 2
Selítrennoye (village) 14
Serbia (Balkan kingdom) 48
Severia (district in N. Ukraine) 82
Shīrāz (city in S. Persia) 32, 34, 41, 67
Shīrvān (province in N. Āẕarbāyjān) 42
Shūshtar (town in S. W. Persia) 74
Siberia (Sibir) 1, 85, 86, 89 note, 101
Sicily 28, 59
Silesia (province in W. India) 60
Sindh (province in W. India) 60
Sinyukha (river in W. Ukraine) 55
Sīstān (S. E. Īrānian province) 41
Sivas (city in E. Asia Minor) 75
Slavonia (territory in C. Europe) 13
Spain, Spaniards 59, 62, 63, 78
Stalingrád (city on the lower Volga) 14, 96
Straits (Dardanelles) 28, 54
Sulṭānīyeh (former city in N. Persia) 38
Sweden 96, 97
Syria *(al-Shām)* Syrians 17, 20, 23, 26, 27, 28, 29, 30, 38, 40, 42, 49, 53, 54, 56, 58, 59, 67, 68, 74, 77, 78, 79
Syriac language 31

Tabrīz (city in Āẕarbāyjān) 25, 28, 29, 30, 31 f., 33, 35, 37, 40 f., 42, 49, 51, 54 f., 67, 74-77, 80
Tājīks (Īrānian people) 45
Talikota (battle of) 73
Tārim (river in E. Turkistān) 2
Tatars 1, 2, 22, 49, 50-56, 80-101
Taurida (Russian province) 99
Terek (river in N. Cancasia) 22, 52
Terjān (battle of) 76
Thrace (Balkan territory) 48
Tibet, Tibetans 21, 65, 74
Tigris *(Dijlah)* (river) 36
Tisza (river in Hungary) 13
Torzhók (town in N. W. Russia) 12
Transoxiana *(Mā warā' al-Nahr)* 10, 24, 25, 26, 28, 32, 33, 34, 38, 40, 43-46, 49, 65-70, 80
Transylvania (territory in C. Europe) 13, 97
Trebizond *(Trabzon)* (port in N. E. Asia Minor) 24, 29, 76
Tripoli *(Tarābulus al-Shām)* (port in Syria) 28
Turcomans *(Türkmen)* (Turkish people) 42, 69, 74-77, 78, 79
Turks 1, 2, 9, 10, 11, 19, 23, 24, 25, 36, 43-46, 50, 53, 54, 57, 61, 62, 63, 64, 65 f., 70, 71, 74 f., 77, 83, 85, 86, 88, 92, 93, 94, 98, 100
Turkey (republic) 100
Turkish languages 36, 50, 50, 57, 69 note, 70, 77, 86, 92, 93, 94
Turkistān 1, 43-46
Turshīz (town in Khurāsān) 42

Ufá (city in the Urals) 93
Uigurs (Turkish people in E. Turkistān) 1, 8, 21, 43
Uigur language 2, 21, 50
Ukraine, Ukrainians 12, 55, 84, 97, 99
'Umān (territory in E. Arabia) 75
Ural mountains 93
Urdū language 73
Uzbeks see Özbegs

Venice, Venetians 28, 50, 59, 76, 83
Vienna 98
Vijayanagar (kingdom in S. India) 73
Vilna (city) 82
Volga (river) 1, 11, 13 f., 16, 24, 49-53, 67, 80, 81, 85 f., 88-94, 96, 99
Volga Bulgars 11, 24, 50
Volhynia (province in W. Ukraine) 12, 55
Vorskla (river) 80

Walstatt (plain) 13
Warsaw 97
Western Asia 11, 14, 18, 20, 26, 28, 68, 69. *See also* Near East
Western Europe 17, 28, 31, 37, 49, 50 f., 59 f., 76, 78, 92
White Russia 55

Yaroslàv (city in Russia) 12
Yazd (city in C. Persia) 41
Yenisei (river) 2

Zagros (W. Irānian mountains) 19, 26, 32

INDEX C

Technical terms

Amīr (commander, governor, prince) 39, 41, 45, 66
Atabeg ("guardian", = ruler) 63
Baskak (Basqaq) (Tatar tax official) 48, 52, 55
Beduin *(Badw)* 64
Beg (Turkish = *amīr*) 45, 46, 66
Bhikshu (Bakhshy) (Buddhist priest) 26
Black Death (bubonic plague) 40, 54

Caliph *(Khalīfah)* 8, 19, 20, 22, 24, 25, 45, 59, 63, 78, 99
Capitulations 60

Duma (parliament of the Russian empire) 93

"Eastern Question" 60

Feudal system *(iqṭā')* 51
Fief *(qaṭī'ah)* 57, 65

Grand Prince (of Russia) 12, 52, 55 f.
Great Khān *(Khāqān)* 6, 11, 13 f., 16, 17, 18, 21, 22, 25, 30, 32, 36 f., 68

Hetman (elected Cossack commander) 97 f.
"High Commissioner" *(Parvāneh)* 27, 32, 34, 37
Hospodar (Moldavian and Wallachian governor) 55, 83

Ilkhān (viceroy) 22, 37
Imām (prayer leader) 99

Khān (commander, prince; title of Mongol, Tatar and some other rulers) 37, 66

Law of Islām *(Sharī'ah)* 6, 37, 39, 45, 54, 56, 58, 63

Mamlūk (slave soldier) 23, 49, 51, 62 f., 72
Metropolitan (Bishop) 12, 47, 48
Missionaries (Christian) 14, 28, 50, 53, 88, 90, 91, 97, 99
Muftī (Islāmic Jurisconsult) 91, 93 f.
Mullā (= *'ālim*; scholar of religion) 92

Naqīb 20

Paper money *(chāo)* 35
Patriarch (Christian) 31, 36
Poll tax *(jizyah)* 71
Pope 14, 15, 16, 28, 29, 50, 53
Post *(barīd)* 7, 17, 37

Qalga 95
Qur'ān 60, 61, 64, 89
Quryltai (Mongol national assembly) 4, 11, 44

Rabbi 31

Sayyid ("lord"; = 'Alid) 71
School of law and theology *(madhhab)* 39, 58
Sermon *(khuṭbah)* 99
Shāh (Persian title of rulers) 76, 91
Shaman (animist priest) 2
Sharī'ah see Law of Islām
Sharīf ("noble"; = 'Alid) 59
Sulṭān ("authority"; title of Ghaznavid, Saljūq, Mamlūk, Ottoman, early Indian Muslim and other rulers, *q.v.*)

Ṭarafdār 73
Tatar tribute *(tysh)* 47 f., 52, 56, 80, 84, 96
Taxation 7, 34, 37, 48, 52, 65, 71, 78, 88, 90

Waqf (pious foundation) 37, 57
Wazīr (minister) 32, 34, 37-39, 69 note, 71, 73, 85, 96
Women 6 f., 14, 16, 17, 39, 40, 44, 63, 95

Yasa, Yasaq (law of Jingiz Khān) 6, 8, 31, 37, 45, 54

INDEX D

Authors cited

Ammann, A. M., 15
Arnold, Sir T. W., 99
Ayalon, D., 79

Ballod, F. V. 50
Barthold, W. V. 18, 99
Becker, C. H. 99
Burbiel, G. 92

Çağatay, S. 92

Ghanī, Q. 41

von Goethe, J. W. 41
Górka, O. 97

Ibn Iyās 79
İnalcık, H. 96

Jahn, K. 35
Jansky, H. 79

Lescot, R. 41

Małowist, M. 83

Mańkowski, T. 98

Pirenne, H. 59
Poliak, A. N. 23

Roemer, H. R. 41

Seydamet, C. 92

Smolitsch, I. 85
Spuler, B. 46, 94
Stripling, G. W. F. 79
Sumner, B. H. 98

Vernadskiĭ, G. V. 6

Wiet, G. 79

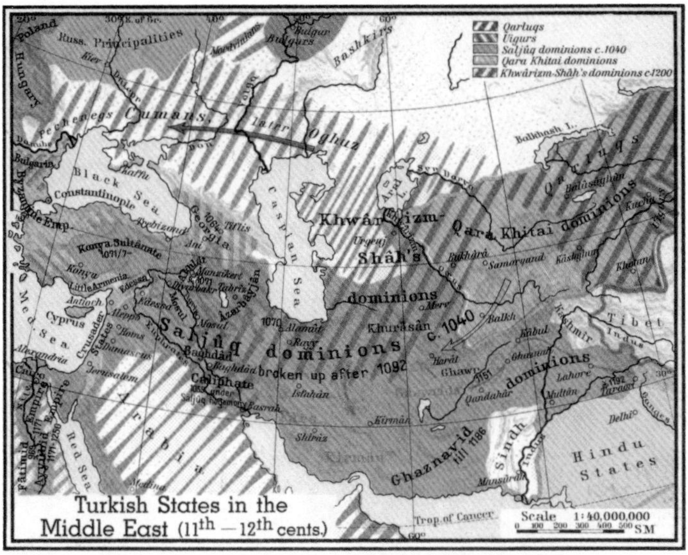

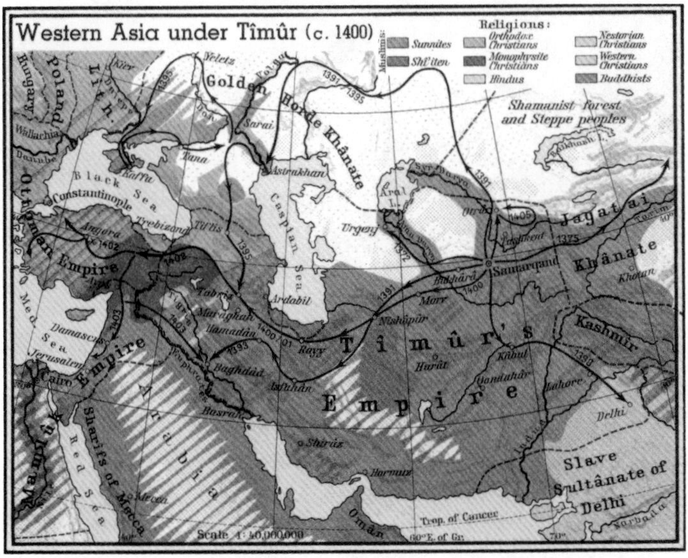

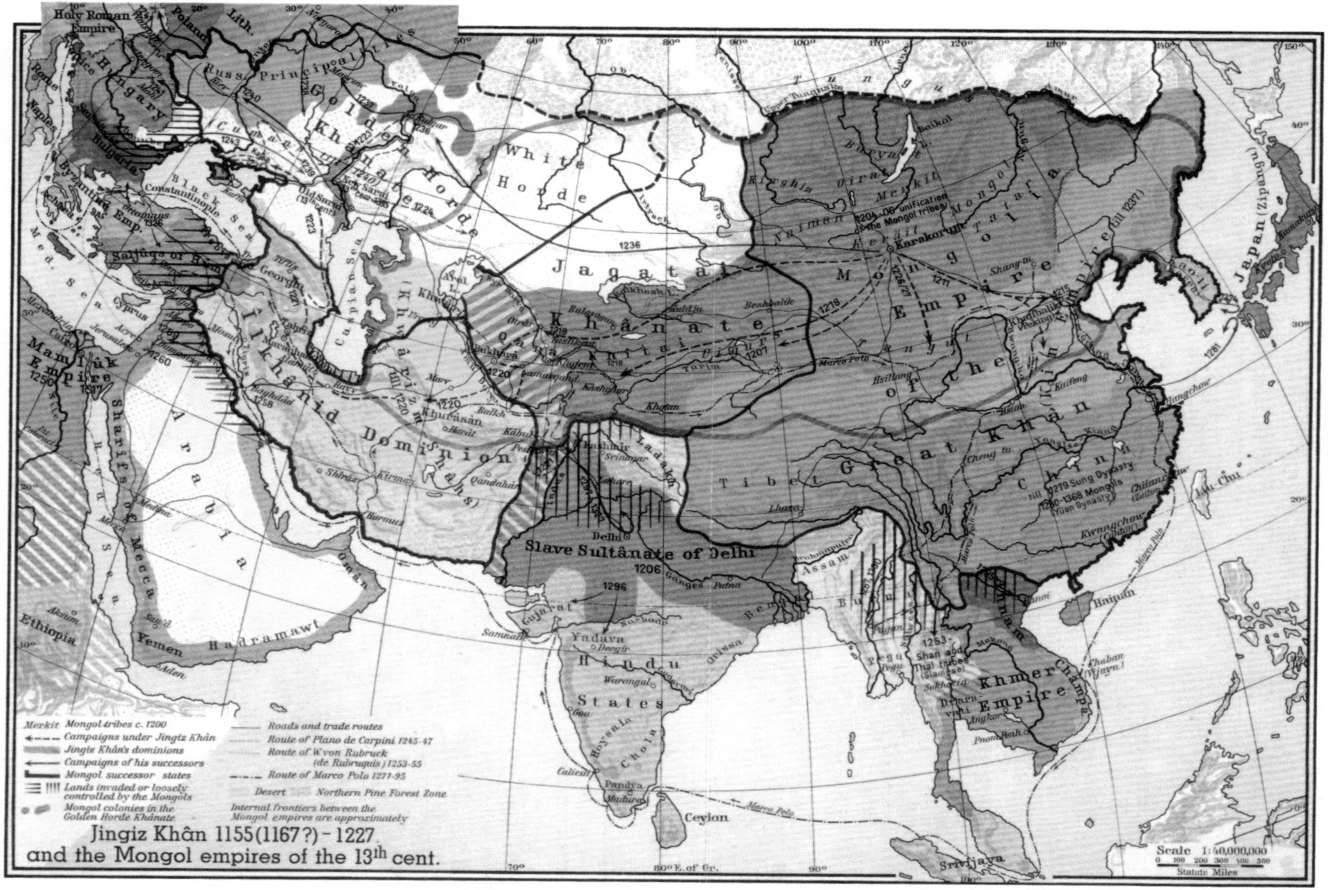

Jingiz Khân 1155(1167?) - 1227
and the Mongol empires of the 13th cent.